GO IN

NINE POINTS
TO CONSCIOUS LIVING

DANIEL J SCHWARZHOFF

Pendum Publishing Company
A subsidiary imprint of Schwarzhoff Media
PO Box 798
Longwood Avenue
Hyannis Port, MA 02647

Pendum and *Non-Contemplative Meditation* are Trademarks of Daniel J Schwarzhoff and Schwarzhoff Media.

For information about special discounts for bulk purchases please contact Nancy Schwarzhoff at: nancylee@schwarzhoffmedia.com.
For information about appearances, speaking and other events please contact Daniel Schwarzhoff Jr. at: djsjr@schwarzhoffmedia.com.
More information available at www.schwarzhoffmedia.com

Produced and printed in the United States of America

Name: Daniel J Schwarzhoff
Title: Go In: Nine Points to Conscious Living

Subjects: Non-Contemplative Meditation, Consciousness, Mindfulness, Spirituality,
Description: 1st ed. Hyannis Port, MA: Pendum Publishing Company, 2017. 203. Print.

ISBN: 9780988911918

With regards and acknowledgment to
Alan Alexander Milne

Table of Contents

Letter.. i

Preface *Please Remain Calm*..iii

> *There are two main elements to what you are about to discover in the following chapters. At first, some of what you read could seem a little scary. But it is all vital and true. Please keep an opened mind and no matter what, do your best to stay calm. The first element is the written narrative which holds a very special message. The second element . . .*

Point Zero *The Introduction*..xi

> *By which I make the case for how this book and the unique method for consciousness proposed in it isn't like anything you've ever seen, heard or experienced before.*

Point One *The First Chapter*.. 1

> *By which you are asked to consider, "Are you really who you think you are?" Probably not.*

Point Two *The Second Chapter* 19

> *By which everything you need for a peacefully whole, productive life arrives effortlessly and automatically, just by giving up the ambitious struggle to get it.*

Point Three *The Third Chapter*.. 39

> *By which you are encouraged to begin a very special kind of meditation and to begin practicing it as if the preservation of your life and all progress depends on coming to consciousness and remaining mindfully aware—because it sure does.*

Point Four *The Fourth Chapter*... 71

> *By which you discover how error and the flawed nature in us all ultimately work toward good and that once becoming still, courage rises to vanquish all fear.*

Point Five *The Fifth Chapter*.. 97

> *By which the nature and origin of resentment are revealed and you
> realize how crucial it is to get free from anger. In abandoning
> bitterness, you cease the lifelong struggle with irritating people.
> Inner peace is possible in this lifetime.*

Point Six *The Sixth Chapter*.. 117

> *By which it becomes abundantly clear just how magical and life-
> altering is the power of forgiveness. As you emotionlessly observe
> defectiveness in others, you begin to experience tolerance, right now,
> in each new moment.*

Point Seven *The Seventh Chapter* 147

> *By which you discover that anger isn't normal for human beings,
> that not everyone gets upset, and how simple it is to discover
> honesty, truth, and peace within, once freed from resentment. The
> psychic clockwork of dishonesty is exposed and you can never view
> the world as you once did.*

Point Eight *The Eighth Chapter* 181

> *By which you see how losing your fear of today, tomorrow and
> yesterday comes quite simply once you take responsibility for your
> actions. Inner accountability frees you from faulty self-reliance and
> you begin to place faith where it truly belongs.*

Point Nine *The Ninth Chapter*... 199

> *By which the compelling case is made that you are never alone
> because God-consciousness can be accessed anytime and anywhere.
> Survival amid all obstacles sustains progress toward fulfillment as
> life becomes packed with purpose and meaning.*

Out Into the World *The Tenth Chapter*.. 221

> *By which you've begun to awaken, watching the world and living
> consciously . . . in real time and in all your affairs*

I Have a Big Problem *The Eleventh Chapter* 249
By which I further make the case that how you meditate matters. It matters so much that I wrote this separate chapter just to address the subject. There are many methods available, but there is only one way to safe and effective consciousness. This is the one

How This Came About *The Twelfth Chapter* 265
By which I summarize my personal story and clarify a few of the credentials that allow me to say and to write as I do.

Just a Brief Backgrounder *About Daniel J Schwarzhoff*.........275
By which you learn some of the basics about Dan's background and life.

And by the way . . . *Why is the term Non-Contemplative Meditation™ trademarked?* 279
When we think of trademarks, what first comes to mind are those little legal symbols used to protect brand names, products or services against infringement by competitors. You'll see one such symbol attached to Non-Contemplative Meditation™.

Would You Like Some More? 283

Errata Grata 285

Hi Everybody,

I am glad you're reading my book. There's no doubt that many of you will do quite well with what I've written. But I'd like to give you a *heads up*. Throughout *Go In*, you'll notice one underlying premise. It is *meditation*. A certain kind of meditation. I do it. I believe you should too, and everything I write stems from this. Through this unique practice comes conscious awareness, leading to the benefits I write about.

But must you meditate to benefit from this book? No, of course not. Disregard it entirely if you like. There are many other ideas you'll find useful, even if you don't fully agree with every single one of them.

Still, as it comes up, the word *meditation* is likely to raise certain images, like controlled breathing, mantras, visualization and mentally stimulating the imagination. These are highly popularized techniques and you've probably seen them all. *But I don't endorse or use any of them and will state right now that neither should you.* The meditation fundamental to my work is very different from those on New Age websites, bookstore shelves or in spiritual cultures and religions. It is a simple, timeless technique, unlike anything you've ever seen before.

I don't hypnotize people. There is no trance. I do not use meditation to indoctrinate subjects into a religion, a philosophical society or New Age culture. As you are about to discover in *Go In*, I encourage quite the opposite.

In the following chapters, not only will I show you how to properly use this very special technique, I will also explain exactly *why* you should do it. I'll give you its background, how I came to develop it and explain some of the changes you'll experience if you will consider my ideas and choose to give this method a fair shot.

I am no guru. I am not a trained counselor or medical doctor. I don't speak with angels, channel dead relatives or alien beings from outer space. (No one does.) I'm just an ordinary man who's lived the way described in this book for the last 40 years, offering extraordinary perspectives on work, business, family, relationships, and just about all of life's affairs.

If you're a seeker, then it's likely you've already come across many spiritual philosophies, the kind found in self-help books, on websites or YouTube. Much of what you'll read here is 180 degrees opposite those, as well as much of what you've been taught by preachers, self-proclaimed spiritual guides and God knows who else. I can offer no apologies.

It's not my aim to tell you how to live or what to think. Introducing this practice and carrying this message to the world is the core component of my life's work. I write simply to encourage others to try it, so they can allow their lives to change through a Power greater than any of us. Thousands all over the world have already been directly helped through my work. I believe that number can become millions. Perhaps as a result of this book you will become one.

If I can't do that for you, then I have failed and you have wasted your time. But I am giving it my best shot and hope that if you haven't already begun to practice this technique then you'll at least consider it at some point along the way. You will be very glad you did.

God bless,

DJS

Preface

Please Remain Calm

There are two main elements to what you are about to discover in the following chapters. At first, some of what you read could seem a little scary. But it is all vital and true. Please keep an opened mind and no matter what, do your best to stay calm. The first element is the written narrative which holds a very special message. The second element...

... is the revival of a timeless spiritual tool. It is actionable. It is practical. It's an exercise. I've given it a name. I call it *Non-Contemplative Meditation*™. You can begin it right away.

Do not let the term *meditation* prejudice you. This is not like anything you have ever seen or heard before. I don't mean just a little bit different, a variation of something you're already familiar with. I mean radically different. Keep reading and I assure you this will become abundantly clear.

The fundamental presentation I intend for this book combines the two elements. You are welcome to use them separately, although to receive the full benefit I strongly suggest you combine them. If you do, the effects, which I'll describe in detail as we go along, will be extremely powerful. Not only is this meditation different from anything you've ever encountered, but so is the message. I am convinced that the world is ready for this right now.

What first began as a thirty-page E-Pamphlet to be written in under a month ended up taking three years to complete. *If it's true that God laughs at our plans, then I guess He must have been in stitches on this one.* This book is the result.

It is not a compilation of some theories or philosophies I picked up in my reading or heard about. It isn't a bunch of ideas stumbled on while surfing the Internet, then assembled like some scrapbook project just because I agreed and liked the way they sounded. You won't find anything in this book gleaned out of preacher's sermons, borrowed from gurus or new age teachings like you might on the *self-help* shelves and *personal growth* websites. I am not part of a positive psychology movement, cult or religious organization.

What you will find is a unique proposal unlike any of those, which if given a fair trial will radically alter the course of your life. You'll experience reality that you don't now know exists and a quality of living that is better than anything you could ever plan for yourself. It will happen automatically and quickly.

What I propose for every reader who will consider it, isn't New Age or New Thought philosophy. It's not a positive thinking scheme, fad, religion or part of any cult. It also isn't hypnosis or a funky new behavior modification psychology. I use no chicanery to convert you to a philosophy or Eastern religion.

I have rediscovered intuitive innocence and how to live within the conscious state. With this comes all the peace and goodness available to any of us in this lifetime. I write about it, and I show you how it's done. It's that simple. Everything in this book comes out of my own personal involvement and experience living within this realm. Nothing is embellished. Nothing is invented. There's no conjecture. I'm a veteran practitioner of what I preach,[1] with over 30 years living and showing mindfully *conscious contact* to others just as described in these pages.

I use terms like *mindful* and *mindfulness* throughout this book and in much of my works. These simple words are also used a lot in New Age philosophies, by cults and pop-meditations, all of which as far as I can tell, derive out of dharmic cultures like Buddhism or Hinduism. Many of these focus on meditation.

They also speak, very smoothly I might add, of being *in the now* and of self-consciousness. Despite this, my books and practice have absolutely nothing to do with any non-duality cult, or contemplative meditation from New Thought, New Age pseudo-religions, or any other religion borrowing these terms from our own English.

The quality of *mindfulness* that I practice and present here is far beyond any of those and not in any way influenced by them. In fact, if you thought this book was about non-duality, Eastern religion or any convention of that order, then you could at first become disappointed. But hang in there. What you are about to discover is unique and so much better, you will thank God for the day you came across this book.

I've done it right and benefitted. I've also done it wrong and suffered the consequences. I have been doing it right, for a long time. All members of my immediate family live consciously too.[2] We're a close and productive clan. My 38-year marriage to Nancy is filled with love and durable stability. It can never end in divorce. It can never disintegrate. I've overcome anger, fear, and resentment, and show each family member how to do the same. This has resulted in two highly successful children, raised within a realm of existence that is so wonderful, you'll want it too, believe me. I'm also very good at helping others find the same. Once they allow it, of course.

This book is for anyone who would like to share in this discovery—who's been to the churches, tried all the self-help gurus, read all the spirituality, personal growth, and self-empowerment books, or perhaps avoided these, sensing that there must be more to human existence than just endless, self-centered egoism. There is more. *Oh, there is.*

Getting to it will require some open-mindedness on your part. Not to the point of gullibility, but just enough heartful liberalism to at least set aside prejudice for me to make my case. This shouldn't be too difficult. After all, whatever the reason, you've already been drawn to this moment, to this book and the message it holds. Right now, this is for you too. If you will give what I do and propose a fair shot, you'll be very glad you did.

There's hardly a single person reading this who hasn't got an untapped, inner capacity for resourcefulness waiting to be unleashed—an energetic force of creativity to effortlessly help solve all their problems, making life more productive and meaningful.

It is the very same source of creative energy possessed by the people you probably already know and admire, from the local business leader in small town America who sponsors charity drives, to the multi-billionaire corporate disrupter, shifting world paradigms through inspired thinking and a prodigious work ethic.

You could be the captain of a billion-dollar enterprise, a part-time cashier at a grocery store or a stay-at-home mom raising a family, wherever you are in life now makes zero difference. I claim that access to the same creativity and intuitive prowess as any of the classic disruptors, big or small, is very simple and attainable. If you'll access it, then as the direct result of consciousness, the future will alter in ways you dare not now imagine.

The exercise accompanying this book is a *catch-all*. Rather than my words centering on any specific concern you may have right now, whether it's financial, health or with relationships, this version is appropriate for everyone at any time, regardless of individual circumstances or concerns. It will be effective with any of these issues and more.[3]

Let's be clear here. This is not a *self-help* book. Nor is it some sort of self-improvement manual[4]. I am never going to suggest that you complete worksheets, attend webinars, seminars and spend thousands of dollars on weekend retreats being hypnotized by me or some equally awe-struck life-coach. I'm not here to dictate how anyone should live. The non-contemplative exercise included is all you will ever need for the rest of your life. I am merely an envoy of sorts.

With every breath of air and every beat of my heart, beginning right now and then with each new *now* to come, I dedicate to remaining awakened and mindfully receptive to God's will through consciousness. I couldn't write what I write or live the life I do if this wasn't so. I'm an ordinary man who lives a consciously inspired lifestyle and it warms the cockles of my heart just to be helpful.

Of course, I'm aware that many people would prefer not to become mindful. Coming out of the dulled state in which they already exist is painful. It can be too tough for them. They may harbor a fear of the word *meditation*, keeping them rigid and obstinate to change. Those are people I am unable to help very quickly.[5] To them, I might be one of those goofy *meditation people*, maybe some New Age guru or Spiritual Guide. With that frame of mind, there's no way they will readily acknowledge the depth, breadth, and importance of this work. At least not immediately.

Now, if you're like me, you might get about this far into a book like this and begin to think, *Oh, boy. Here we go. More dharmic gobbledygook. Another urban Buddhist or New Age crony from some self-help cult who's spent a week at a hermitage or attended a personal empowerment seminar and now sure he's found the secret to happiness 6.* Oh no. Not in this book.

Mindfulness, Consciousness, Meditation, these may be words that are common to many popular egoistic pursuits, but that is not what's going on in these pages at all. This book is quite different.

As the opening in my "Introduction" says, what is offered here *isn't like anything you've ever seen before.* I mean exactly that. I am not going to become your *life-coach.* You can't hire me to be your mentor or spiritual guide. There's no course that I'm trying to get you to take, nothing to remember, learn or study. There aren't any phony credentials to earn. There's no school for you to enroll in. I am not looking to indoctrinate anyone and I'm certainly not the minister of any church. This book isn't designed to cultivate followers[7] and if you try to become one I'll just *shoo* you away, anyway.

I have written *Go In* only to share the most profound discovery mankind has ever known, a gift that you can take into your life without any attachment to me whatsoever. I've devoted my life to this cause.

To get the most out of this book, I suggest you first begin practicing my Non-Contemplative Meditation exercise. This isn't mandatory of course. *But kind-of.* Put it this way, *it is highly suggested.* It's complimentary and easy to find on my website.[8]

Then, once making that beginning, start going through the book a little at a time, taking some time to pause every now and then. It isn't a novel. There's no plot or story arc to follow. There isn't any finish line. This isn't an academic course. The ideas presented here are too simple and rich for the intellect to grasp and hold by rote anyway.

Here is a kind of information that absorbs into the psyche through spiritual understanding, not by learning. There's no need to hurry. There isn't any surprise ending, just truth made bare by words, and revealed as you awaken to them. *Oh, and the endnotes? You'll find this to be a good book without them, but if you want a little extra, read those too. Think of them as bonus material.*

This is an experience you'll be eager to tell others about. Once you're practicing what I propose, the example set in your own life will help amplify a progression of consciousness, first within you, then extending to your children, mate, and ultimately to everyone in your life. Yes, in this regard, peace, security, and confidence are contagious. You'll become a carrier of *wellness.*

You may ask, "Is this really necessary?" After all, why should anyone have to go through the trouble of meditating to become conscious? "Can't life be good enough just as it is?"

My answer is an emphatic, "No." Life is not good enough just as it is. Despite what you may think, you are not doing just fine as you are. Yes, you do need to hear this. Everyone needs to awaken and live consciously, even if not everyone will. Although our lovely earth was once paradise, mankind has blown it. Now the earthly existence has been re-formed into a treacherous course.

With this book and all subsequent works and articles I write, maybe that can change. I can show the world how to discover true, mindful consciousness through proper meditation so that people can share in this discovery. In this regard, I'm a one trick pony, devoted to carrying this single message to others, beginning first with my family and then to anyone who can hear it. I am defined not by my own will but through a will that comes through me.

Hopefully, I've made it abundantly clear that I am not asking you to join or belong to anything and that I don't want your personal allegiance. What I propose in this book is for you to freely take an independent journey and rediscover what I have—a state of existence we all know first as children, but then soon lose.

There's nothing especially exotic about any of this. You'll find this approach and means well-matched with our western way of life.[9] It's the way of living intended for all from the beginning. Your life is about to change in ways you could never have imaged, but first, allow me to present a bit more. Please go straight on to my *Introduction* to begin at "Point Zero."

— Dan

Point Zero

The Introduction

By which I make the case for how this book and the unique method for consciousness proposed in it isn't like anything you've ever seen, heard or experienced before.

The Vietnam War raged. Pony cars and family sedans built in the USA lined the streets. Under-dash car-stereos blasted Beatles and the Stones. Our lower middle-class neighborhood in the North-East Bronx vibrated with a wealth of social diversity and culture. But there was also danger and intrigue. Not all of it was out in the borough streets. In fact, most came under our own roof. No one knew it. It wasn't the Bronx's fault. Had this been the open spaces of Iowa or a small town in the Rockies, I'm sure it would have been the same.

It's clichéd, I know, but raised in the big city a child does grow up hard and fast. Just like every kid anywhere else, I needed guidance. There had to be some template for survival to go by. I craved another human being I might emulate, someone who'd been through the same hazards and endured. I needed to see what survival looked like on a successful man. And I needed it badly. But raised by a single mother without the benefit of a father, that kind of fulfillment at home was impossible.

Where could I find a role model?

There was my mother's part-time, live-in boyfriend. But he was a violent drunk who terrorized us all, including my two little half-sisters. We were all scared to death of him. There were some male teachers in grammar school I might have looked to, but they seemed angry so much of the time. As you can imagine, suitability was a key issue. I found no one.

But not all was lost. After all, these were the 60s and 70s. We were the TV generation, suddenly given access to an expansive knowledge base and new experiences. It was a society becoming overwhelmed by electronic media and entertainment. I didn't have to go very far to find as many substitute dads as I could use. They were right in our living room and at the local movie theaters. On the silver and green screens[10]. I discovered men of honor and integrity who never failed to triumph over seemingly impossible obstacles.

Their names were James T. Kirk, Superman, and Bond . . . *James Bond*. And boy did these guys ever know how to get things done.[11] Adopting celebrated heroes as role models was irresistible. Each had a commanding approach toward life that brought brute logic and security to senselessly unsure situations. People respected them. They wielded authority over evil doers. There was safety whenever these manly mainstays were around. *If I could just become like them, my world could become safe too. I would make it so.*

There was just one problem. As delightful and terrifically encouraging as those cinematic images of courage were, they weren't real people. Entertainers cannot possibly fill a boy's need for genuine, paternal contact. Here, substitutions fall flat.

Oh, sure, I can tell you about *truth, justice, and the American way*. I've learned about *duty to queen and country*. I am also painfully aware that a man must be prepared to *blow up the Enterprise* if necessary. These are admirable tenets of virtue, certainly. But in the final analysis, my *cinema dads* were, after all, just characters—synthetic figments spilled out of the creative minds of professional screenwriters.

And so, I never did witness in *real life* how to safely meet *real stress* in the *real world*. No matter how hard I pretended, I still never felt genuinely safe or truly prepared. Worse, I resented it. Not my fictional Hollywood heroes, but myself for failing to measure up to them.

I still tried. Eager to abandon the insecurity of our broken Bronx home, I went barreling into the tough, unpredictable business world like I owned the place. Frustration fueled raw ambition. My mind filled with fantasies, and it was easy to mistake them for *The American Dream*. [12] I was unprepared for the stark realities that awaited.

Pressure mounted. Fear set in. Life was soon imploding. Dream turned into nightmare. Though still only twenty-something, stress took my health into decline. Thinking turned headstrong and I was soon tormented by chronic anxiety and depression. [13] But there was relief available. It came through obsessive eating and binge drinking. Drugs, music, and sex entered the scene.

Handicapped by these distractions, but still brimming with piss, vinegar, and cockiness, the self-propelled endeavoring to conquer the world was all about *getting*. I developed an attitude that nurtured blind ambition. Greed, really. Soon money was my God. Business, a temple of worship. There is a healthy way to prosperity. This wasn't it.

There was a constant, underlying feeling that something was not quite right. Because what do British spies, Starfleet Captains, and alien Superheroes know about business anyway? Do they know about getting rich? Not as far as I could tell. They had to be fired and replaced.

Once again, all was not lost. Suitable replacements were readily available. There were the real live, celebrated leaders of business and finance to fill in. Giants whom I admired. No, they couldn't bend steel with their bare hands, command a starship or save the world from evil geniuses bent on destruction and mayhem. But what they knew about enterprise promised to deliver what I really wanted. Power and money. These I equated with the safety I so desperately craved.

The bigger than life, corporate front-runners and CEOs of major companies wrote books about their achievements. They were frequent guests on TV talk shows and the subjects of radio interviews. They wore authority on their sleeves as conspicuously as their bedazzling cufflinks. Most importantly, they seemed so secure. *Oh, God! That is what I want.*

To heck with the TV and movie characters. Guys like Donald Trump and Lee Iacocca were my new heroes. I came to revere the likes of John DeLorean and Bill Gates.[14][15] The lifestyles and examples set by these remarkable men supplied such appealing imagery. I was sure if I did what they did, I'd get what they got. And so out of the annals of celebrity entertainment and business chiefdom, I assembled a secret cabinet of personal motivators. The effect was gratifying and immediate as money, applause, and power arrived in fair measure. *My God. It was working!*

In time, it seemed I was indeed becoming successful.[16] And yet, I never truly felt like the rightful owner of my own accomplishments. Instead of living my own life, discovering my own way on the path to security, I had surreptitiously profited from someone else's ideas of achievement. I hadn't come up with some fabulous invention with which to change the world. There were no enlightening ideas to write about or publish. I didn't even have any practical experience in business, finance, or life. I had no real product to sell. All I had was my panel of personal gurus and fake role models and the fabricated illusion that I was on the path to success.

I'd come under the classic, mistaken notion that sheer enthusiasm and passion were enough, that achievement would alert the world to my *wonderfulness* and people would beat a path to my door, showering me with praise and money. I'd be *discovered*. Well, that didn't happen.

Oh, I was passionate all right. Passionate about achieving prestige and security without the discipline to carry it. Not yet 25 years old and already a fraud. My self-centered entrance-strategy into the highlife was already failing. Miserably. As much money as I could gather, it was never enough to buyout the fear. The plan just never quite came together as I'd hoped.

Poor me. Poor me. Right?

Oh no. Not in the least. The error and the misfortune of my upbringing forced me into something unusual. I stopped looking toward worldly, substitute dads who were appealing from the outside but were short the metaphysical advantage that only a real father can deliver. Instead, I went within. There I found the paternal link and discovered the Source of direction. I became a survivor. Survival gave way to growth, and then to the discipline I had lacked earlier on.

This is not something that happens to everyone. I realize that I'm one of few. Nevertheless, it did happen to me. Everyone receives gifts. I regard this as one of mine. I know it is from God. Dire circumstance has delivered astounding fortune. It is the blessing of *consciousness*, a treasure that endures to this day.

If I could tell you what life is like for me, my wife and children today, it would sound like boasting. I'm not a braggart. But trust me, you'd want what we have—in health, finance and relationships.[17] Subsequently, I've dedicated my life to showing others precisely how they can have the same experience in their own lives.

Does that make me one of those "How To Be a Success" experts, the kind we see all over media these days? Well, yes, in a way, I suppose. I am an authority, but not in the sense to which you may be accustomed. *Some approaches are best left to the prosperity preachers, self-help gurus, and management consultants.*

I am not getting rich selling pickaxes and prospecting pans to gold-diggers. I've really struck the gold myself. I'm well onto the mother lode and begun unearthing the riches of the find.[18] This book is simply a way to share unconditional, free access to the same discovery. Come and get it, anytime. No permission from me is required. *You want what I have, believe me.*

Still, there are those who will be persistent and want to know directly, "Can what I experience through this book make me rich?" Absolutely it can! It already has for many. This book deals with human attitude, showing in no uncertain terms how to discover natural leadership from within and how to let that inner guide steer you in the direction of what is right, good, and yes, even profitable.[19]

Consciousness, at least the kind arrived at by the ambition-free means I'm proposing, will activate the mindset to such a state that yes, you could safely become a multi-billionaire. Many people have become fabulously wealthy as the direct result of what you are about to discover in this book. But I don't lead with a *How to Get Rich* pitch, per se. I'm no prosperity guru. That would appeal to something in you that I have no interest in tempting. In fact, I would much rather see it smashed.

I could just as easily have titled this book, "Meditate Your Way to Riches," or maybe, "Use Your Mind to Make Billions." Catchy, wouldn't you say? The narrative could be easily adjusted to fit this attractive premise. I'd design a mesmerizing meditation exercise to stimulate the pleasure center of the brain, inducing bliss and a positive attitude. And I would sell millions of books. I'd also make millions of dollars. So would many of the more suggestible readers seduced by such titles. But being improperly motivated, they'd also end up very unhappy and ill.[20]

Look, you could become fabulously wealthy or increase your existing affluence through the consciousness I propose. Either is likely. Still, neither is my primary aim or *hook* at this time. The book you're reading now, *Go In*, doesn't focus directly on the material realm. It is a metaphysical proposal. It will drastically affect your material bearing nevertheless. I present both the tool and method that will escort you to the threshold of the door to understanding—beyond classical, personal growth philosophy or spiritual theory, to something much better.

I am going to show you precisely how to access pure and simple consciousness. Once you do, wonderful things begin to happen. Intuition elevates. There's an instant release of resourcefulness such as you could never access before. You won't be able to help but spill creative, positive energy into the stream of life. The great difference between ambition and enthusiasm becomes crystal clear.

In a short while, you'll look back to see how the world and the people around have modified to accommodate your new state of being. Then, going forward, you'll find that you are more productive than you've ever been. Your intellect will ease, giving way to free flowing, inspired reasoning. You'll begin to integrate God-given brain power with intuition as never before. You will even begin to experience unimaginable leverage in personal relationships, not by taking undue advantage of others, but in naturally outmaneuvering their attempts to dominate and control you. As acquaintances polarize around you, it will become clear who your enemies are and who are true friends, without casting judgment on either.

Please bear in mind, this idea is nothing new. It is simple transcendence in its purest form.[21] It's been around for centuries. I didn't invent it. All I've done is discover a simple way to tap into the universal stream of goodwill through consciousness, allowing it to happen. Our world has many mindfully productive people leading useful, inspired lives. These are the business and social disruptors, the inventive captains of innovation. They include certain heads of state, great legal minds, and other celebrated personalities, who while at the top of their games project *awareness* like beacons.

Don't think for a moment that such people are just lucky elites or privileged geniuses born with silver spoons in their mouths.

They aren't overachievers either, high-flyers who've read up on acquiring charisma or, *how to get ahead.* These are individuals who have a special energy emanating outward from inside them. You can sense it. It sets them apart, even from other apparently successful types. How did they get this way? How does that unique energy get inside them? That is simple.

It's so simple in fact, that even before you are through reading this *Introduction* I'm going to show how to discover it for yourself. You'll learn how to connect with a force within that'll allow you to do what you could never do before. This connection will so drastically change your attitude and approach to living, you'll hardly believe it is so.

Not everyone can end up on the cover of next years' *Time* or *Entrepreneur Magazine.* But someone will. You might not wake up one morning to find yourself standing at the helm of a multinational conglomerate. But in time you may. Where you're taken on this journey depends on from where your awakening begins.

Everyone gets a conscious start at birth, that's true, but each life-trip is unique. We all get thrown off course and must experience many new beginnings along the way to help us stay on the path. These fresh starts happen at different junctures and in different ways, but despite what anyone has told you previously, this lifetime *is* a race. Progress has to be made. Let *now* be your time to move forward in a way you would never have thought possible.[22]

No matter what your station in life is right now, mother, father, student, manager, laborer, CEO—simple *consciousness* will place you at the top of your own game, whatever it is. Live consciously and inner brilliance you could never have originated will project from within. You'll accomplish much and experience a fulfilled life from inside your unique wheelhouse. You may even discover an entirely new platform that's different from the one you're on now.

This is quite a claim, is it not? I make it with absolute, experiential confidence. If you go with me on this, everything changes. I mean all.

There is more here than first meets the eye. Along with the extraordinary ideas conveyed in the main narrative of this book, I've also provided an essential tool to use that goes far beyond the face value of the written words. I've included instant access to a simple, consciousness-raising audio exercise that you should begin right away. You might recognize this as a form of meditation, but I assure you it isn't like any *meditation* you've ever seen before, until now.

I call this method *Non-Contemplative Meditation*™. It is a tool that will allow you to live and work at the highest level humanly possible by reconnecting you to the original guidance Source. Through this indispensable metaphysical exercise, you'll be able to experience life-changing *consciousness* while reading along with the book.

I sometimes like to introduce it by making a comparison to the personal computer.

When I was starting my first business the desktop PC was new and widely argued as nothing more than a glorified electronic file cabinet. Some said, "The average person would never embrace it."

Others saw it as a miracle device with the potential to alter the course of the world, destined to become as ubiquitous in the home as the electric toaster or television set.

We now know which of these opinions was correct.

The personal computer is a tool bringing us special technology that frees us from many of life's drudgeries so we can better employ our personal resources. It allows us to live and work in a realm where individual creativity amplifies. It's had a profound effect on all our affairs.

Non-Contemplative Meditation is also a tool. It brings us to a distinctive consciousness that frees us from the drudgery of resentment energy so we can apply intuitive resources without stressful interference. We are released from the bondage of a lower Self, to begin living and working within a realm of existence where understanding is profoundly amplified. It affects us and everyone whose lives we touch. Subsequently, we experience a life that we could never have dreamed possible and contribute toward making the world a better place.

Like the *technological progress* made by the personal computer, it is my vision that *conscious progress*, through personal, non-contemplative meditation, will also become commonplace in every household. It is truly a miraculous metaphysical device that will alter the course of the world as surely as does the computer once it is widely accepted.

You will soon discover that what you're now reading is something special. Treasure it as you would a priceless diamond. Consider and use what you find within these pages, and you'll experience a special form of mindfulness supplying the answers to all issues, bar none.

As you begin to live daily in the awakened state, a new understanding will begin to penetrate and you'll begin to deeply comprehend what is presented in each chapter. Don't rush. Take it one line at a time. One paragraph at a time. One idea at a time. Skip around the chapters too. Resist the silly Ego's tempting to wrap Itself around concepts or to intellectually analyze. Just notice both the comforting and the discomfiting ideas[23] you encounter without becoming emotionally attached to the words of either.

This isn't a book to plow through, gathering material to be pulled out of memory later. You won't be able to. Even if you could, it would be a useless exercise. Go slowly and practice the meditation technique as you proceed.

This book could very well become a bedside companion for a very long time. Just meditate and read a little each day and each new moment will contain fresh disclosure. Many of these will seem to parallel with your reading.

***

I've been very fortunate. Over last several decades, I have witnessed my work alter the course of lives all over the world. This hasn't been by preaching to folks, I am no preacher, but by showing them how to find consciousness through Non-Contemplative Meditation. It's been astounding to watch individuals begin to practice, change and then introduce their families to a new, conscious existence. They've become the real people they were born to be, enhancing the quality of life for themselves as well as their loved ones.

Many are resourceful, successful people looking to boost creativity, improve their professional efficiency, or enhance the quality of their personal relationships. Others are individuals who simply want to enhance their physical health and improve mental outlook. Then, there are those with life threatening compulsions who engage in obsessive behavior for which they've been unable to find a solution.[24]

Whichever is the case, once shown the method I'm going to show you in this book, these individuals discover within themselves an intuitive, regulating life-force. They become effortlessly guided through each moment of each day, with natural insight answering and remedying all their concerns. It's as though they are suddenly un-hypnotized, released from a trance they didn't even realize they were in.

They find they can effortlessly quit smoking or lose weight without dieting. Lifelong compulsions and addictions to substances, certain foods[25] and chemicals are broken. Strained relationships heal. They become naturally healthy in body and mind. Childlike enthusiasm for progress replaces willful ambition. Life peacefully and easily unfolds without struggle.

Of course, you may not have issues as drastically distressing as some individuals. Maybe you're instead driven by a vague sense of uneasiness, some aspect of life you sense could be a stumbling block to further fulfillment. Or perhaps you already lead a productive, contented existence and are just looking to maximize personal output, to become a more effective parent, worker or boss. If this is the case, you are going to be glad you came across this book.

I will show you exactly how it's done, as I have done it and experience the benefits in my own life and in the lives of people I've worked with over the last several decades. Whether your concerns are big or small, terminal or merely inconvenient, I maintain that the resolution to all of them is to simply *become still to discover the answer within.*

For this reason, I've titled this book *Go In*. As the title implies, it's to point you toward your *within*, showing in no uncertain terms precisely how to awaken, but just as importantly, *remain awakened* so you can proceed mindfully forward to have a wonderful life.

I've organized this book into a numerical format corresponding with Chapter numbers. It's *a multi-point proposal*. These "points" aren't rules to follow. Think of them more as predictions, each a token preview highlighting how you might live once you accept the primary proposition. Simply put, this is *to practice the special Non-Contemplative Meditation exercise and becoming God-conscious as the result.* Then, stand back and do nothing. Allow Him to take care of the rest of your life without any further interference from you.

So simple, and yet you will not believe the power and magnifying effectiveness of this idea. It will place you on a plane of existence altering how you interact in this world. It will never be the same. At times your awareness will seem at odds with other's world views. Like a pebble dropped into a pond, you'll disturb the surrounding waters. Some will appreciate it. Others will feel threatened by your vision, but ultimately the waves you make will be for good cause and have a positive effect.

We need more disruptors and innovators. We need more brilliant, invigorated beings whose presence changes the world. My hope is that you and others will embrace this lifestyle. If this were to happen, each individual's personal awakening experience would project inner change outward into the world around. It would form a global collective of blessings. This is the kind of world I want my children to live in. It's the world I want to live in. I'm sure you do too.

Writing this book hasn't been my first rodeo. I've been working this vocation for many years. During that time, I've come to see how some of the ideas I present go very much against the grain of what many people have already been told and believe. Some become upset and even angry with me. (I will reveal the surprising reason for this in a following chapter.)

But I've also seen people experience a sense of identification such as they've never felt before. Once giving this approach to consciousness I've discovered, they take it to heart, give it a fair shake, and the truth transforms them. It is my fervent hope that this book will expand my own usefulness as even more discover my work and find it useful. God willing. The world needs what I offer and it will change because of it. I've committed my life to this cause.

I am a professionally trained, exquisitely experienced salesman. I can sell a product and close a business deal better than anyone. I mean *anyone*. Still, I don't believe I possess the persuasive skills needed to convince you of the need for this. I would love to, but it simply cannot be. It'll have to be your choice. I know that somewhere within, you can sense that there's something exceptional in this book. I am also aware there's something inside saying, "No way! You're doing fine just as you are. You don't need to hear what this Schwarzhoff guy has to say." Still, all I can do is point toward the option.

Each bump in the road exists so we can overcome the rough spots, discovering peace for ourselves by the stress of living through it. Perfection hasn't been handed us on a silver platter. Perhaps for the first man it was, but not for us. He blew it and now we must earn individual perfection for ourselves, then eventually the world, while we can. *Somewhere in the universe, there is a cosmic clock ticking away. Surely, you can sense that.*

Spiritual progress develops with practice. With this book you have the opportunity of a lifetime, for within its pages you are shown the means to safely endure that arduous journey back to the place of our original inheritance.

Through consciousness, your life-path changes. You develop perceptiveness permitting you to realize certain aspects of the past, present, and the imminent *now* you never dreamed you could know. You gain insight without anyone telling you what it is or what to believe about any of it.

At first, some of what you realize may seem a little disconcerting. Some of it won't be. All of it will be truth. If truth is what you're looking for, it's well worth some initial discomfort. Endure. What is at stake? Enlightenment, and a way of life leading to a productive, peaceful existence beyond anything you could experience prior to waking up.

What we call *enlightenment* literally means to *make illuminated* inside, to *in-lighten*. It's simply an English word describing the state of conscious awareness where we are metaphysically severed from a connection to the intellectual Self and instead experience intuitive reconnectivity with our Creator's will.[26]

As you begin to increasingly live in the awakened state, you become impervious to despair, fear, anxiety, and depression. Health improves. You know physical, mental and emotional wellness. Behaviors regulate. Latent virtues are enhanced while simultaneously, imperfections of character begin to diminish.[27] These are the benefits of true enlightenment. It isn't knowledge. Neither is it the mere elimination of ignorance. It is much more powerful than either of these.

Enlightenment is independent of the thinking mind. It isn't a feeling. There is no emotionality about it. We aren't looking for a sign that we are reacting the right way, doing the right thing. We aren't straining to hear the voice of God as though He might motivate us by whispering uplifting words into our minds. We don't feel *holy* or *spiritual* once we've been enlightened. Enlightenment works inside in a subtle way, barely noticeable to us in real time.

In practicing God-consciousness, Light enters, becoming a noticeable energy within. This is the *inner light* spoken of by ancient mystics. It's real. You feel it. You see it. This Light is not a metaphor for knowledge. We literally *light up* inside with understanding. Intuitiveness flows via our connection with the Creator's expression of His will on earth, through us. As this occurs, we are *enlightened*. We become full of grace. This sounds wonderful, of course.

But no words can adequately describe the experience. This goes beyond the meditation practice, flowing daily into all our affairs.

Through *enlightenment*, life becomes more ordered and peaceful, not artificially by willful conduct, but truly and automatically, without any of our own efforts. Once awakened, we simply go forward with our daily living as we did before.

It's only later when we look back do we see how propitious our course has become. Going through life, trudging faithfully, we experience optimism and gratitude, but we never feel special.

Non-Contemplative Meditation activates consciousness, opening the human psyche. This is the metaphysical gateway through which enters all understanding. True insight and solid, internalized education is the result of us becoming receptive to God's will through consciousness.

Intuitiveness, creativity, and vision correspond with a new, heightened sense of awareness. It restores the natural condition—an innate connection with the original Source. It doesn't take much to reach this state. But it's so simple that until you've practiced Non-Contemplative Meditation it can seem challenging.

Do not assume so. Because despite this paradox, I'm going to show you something no one has ever been able to show you before. Follow the straightforward, simple directions, and I predict the results will be what you've always needed and yearn for all of your life.

This is my second book and since writing is my livelihood I will likely produce many more. I hope you become one of my regular readers. Before that happens, it may be appropriate to answer a question I'm often asked, "How do you know this?" *I know this* the way *you will know this* too, if you take me up on the key proposal of this book. Once we become awake, aware and conscious, we perceive truth as understanding downloads into the psyche as streaming, divine data. It's wordless, emotionless and subtle. Once you become still, you'll know too.

If you are now ready to return as a little child and discover how to refurbish and maintain the misplaced gift, you'll find it's as simple as becoming still and looking inside your own psyche. It is there that all answers await.

Please take advantage of what I offer. If you do, you'll begin experiencing life changing, mindful-consciousness from the first day you begin. Family, work and social milieus follow in kind, corresponding with your inner being as you transform from within. This will happen without any effort other than beginning the Non-Contemplative Meditation™ practice I propose.

See What I Mean?

You are about to learn of an incredible journey you didn't even know was possible. You are invited to take it right now and if you do, the experience will change your life in a way that would not be otherwise possible.

Right from the start...

You'll become more productive through inspired reasoning, exploiting brainpower as you never have before.

You'll experience incredible leverage in all personal relationships. They could be business, romantic or social—each will improve drastically.

Your intuition will reach new heights. An unseen, positive power affecting others will emerge from within. It'll flow through and out from you automatically in ways you won't always see and much of the time need not know.

Before long, you'll see how the world and people around have already modified, accommodating your new state of being without any pressure from you.

The life choices you make can ultimately never be wrong once they cease being decisions at all, but are clear choices unfolding on an obvious event path.

The path you are on is different from any other you could imagine or create for yourself. It will open to you once you learn how to go within in a very special way.

As you proceed through this book, read without prejudice. Feel free to peruse at first, to meander. Perhaps pick up on something resonating within, causing you to realize, "Oh my God. Consciousness is what I need. I want to awaken and stay awake for life!" Then allow me to show you how it's done.

All it takes is a few minutes each day. It's amazingly effective. It's fast acting. It's outrageously simple. I've done it myself. I'm still on the journey. I live this way. Perhaps it is your time now.

If you feel you're ready then come join me, will you? Let's get straight onto the first chapter to make the first Point.

Point One

The First Chapter

By which you are asked to consider, "Are you really who you think you are?" Probably not.

Steve Jobs didn't have to take classes to learn how to become Steve Jobs. Neither did Jeff Bezos. Mark Zuckerberg, Ronald Reagan, Donald Trump. Whether you like their personalities, agree with their methods, share in their world views or not is irrelevant. These are people whose unique brands of natural brilliance have each altered the course of the world.

They're visionaries in their respective fields, who've challenged the obvious paradigms[28] and opened doors we don't even know exist. The internal intensity and influence they wield aren't part of some charade. They don't force or strain to push their inner drive or inspiration. They aren't mimicking anyone else. Nor is the essence of what they demonstrate a learned behavior, injected through study and training. They are themselves, and all for which they're known comes naturally. The force behind what they do and how they exist can't be learned or taught. Some people just have natural brilliance which they carry into any situation. They stand out even among the already outstanding.

Individuals like these bring to the table a quality others never can. It is the projection of a light existing inside them—a brightness from within, shining outward onto us. It illuminates our world and the brilliance changes us. Through their personal endeavoring, we become the fortunate beneficiaries of what could never have been foreseen. Ironically, not even entirely by them. Even visionaries see ahead only so far.

They aren't egomaniacs straining to become world-class leaders in their fields.[29] True, oftentimes they become *bigger than life* characters. But what distinguishes these people from over-ambitious, highflying *also-rans* is that instead of being driven by raw ambition, they aspire to reach their full potential in each moment, living in the present. They're just people pursuing their own personal interests, *now*. They progress on their life path one moment at a time, and to them, each step in the journey is the only obvious next one.[30]

Bezos didn't set out to create the Amazon.com we know today. He simply wanted to be in the online bookstore business. Steve Jobs was a middle-class schoolboy who needed to build an electronic frequency counter for a class project. Ronald Reagan was a radio sports announcer and just showed up for a Warner Bros. screen-test one day.

At this very moment, some unique individuals armed with the yield of their abilities are ushering humanity beyond the moon, into the far reaches of outer space. They will expand human presence and enterprise into the cosmos the way voyagers like Cabot, Columbus and Vespucci helped lift humanity's quality of life, expanding European culture around our world.

Right now, someone is pounding away on a MacBook keyboard, writing the next great novel that will spawn an avalanche of sequels, lunch-boxes, action figures and theme parks, not to mention a multi-billion-dollar franchise of movies and a legacy of yet unknown actors whose fame will span decades.

Another person is, right now in the throes of inventing a new technology none of us have ever heard of before. It will forever be remembered for playing a pivotal role in world history and changing how future generations live. It will be as earth-shattering as television, personal computing, Smartphones and electric light.

When we live moment to moment, each second mounts into minutes, the minutes into hours, days become years. Eventually, we have the construct of a lifetime. If we've lived consciously, those days comprise a level of personal productivity that to others, seems extraordinary. To us, all is *just in a day's work.* From those who live this way, we see earth-shaking achievement like advances in medicine, world peace, Smartphones. Even an Amazon.com or a SpaceX becomes possible.

Through a force springing out of a notable few, the future of the world will continue to bend and modify for the benefit of many. These are not holy people or hapless benefactors of good luck. They aren't supermen and women. Neither are they saints or perfect human beings. They are simply conscious. And they are rocking our world.

We can respect how these creative geniuses rearrange common ideologies like magic. There are practical lessons we can learn from some of their methods for sure. But try as they might, no politician will ever be able to duplicate what Ronald Regan did as President of the U.S. and in the world political arena. There will never be another *Beatles.* No one will ever be able to create a behemoth class of Internet retail business that Bezos is building.

You cannot truly become like another person through study and emulation. Try it, and all you'll ever be is an inferior knockoff of another human being.[31]

No one will ever decode Apple's *secret* management system and begin knocking out ridiculously useful consumer products the way Steve Jobs did. That's because there's no code to decipher. There isn't any secret business strategy or marketing approach to purloin. Even sophisticated business people cannot fathom how Jobs accomplished what he did with Apple. *They try. Oh, they try.* They are wasting their time.

No one, except those who discover what you are realizing now through this book, will ever know how any of the truly inspired masterminds do what they do, as well as they do. That is because what they do comes from within their being. It isn't rooted in intellectualism. It's a reflection of human consciousness that cannot be recreated. All attempts can only produce counterfeits.

No matter how useful and wonderful the products, if it weren't for the consciousness of Steve Jobs, there would be no Apple today. No iPhone. No iPad. No MacBook.[32]

Those who tap their inner source for energetic vision work independently of the paradigms we typically associate with triumphant success. What energizes this type of individual isn't self-generated or faked. It's a magical force, the fruit of which can then be shared with the world.

Magic is real. And it isn't limited only to the world's most eminent figures. There are multitudes of individuals who aren't in the public eye, living and working in smaller social milieus. There are probably some remarkable people in your life, not in the least borne of privilege but who still exemplify this quality. Consider certain teachers, employers, friends you admire—or perhaps even some people you don't admire so much. They're raising families, running small businesses and serving the communities in which they live.

These are the exceptional personalities we all know, people we meet in business and social settings who project natural clarity and brightness. You can see it in their eyes. You can hear it in their speaking. It is even reflected in the lives of their children. The personal magnetism of these attractive individuals expresses through the creative thought of anyone who is not a slave to their thinking mind.

They've discovered how to access intellect without becoming inexorably attached to reasoning and thus, developed a keen knack for conveying intuitiveness. Using language and an energetic force from within, inspired reasoning drives outward into the surrounding world.

This isn't mere spillage of thought. For these people, mind, tongue and communication skill all merge into one simple projection of dynamic creativity. From within, inspired essence forms a very distinct bundle of *genius*, coalescing out of consciousness rather than out of pure intellect. A virtuoso nature arises and a productive domain naturally forms around them. It isn't just *smarts*. It isn't will. It truly is magic, and it evokes out of *consciousness*.

These types use the mind as the practical apparatus it is intended to be, not as a source of information but as a means for transmitting information they don't even know they know until they know it.

Then they tell us. If we're lucky.

Once intuitiveness combines with a desire to be helpful and improve the world, profound creativity pulls out of pure consciousness. This is how God uses us for His good. Though it may appear to other people that we're accomplishing extraordinary things, we aren't. But He is.

The question is, "Can you become one of these prolific types?" My answer is, "Yes, you can, and, yes you will," if you choose to take me up on the proposition offered in this book, to awaken and become *you*. Not some picture of yourself fabricated in the mind. Not who parents, teachers, gurus or mentors have told you—but the real you, who exists only *now*.

You can become an authentic *you*, as creatively inspired and successful as the world-renowned visionaries. But you'll emulate no one. Not their achievements. Not their lifestyles. Not their personalities. You'll just be you. You could become famous or remain a private success. That will depend on career positioning and the lifestyle path you take. But once becoming who you are for real, you will be one of us. Ironically, as genuine prosperity spans the spectrum of human affairs you'll also become a subject of emulation for others.[33]

That cannot be helped.

Whether you're a celebrity, rich or poor, man, woman or child—we each carry the same spiritual DNA in our make-up. We're all brothers and sisters sharing a single metaphysical code of human composition, permitting us to awaken, bringing forth into the world power and positive energy from within.

John Lennon once wrote that all we need is love and that through love we can learn how to be who we really are and realize where we belong in the universe. He was correct on all three counts. But there's one essential piece to this perennial rock hymn John left out—there is a prerequisite to love.

Realizing our true identity and the place each of us has in the order of creation requires we first come to consciousness. Without that, we'll never know what love is nor will we experience it. Consciousness clears the way for love to enter and fill us.

Once it does, all heaven[34] breaks loose in our lives. We become conduits for goodwill and grace. Our life's path changes course, altering the nature and quality of the journey in unimaginable ways. Rather than struggling to create happiness and bliss, as it turns out all we need is to awaken. Then we know true serenity and peace.

Either we dedicate our existence to living within the realm of consciousness, becoming prodigious winners, or we don't. Unless we do, we'll remain unconscious subjects of fate, fraught with mediocrity and dissatisfaction. Then, the world cannot possibly benefit from our best. No matter how hard we try, we'll never experience the creativity or high energy essential to working hard, naturally and humbly toward a successful life. Nervous energy will run us ragged, into an early grave.

In committing to consciousness, we move beyond thinking and wishing or praying for success and happiness. Instead, we begin to effortlessly experience the security we once chased. First, we discover within us a courageous energy to make the single epic choice that every human being must face in this lifetime. Then, in choosing correctly, success becomes instantaneous.

The more we continue living by that choice, the longer success endures and the wider the positive influence our fortunes will have in the world—through us.

There aren't any *keys to success* in life. Search for one and you won't find it. If anyone tells you they'll sell it to you, they're disingenuous. All the so-called "keys" to success are counterfeits, just fabrications of metaphoric fantasies created to open an imagined lock that doesn't even exist. The capacity for success is already within you. Simply step up to the door. Choose to enter. It's never locked.

What I propose is that you make that choice now. Let the same brightness that the innovators possess also flow into you. Then sit still, allowing that Light to purge whatever might prevent you from being *you*. Begin right now. It's so simple.

It isn't tied to any religion, culture or tradition. It doesn't belong to any exclusive, spiritually elite class. There aren't any elites. There aren't any religious gatekeepers. There are no legitimate gurus either. All spiritual cults are fraudulent.

The benefits of consciousness are for everyday people like you and me. We only need to access it as we once did when we were still children. Being awake allows Light inside to drive out darkness. It cleanses. It removes anger. It restores your original virtue, free of the emotional imbroglio of resentment. You become as a child once more. Before the world surrounds them to snuff out their inner Light, children are the most enlightened beings on earth. Who wouldn't like to get back to that?

***

It's likely that you are very curious by now. So, what follows is a brief metaphysical primer on the reason why what I propose in this book works. In the next few paragraphs, you will learn of an incredible truth. Don't believe it. Don't disbelieve it either. But since all else in this book depends on this understanding, then at least please know that I believe it. Simply acknowledge how my belief allows me to write the things I do. This is necessary so that what you read in this book will make sense in the way that I intend. Otherwise, everything revealed here will take on a different meaning.

Be forewarned. You could be in for a bit of a shock, especially if you've been a *seeker*[35] for a while and already done a bit of investigating. You won't find what you are about to read anywhere else. Look to spiritual books or self-help pundits for validation of what you are about to learn, and you will not find it. They don't know, and if they do, they certainly won't tell you. That would mean losing their loyal following.

If what I claim is true, then much of what you've ever been told about life and living, death and dying as well as all human purpose is about to receive a major overhaul. For the moment, make no judgment about what I am about to disclose. You may have already suspected a good deal of it anyway.

Were you to read nothing but these next five pages and practice the exercise proposed, in a very short time you'd have the whole thing. That alone would germinate into a body of wisdom and understanding comprising all you'll ever need to have a wonderful life. Your course would change for the better in ways you cannot now envision.

In hopes that you'll begin practicing right away, even before you finish reading this book, allow me now, right here at the start, to give away the elemental secret to *consciousness*. It's simple to grasp.

You see, you were born into an imperfect culture, flawed and often hostile. You could have been an infant king thrust into royalty, surrounded by the splendor of a regal palace, or you may have been an unwanted child, born in a third world ghetto. It would make no difference. By its very nature, all the world sets up into environments teeming with both negative and positive energy. Then, through no fault of your own, the negative energy in your surroundings got inside you. You were infected.

By *no fault*, I mean to say the instigators of negativity were other people whose selfishness overwhelmed your innocence. It was most likely a parent who first did it. The moment anyone or anything caused you to become upset, you were at once imprinted with the brutality of a tormentor. It breached your inner security, rendering you traumatized and sensitive to the cruelties of the world beyond the initial event.

Once infected, uncertainty spread within you. We are all born with a natural, spiritual guidance system, but now you underwent a systematic disconnection from insightful direction. Your intuition was impeded and you began to doubt yourself.

You didn't know this was happening. You felt uncomfortable and in defense, retreated into intellect, becoming entangled with thoughts inside your head. This marked the beginning of a dulled state of consciousness that left unchecked, will haunt you till your dying day.

Even now, as you are pulled into thinking, you believe you've been successful at managing life. It isn't true.[36] By exacting strings of little traumas, influencers learn to ensnare and manipulate you in ways you do not know. They are family, loved ones, people you work with. Among these include counselors, psychiatrists, preachers, and teachers. On a larger scale, they are the politicians, governments, and media.

Each causes you to react. In time, you become conditioned to respond emotionally with resentment. This is the well-known "people, places, and things," problem with which so many people identify.

Come back from the intellectual apparatus of your thinking mind to receive inspired reasoning. Return from the past and future to *now*, where you discover how simple it is to stop hating the unfairness. Wake up. Then problem people and situations cease being problems. Instead of others controlling and manipulating your course through their lack of kindness, you'll now begin to grow in tolerance and patience, meeting each cruel encounter with grace. No one can intimidate or upset you when you are grounded in conscious awareness.

Many of us have been trained to think of the Ego as a part of us—just one of the multiple facets that comprise the complex human personality. Counselors, clerics, and teachers believe this. Your doctor believes it. Everyone coming out of the universities believes it too.

Despite the prevalence of this idea, their beliefs are only theoretical—incomplete at best. They have no idea what the Ego is and their speculating about It has led to much misunderstanding about the nature of human suffering.

The word ego just means, "I myself." It is taken directly from Latin, first coined by a German physician named Georg Groddeck, who was an early 20th Century pioneer in psychosomatic medicine. Professionals like Groddeck, examining the human psyche have long recognized that *some Thing* is there and whatever that is, it holds enormous command over thinking and human behavior. But they haven't been successful in identifying its nature or very much of its enormous significance. All they have is the label they've put on it. They've dubbed it, the "Ego", but have no idea what it is. With few exceptions, everything you've ever read or been told about the Ego has been untrue. That is, until now, the day you've come to discover the truth in this book.

We can still use their word. There's nothing wrong with it. But we can also discover what it is, and we had better because Ego is not some psychological aspect of the human mind as many suppose. It is far more nefarious.[37]

What some term as "Ego" is a metaphysical identity. It's the dark, alien nature of *Something*, sometimes pegged as *Pride*, expressing inside each of us. It is a lower *Self* that's taken up residence within our psyches.[38] It pretends to be us, or at least some fragment of our human makeup, but It is neither. It's a parasitic foreigner, an inhuman entity having no life of It's own except that It lives vicariously through us. It even speaks to us, uttering by way of the thoughts inside our heads, as we mistakenly identify with It.

We believe It to be us. Thus, we are fooled by a terrible ruse— our eyes, our ears, our bodies cease serving our Creator's will and we begin to serve the will of Darkness, totally unaware that we've been deceived.

This dark, intrusive intelligence carries on the charade for as long as we remain unmindful of It. Meanwhile, It feeds and nurtures off whatever resentment energy It can instigate through our thoughts and actions. Our life becomes It's life. We go from innocent and childlike to angry and judgmental, God-separated beings. Left alone and rudderless we are lost, without discipline, direction or intuitive guidance. The quality of our lives becomes pitted with ailment and heartache when it could be characterized by well-being and joy.

This is part of a metaphysical etiology out of which all the troubles of mankind stem, originating with the psychic infection of resentment. This is the very description of what is often termed as "spiritual disease."

While our spirit entity remains intact in this realm, it is the spirit's conscious connectivity with God that has become infected, damaged and unable to communicate with Him. A Dark Phantom Self rises to take charge. As life goes on we become increasingly desensitized to Its presence, until one day we can no longer distinguish where we begin and It ends. Our true identity becomes blurred and we slowly go mad.[39]

This creature will do anything to make sure that you or anyone reading this right now do not believe what I've just told you. It perverts religious teaching, psychological analyses, and spiritual philosophies to conceal and invalidate all of this.

It will mutter in your own voice, or perhaps the voice of a parent, discrediting and castigating anyone who dares reveal this to you. It rebels against truth because It needs to remain undetected or at least mischaracterized so as to continue replicating Itself in our children and our children's children.

The Ego is an inhuman, spiritual entity, projecting the nature of a nefarious intelligence. It is not a psychological feature of humanity. Do not be misled by whatever suppositions the proponents of such theories advance. Without this base insight, all views stemming out of conventional theory will be erroneous. Any book you read, any lecture you hear, any philosophy you learn of, any motivational speaker who speaks of Ego without this understanding, is worthless.

It's likely that misconceptions have already occurred. If that is the case, then please observe any insolent attitude that may arise from this moment on. A whole new set of sensibilities is about to come into view. Your perception of how you've lived up until now, of the world and its people will begin to make more sense than it ever has. You may even discover that many of the secret suspicions about life and the world you've dared not ever tell a soul have been correct all along.

As you can see, most of us aren't who we think we are. And don't know it.

Psychiatric wards and prisons are filled with highly perceptive, but overly sensitive people who've gotten a glimpse of the truth about the inner human condition. They simply haven't been able to break free from the controlling influence of the Dark Self within them. And so, they're driven mad by the conflict of knowing but not accepting the truth of what's gotten ahold of them.[40] It's taken over their thinking and behavior to such an extent they've become a danger to themselves or others. People who commit murder and suicide are frequently highly intelligent. As Aristotle is thought to have once observed, "No great mind has ever existed without a touch of madness." Some become more *touched* than others.

Unless we awaken, an unholy nature within continues the masquerade, pretending to be us. The imposter turns us into Self-centered, spiritually sick wretches, wreaking havoc in our lives and the lives of those unfortunate enough to have anything to do with us.

Got it? Good. Because unless you do, *It* will *get* you. I do realize some of this may sound like a science fiction movie script or a tale out of Stephen King's nightmares. But this isn't fiction. It's all a terribly true scenario into which we're all born.

You may have heard religious people refer to this as being "born in sin." What I've just described is all that this expression means. It's a curse upon all mankind. Until you have the means to reconnect with the Source of inspired guidance, it is impossible to reverse. Yet once you discover how to become mindfully conscious in the special way I will show you, the curse is broken.

This is why it is so vital that you know who you are, allowing the Light of consciousness to illuminate and separate the real you from the dark *not you.*

Each time you practice consciousness, you become released from the confines of the thinking mind. Non-Contemplative Meditation works by placing you in a protective state of neutrality where you are the observer of thinking, apart from the constant stream of thought.

You become free to understand beyond sheer intellectuality. You become *you* once again, as you were when you were a little child. This is the spiritually awakened condition people often call *the 4th dimension of existence.* It's an elusive place many speak of but precious few ever seem to truly experience.

But now you will experience it. It'll change your life and the lives of everyone you touch, beginning the moment you first meditate in the manner shown. Then if you continue, for the rest of your life.

With just little practice, rather than drowning in the stream of thought, consciousness begins to rise above thinking and intellect. It's much like a surfer who rides an energy packed ocean wave. He doesn't tame the wave. He doesn't become overwhelmed by the wave. He is the rider atop the wave, exploiting natural waveform. He doesn't move forward by his own power. The surfer maintains stillness, intuitively balancing natural forces contained within him with those of his environment. In exploiting energy rising from within, he is kept dry and elevated, driven safely forward through time and space.

Likewise, God-consciousness converts the destructive energy potential packed into hectic and morose thinking into a new resourcefulness promoting progress effortlessly. Once we rise above thinking, we gain insight. We become mindfully vigilant of our existence. We perceive everything around us with clarity. The irrelevance of our old thinking is seen through new eyes. Our vision unites with His. Activities once requiring the exertion of great energy become effort-free. We move forward, propelled by the same pressures that might otherwise overwhelm and ruin us. A creative force that's not of our doing emerges from within.

To experience this unbridled resourcefulness all we need to do is be awake for it and allow a new state of awareness to safely lift us away from stress—to *save us*, so to speak. Now, the pressures of daily living placed upon us transforms from stressfulness into ingenuity.

Effort is the human spoiler—faith, the divine restorative.

Brainpower combines with intuition, both now serving their intended vital functions. Our finite brain can no longer override the infinite spirit. We recover once lost divine reasoning. We experience a re-prioritizing of power within, inspiring the fulfillment of all human purpose. Along with the spiritual utility of inspiration also lies our willingness to accept the gift of consciousness.

This is the *where and how* of all inventiveness and fruitful production. The mindful state establishes a perspective from where everything is obvious and there aren't any decisions to make. There's no fearful fretting over imagined errors. There isn't any fantasizing about the glories of impending achievement either. Each moment serves in its own time, *now*, revealing God's vision for us in *the present*.

The knack for existing in this state is an inimitable quality that all true visionaries possess. The innovator maintains a predisposition for knowing just what to do in each moment, free from the drag of emotional ties. He does not foresee the future as much as he allows for consciousness, so he experiences each event as it unfolds before him. As each moment comes, he's ready for it.

Jobs is only Jobs. Zuckerberg is only Zuckerberg. Bezos is only Bezos. Trump is only Trump. Likewise, you are meant to be only you. Try to be anyone else, through emulation or by sucking on their energy and your failure is immediate. Remain true to your genuine identity and failure is not even possible. You gain the vision to spot opportunities as they pass before you, whereas before, you would never have noticed them. *You are ready.* I've just outlined the complete secret of dynamic creativity. There's nothing else to know about it.

To the extent that we remain mindfully aware people, we live mentally and physically robust lives. We're clear from the debilitating outcomes of negative emotions as our fears fall away like dead leaves off an autumn tree. A powerful immunity to stress evolves within and we discover freedom from the damaging effects of emotionality. Compulsive behavior and obsessive thinking become a thing of the past. We aren't stepping on the toes of our fellows, causing harms wherever we go. We don't make strings of poor life decisions. We have solid, enriching relationships with others—whether romantic, business or social.

We are without morbid habits like chronic overeating, over-sexing, smoking, drinking alcohol and drugging, not because we're forced or coerced not to do these things. We just lack any need for them. For us, there's no longer any therapeutic satisfaction to be found in nicotine, alcohol, food or indulgent behavior because we aren't demanding fulfillment out of the world. Our fulfillment is already here as we exist moment to moment.

16

We don't need antidepressants, therapy or counseling to assist and make us feel better. We exhibit intuitive discipline, without emotional encumbrances, making our way peacefully and with confidence on life's path. We display a brightness, outshining all our human defects, not demanding sainthood or the immediate perfection of character. All it requires is a conscious awareness, continually improved through regular exercise.

The subject matter in this book is not to be trifled with. I cannot overstress how important it is that you appreciate this. Consciousness through meditation isn't some plaything to be tested by whim. What you will find here goes to the realm of powerful metaphysics where the unbiased observation of the world can be startling. You'll become aware of certain forces, some of them quite ugly, which you've never noticed before. Or if you have, you've compulsively suppressed any annoyance and frustration. But be assured that if you're earnest in yearning for spiritual progress and truth, you'll recognize it when you see it. You'll meet these in safety.

Mindful consciousness through Non-Contemplative Meditation™ safely accesses the most powerful force in the universe. You'll experience a spontaneous release from hypnotic influences you haven't yet realized have already gotten ahold of you. The exercise will free you from all prior suggestions placed upon you through the exciting clamor and stress of the world, both seen and unseen. It'll unhitch your thinking, perhaps for the first time in your life, allowing you to fully grasp what is written in this book at a level beyond intellect.

I would like the chance to show you exactly how it's done.

Consciousness is synonymous with awakening. It's a metaphysical experience where we emerge out of a psychic trance we don't even realize we're in. Once it happens, we see. We change. Now exposed, the false Self shrinks, losing It's gripping influence over our thinking and behavior. We become who we were born to be, and thereafter cannot help but exhibit goodwill. We wordlessly sense truth, receiving the power to live confidently, carrying positive will and vision into the world without effort.

Where previously we justified a strange attachment to instinct and reaction, we now live by wordless intuition, free from the burden of painful emotions. Other people lose their power to control us. We are liberated from our tyrants. *They hate that.*

What once stressed us toward death, anger, fear, and remorse, now gently coaxes us toward life as we overcome their fatal effects on our mind and body. This is a completely new lifestyle—a metaphysically healed existence. We're no longer spiritually diseased. Health spontaneously restores. Even life-threatening ailments are reversed and cured while the body's immune system maximizes.

Relationships mend in response to selfishness dropping away. Vices and gross addictions fall while obsessions mitigate and dissolve—as if into thin air. We grow in usefulness to our Creator and to others. It's mystical. Call it magic if you like.

Know Who You Are. Be You. Only You

Who are you? Consciousness places us into a mindful state of neutrality where we separate from the confines of the thinking mind. We reconnect with inner vision. In realizing your identity, you gain an uncommon understanding of yourself and others. Who you are and what you are to become is revealed. Strengths, as well as shortcomings, are exposed. This is truth. It's real. It's vital. It's magical.

18

Point Two

The Second Chapter

By which everything you need for a peacefully whole, productive life arrives effortlessly and automatically, just by giving up the ambitious struggle to get it.

We spend all our lives facing challenges and overcoming problems of all kinds. There are financial difficulties, bad relationships, and health issues. There are also satisfying financial dealings, stable relationships, and fine health. Life is a mixed bag, presenting degrees of challenge. Unless we meet each kind of encounter properly, they interfere with our emotional stability.

We may not even be aware that we've been upset until symptoms appear. Behavioral difficulties crop up. We acquire bad habits, addictions and even worse, debased lifestyles we know are causing us to become unhealthy and unhappy. Yet despite the harms we inflict on ourselves and others, no matter how hard we try, these behaviors seem impossible to conquer.

Unmanageable obsessions develop. We do what we don't want to do and then continue to do them even though they're harmful and undesirable. Obsessive thinking leads to mental confusion. The consequences can vary. Sometimes these obsessions wreak outright havoc in our lives, other times just mild frustrations. Either way, there is discord and unhappiness. To restore order, these obsessions must go. But before that can happen it will help to know exactly what these overpowering modes of thinking and behavior are.[41]

There is more than one way to use the word *obsession.* Psychologists have their clinical definition. Romance and mystery novelists often have their own tawdry portrayal. When I use the word *obsession* I describe each of these at once, but then some.

There are certain behaviors, *you know what they are,* that you are unable to stop, which seem more to be *doing you* than you are *doing* them. It is my intention to introduce an extraordinarily simple technique that will change that, beginning right now. Keep an opened mind,[42] and not only will you soon discover how to overcome obsessive behavior, but also just about any challenging issue you might have.

First things first. No matter what is testing you now—it could be a stubborn vice like smoking or overeating, the pain of a failing relationship, a financial issue, substance abuse like binge drinking or a drug addiction—the only way you'll conquer it permanently is to stop trying to overcome it.

I realize how counterintuitive this sounds. The fact is that nothing will ensconce a difficulty into your life more firmly than struggling against it. If you would like to overcome emotionally induced conditions like anxiety, worry, and depression, again I say, "Stop trying." What I'm asking you to do from here on in, is to set aside all willful effort to solve your problems—just for the time being. If you've been very ambitious in the past, giving up *trying* may prove to be difficult at first. It'll feel unnatural to you.

However, once you acquire a simple knack of least resistance it will become easier and the answers to so many problems will appear all on their own. Solutions to even the most daunting situations will become plain. From major calamity to minor nuisance, by eliminating struggle, you'll discover inner access to answers you never had before. The cause of any issue will lose whatever impious grip it has, if you'll just follow the directions given.

When I say, "Stop trying" I mean it literally, in both a physical and a mental sense. Should you become an apathetic do-nothing? Of course not. Life should be active, full of accomplishment, failures, setbacks, and triumphs. It is only the willful way of approaching problems that cannot stand. I teach my children to always *swing for the fences* because it is the attitude behind the action that makes the difference—not in the outcome, but in whether one survives the endeavor with their integrity intact, or not.

Look, there's no denying that human effort works well in many situations. It can be properly used for solving math problems, making money, weight lifting, or marathon running. It takes patience and lots of energetic moxie to start and run a business, raise a healthy family, or effectively manage a staff. Heck, you can't get a driver's license, an engineering degree or learn to cook in a restaurant kitchen unless you take positive action.

But when it comes to overcoming behavior, specifically those caused by obsession, any ambitious effort to defeat objectionable conduct always fails. Struggle succeeds only in distracting us away from seeing the real cause and unless you get to that, the chance of truly solving any obsessive problem remains nil.

This is why nearly all those who go on elaborate weight reduction diets ultimately end up heavier. It's also why so many smokers trying to give up their drug will end up increasing nicotine intake. They try to scheme or outwit a lover to repair a failed relationship. None of it works. It's an odd paradox. You become worse through effort. Many people have bitter experiences with this frustrating phenomenon, but as you read on you'll be introduced to a better way, one that works for eliminating all obsessive behavior.

The reason *trying* ultimately makes us worse rather than better is because our efforts are too often built on a flawed understanding of underlying causes of the problems we are trying to solve. We've all been preconditioned to seek wrong solutions to life's obstacles.[43] We are compelled to grab the bull by the horns, as though we might wrest problems into compliance.

Human effort of this order imparts willfulness into all we do. It is the metaphysical contaminant that spoils everything. Where we try to bring order, there comes disorder. Where there'd otherwise be harmony, there is discord.

Whenever we are willfully ambitious, irresistible impulse rises within. We're compelled to shape and mold circumstances to Self's satisfaction, feeding a primordial hunger to feel like God. Even with the best intentions, any effort to do good can never finish well. It only fuels selfish motivation by negative energy, validating the Ego Self's longing to control—as God controls. Ultimately, this *playing God* brings suffering and despair to anyone attempting to assume the role. We may believe we are serving God, and in a way, we are. But it is Self, *as God* who receives our loyalties. We begin to serve Self alone.[44] What a desolate, dark existence this is.

In America, we hold a rightful reverence for the "self-made" man, who's relied upon ingenuity and discipline, aspiring toward success by the sweat of his brow. His achievements bring security and fulfillment to himself and others. It's true that some of us become quite self-serving in this capacity but many others do not. Success does not automatically mean an individual is a greedy, selfish glutton for personal enrichment. It cannot be denied that ambitious people do seem to get things done. Recognize the great difference between aspiration and ambition. It is found in attitude.

The building of wealth and business assets from the ground up is not the problem. In fact, it's wonderful. However, it is the hidden nature of ambition that contaminates otherwise worthy vocations. Ambition draws energy up from a dark place. Not everyone who's successful deserves it, especially when wealth has been reached in the ambitious service to Self. Even when it appears that short-term progress has been made, there is a long-term degradation of character within the individual who abandons virtue to bask in success.

You see, once ambitious, you disconnect from the inner Source of guidance. Then there's no alternative but to seek substitute sources of motivation. This often works, but only for a while. Despite initial success, ultimately *playing God* never succeeds. Then, after your efforts have failed, you're left holding the bag, dejected, unfulfilled and aching for a fresh fix of new *self-esteem*. There is none to be found. With nowhere to go for answers, this uncomfortable position becomes a moment of truth. If you don't run from it, the pain now becomes a great blessing.

You could turn to people for direction, but no one has legitimate authority within them to provide answers. There is not a person on earth who can give you the emotional security you hope for. Ironically, in transferring reliance for the incentive to do well onto others, you discover that you're becoming even more insecure than ever.

Hidden doubts harbored by counselors, gurus, preachers, friends, motivational speakers, even book authors, project out of them and into you. Their fears become your fears. Dread becomes a constant companion. Soon you are compelled to cling even tighter to them, lapping up their essence looking for strength they also lack. True confidence to deal with the daily demands of life can only come from *with-in*. It can never come from *with-out*. It will never come from people.[45]

Never underestimate indecisiveness. It's nothing to fear. There's power in *not knowing* what to do next or how to control events, without getting bent out of shape over it. It's humbling. Just wait patiently, not resenting *not knowing* and the answers come. Inner direction uncovers the next right thing, and even short-term errors ultimately turn out to be correct, because you aren't making decisions at all. Instead, you effortlessly travel the real-time path as events unfold before you. Choices become obvious and for you, stressful decision making does not exist.

You don't solve problems. They become solved. To observers, it seems you are the miracle worker—some human dynamo of accomplishment. It isn't you. Something coming through you is to be credited. Of course, unless you have allowed that inner direction in and the power to flow, all bets are off and you become subject to chance. You no longer look so smart. Chance is a cruel idiot.

Equally important, know that confidence cannot come from Self. A person who is lost in thoughts, unconscious and unaware cannot be confident and can only be arrogant or cocky.[46] *Selflessness* is vital to peace and survival. In giving up ambition, you abandon a selfish attitude in experiencing true contentment. This isn't to say you should disregard all concern for personal well-being.

For example, you should always drive your car defensively. You should still exercise caution when crossing a street in heavy traffic. Or in business, you must terminate the disloyal or unproductive employee. In raising a child, you need to issue corrective discipline. If performed without rancor, these remain neutral, unselfish positions, allowing us to safely navigate through life with total fairness.

It is the unfair Ego-self that favors only Its own well-being, by placing comfort ahead of any regard for others. While It masquerades as us, we become absorbed with It, cultivating an ego-centric predisposition that seems to seep into all our affairs. Every human being has experienced this kind of despicable selfishness.

Once self-seeking at the expense of other people becomes our custom, honesty in all our affairs evaporates. We become egocentric creatures of habit, operating without ethics in business or personal relationships. People start to catch on. They don't say anything, but they begin to have misgivings about us.

A stubborn fidelity for Self begins to form, assuring that we care for no one before our own security. Others will sense the narcissism emerging from within us. We'll lose all good reputation. Even our own children will come to see that they can't trust us to the end. It traumatizes them, as we were once traumatized by our parents.

So, am I suggesting we cannot have *nice things* or experience the benefits that come from ingenuity, hard work, and good willed tenacity? Be assured I'm not. Where would we be if not for creative genius and innovation sparked by the base need to eat and have a place to sleep, to drive a nice car and live in a desirable neighborhood, to fund a superior education or expand an existing enterprise, to compete in the marketplace, launch a new product, or introduce a new technology to the world? America would be a Third World country and the rest of civilization would be denied the fruits of our national resourcefulness.

Certainly, there's room to aspire. At the very least, we all have a natural desire to live a comfortable lifestyle without the heaviness of impending poverty or the strain of bad relationships in a home infested with rancor.

What needs to be questioned, however, is what moves us toward achievement. There *is* a realistic drive for success and growth. It's a natural energy embodying the sweat and payment for humbling oneself in toil. In this instance, we become supernaturally employed. We're put on the payroll of the greatest capitalist venture ever conceived, *Creation, Inc.*, with God at the helm of the Divine Enterprise.

Acquisition and material development become wholesome once we've been freed from covetous longing. There's a sense of accomplishment and security that permeates our work and infuses into family life. In the absence of all greedy influence from a lower Self, we experience personal stability.

But a lust for achievement leads to envy and dishonesty. We may become rich and powerful and yet fail in virtue as human spiritual beings. When the fruits of honest labor are legitimately earned, success becomes healthy, benefiting the individual as well as the world. Contaminated by the slightest deceitfulness, success, whether in business, career or relationships, always devolves into ultimate failure.

Certainly, we can experience a balance between material comfort and spiritual condition. Under the right circumstances, wealth coexists well with human virtue—but it cannot be an artificial, arranged marriage. It's got to be a spontaneous union, absent of pretense and avarice. When creativity and intuition blend, they fuel the human-spiritual engine.

There rouses a seemingly endless supply of physical stamina and productivity. The corporate manager rises to the top of his organization, inspiring others. A CEO leads a company to profitability, becoming the darling of shareholders. A political groundbreaker spearheads policy decisions lifting a nation out of economic chaos, into a prosperous era. There are no limits to where this kind of moral dynamism can take a person, a business, a family, or a nation.

Consciousness allows natural equilibrium to develop between physical comfort and self-sacrifice. Then, true confidence overrides the need for ambitious effort. Rather than struggling with decisions, the obvious path unfolds before our eyes. In the present moment, selfish desire simply cannot rise to denigrate the virtue of a humble heart.

Once we're no longer overrun by self-centeredness, the absence of ego-centric intention gives rise to an unwavering expression of boundless creativity. It wells up from within. We begin to think and act for the benefit of the world. We still have to remain on guard for others who cannot live from this realm. There's deceit, greed, and outright wickedness that come to challenge our innovations. Others would quickly rob all from us if not for the protection of conscious awareness.

Have you ever found yourself doing business with a crooked business person? There are people who would just as soon lie and cheat you out of all you own as engage in a single honest transaction—who cannot ever tell the truth because there's none in them. If they ever are straightforward, it is only for the furtherance of deceit down the road.

Do you know anyone who seems compelled to embellish narratives of otherwise average aspects of their lives?[47] Everything they do is such a complete exaggeration, just to hear the drama becomes a grueling exercise in patience. Or surely, you've encountered people who constantly redirect all discussion back to being all about them, rendering most conversations one-sided and unproductive.

These are some of the characteristics that point to an ambitious nature within. It may be a craving for money. It may be a lust for power. It might want attention. Whichever, be cautious around such individuals. They're people who harbor an overdeveloped Ego personality with an insatiable hunger for *living large.* The larger It gets, the larger the doses of appreciation and approval It needs to maintain a glorious image of Self.

Something dark motivates these individuals. It has no regard for your well-being. It's sense of security will always dominate.

This is a nature that fuels a greedy work ethic and lifestyle of every Wall Street charlatan, political power grabber, and bureaucratic potentate. In time, there will be no low to which such a person won't sink in the furtherance of self-interest, self-development, and empowerment.

By remaining awake and conscious, we are protected from harm by these individuals. Forgive them. They have not learned the secret of life sans ambition. It's a lack of wisdom that eventually causes the demise of every ego-centric personality.[48] The life of an awake person becomes a conduit to do good for others, instead of a manipulating tool where the good works only serve him.

Hollywood celebrities, flamboyant religious leaders, and other media *stars* often experience the influence of corrupted spirituality that comes with ambition. Left unbridled, it can spell personal tragedy, altering behavior in absurd ways and placing them in harm's way. This is why drugs, alcohol, infidelity and emotional disorders are so rampant among entertainers and public figures. It isn't the fast environment. It's the *in*-vironment, a condition within themselves, corrupted long before they become rich, famous or influential. They get sucked into a dark, approval seeking, daydream they don't realize they're in. Their bank accounts and lifestyle may scream "Success!" They are still miserable failures.[49]

Truly successful performing artists in theater and music, creative folks of all kinds discover how to remain true to their inner connection. Star athletes, business leaders performing at the top of their game are productive and creative, good works flowing through and out of the consciousness of the individual.

Creatives and star producers of this ilk have access to energy and the inspiration to *go the extra mile* without ever placing themselves on a pedestal. Though they accomplish great things, they never feel greatness. They don't bask in the glory of their success. Not even in secret. The moment a person feels he is above other people, he becomes a *winning loser*. Progress as a human being ends.

Those who are apparently, but not truly successful, access a different kind of energy. On the surface, they may appear to be creative and happy. They might be active and highly visible in their respective fields of endeavor, garnering acclaim, generating large amounts of cash flow and prestige.

Yet, beneath a veneer of triumph, something sinister goes on within the psyche. These are people with such a deep need for approval, they've *turned pro* to get it. Unlike the truly successful, these *failed successes* hunger for greatness to meet their exaggerated expectation of self-worth. They are compelled to bask in usefulness, in being needed, and then recognized for the deeds they do. It could be public gratitude or tacit self-respect. Either will do, depending on the setting. The depraved need for appreciation develops into martyrdom.

To ennoble themselves, we sometimes hear people in business or entertainment say, "I bring people happiness." A comic will validate what he believes to be his life's purpose, proclaiming, "I like to make people laugh." A sports figure or a rock star may think, "I provide people with a good time." A salesman will take satisfaction in knowing he can, "Give people what they want and need."

Servicing neediness in people who're as equally obsessed with escaping their conscience as we are, comes easy. This is not to imply that there's no value at all in these professions. There can be plenty. But for the "professional" approval seeker there is no authentic altruism. Even a job well done only serves a need for relief, evolving a disingenuous ache within. The discomfort grows, blocking true contentment, encouraging additional need for even more relief. Serving others becomes a debilitating addiction, no longer a vocation.

It's true, there can be wonderful value in engaging others. Entertainment and recreation each have their legitimate benefits. So, does filling the needs of others through entrepreneurial undertakings. However, many people don't enter business, the performing arts, or sports for love of the endeavor or humble amusement. They are drawn by a deeply imprinted need for the recognition, power, and comfort these activities provide. They might possess a special skill or aptitude, and discover how to leverage their abilities, fetching the stratospheric level of acceptance they crave—more than anyone could ever possibly deserve.

Athletic, musical or dramatic performance is a lot of hard work. It places enormous demands on the mind and body. Aside from talent, success requires an enormous sacrifice of time, perseverance, and energy. Those who outshine all others are folks who stumble upon creative outlets they enjoy and develop impressive skills but who also take those further than anyone else. They make greater sacrifices, honing talents to the delight of others. Most people are not willing to go the extra lengths needed. Some do, reluctantly. But then it becomes a dangerous living. Celebrity and accomplishment are easily abused.

The overly-hard application of natural ability can numb a lot of suppressed pain. But as the anesthesia is administered, there is also the construction of a spiritual barrier. Performance can enable a broken personality to beg for and receive the people-approval he craves to feel whole. For those seeking to anesthetize the inner pain of a conflicted conscience, *the show* becomes an opiate, inducing biochemical pleasure responses in the brain. Approval grows into virtual drug addiction. This is why those in the performing arts are in such great danger of substance abuse. It's the cause of many tragic ends for those dedicated to this kind of co-dependent existence, turning innocent performance into servitude to the audience.

A performer who derives life-force this way has a great need for relief and soon comes to depend on the soothing supportive energy transferred by an approving crowd of admirers. Applause is more than an expression of appreciation. It is a projection of approving vitality that in effect quickly becomes a narcotic in the brain. An entertainer will work hard for it.

Likewise, rising to the top in business and commerce takes an extraordinary commitment to overcoming fear and obstacles personal to everyone. Not many can do that either. Life in the public eye, performing on stage or in the boardroom, can be either humbling or empowering. Whichever spells the difference between coming to life or moving toward death.

A talented performer who takes the stage[50] to suck approval out of an audience will suffer a slow madness and consequential death. A successful business person who derives self-worth from sycophantic self-seekers is on the same treacherous path.

Are all the celebrated rich and famous this way? Certainly not. But all have experienced the approval-reward phenomenon to some degree. Some to a very great degree. Many celebrities we see today at the tops of their fields are more of a combined breed, becoming as dependent upon supporters for a sense of worth as they are addicted to their own brand.

They can exist for years, amassing acclaim, property, and high net worth, but in time they also come to feel unfulfilled. Under a veneer of financial security and comfortable lifestyles, there comes mounting despondency. An uninhibited ego grows freely to rise above increasingly unpleasant emotionality.

Ego identity evolves and the eminent "star" transforms into a self-generated caricature—not a true person, but an image created through the collective dreams of his *publics,* as well as his own ambitious nature. He gets antsy and self-centered. The greater the restlessness the more absurd life becomes. The egocentric natures of some of the most highly acclaimed individuals are legend. For most secret approval seekers, the peccadilloes, and bizarre idiosyncrasies that exist are never revealed to the public at large.[51]

***

Productive lives are busy lives. It often requires scheduling. Without a flexible daily agenda, too many moments of each day can be wasted, amounting to a chaotic lifestyle. We live in a time sensitive, energy sucking world. It takes a tough resilience to stress just to survive, but there is a fearless dynamism in the well-organized business person. Efficiency imparts courage, placing him at a huge advantage over others.

An unscripted, spontaneous person who's connected with intuitive direction exudes poise. He commands authority because an unselfish nature conveys undeniable confidence. He radiates an energy which at times may frighten those who see his presence as a threat to their self-centered quest for control. Egos sense when they've met their superior. To them, he seems an enigma. Once they see that they're unable to win through guile or manipulation, they turn bitter and frustrated. The free attitude and frankness of an honest, spirited personality outshine the unnatural polish of a rigid, goal-setting intellectual.

There's a huge difference between the tabling of one's time into a schedule and ambitiously chasing self-seeking objectives. Setting daily priorities keeps a calm handle on projects and tasks due. It is a sane and sound practice, maximizing efficiency. Importantly, it also safely thwarts the temptation to worry. Without worry, personal energy is preserved, and we don't tire so easily.

To benefit from success and remain free of corruption, the acquired fruits of personal ingenuity must be free from selfish aims. Without the strain of goal setting, material comfort, health, and emotional security become the natural byproducts of a life well lived and jobs well-done—not the spoils of war with the world.

Flights of imagination about the past, present or future are a threat to spiritual growth. Each jaunt of mental fantasy removes you from the present moment to where awareness is lost. Any distraction interfering with mindful consciousness places both soul and sensibility in jeopardy. Those suffering from what is often called ADD or ADHD know this experience well. These conditions are not actually mental illnesses and they do not have physiological origins. They're just names of symptoms doctors have assigned to the metaphysical disturbance caused by spiritual assault within. The only antidote is consciousness.[52]

Time spent inside the imagination, apart from the conscious awareness of *now*, is time lost that will never be recovered. On hearing this, you may ask, "I can dream, can't I?" I'm sorry, but no. Not in safety, you cannot. When you do, you place your life at risk. I know this goes against much of the success rhetoric you've heard, but it is wrong. True success does not ever happen in the future. It coalesces *in the present, now*. When it happens this way, it's huge.[53]

A narcissistic attitude supporting the lower Self emerges out of fantasy and rumination about the future. Outcome-based activity and thinking fueled by ambition block clarity. The "next right thing" always turns out to be ultimately wrong. The thoughts of egoistic achievement surround us in a soothing miasma of make-believe. It's addictive. We could become preoccupied with *self-improvement.*

Do not reject this idea for fear that I'm am proposing a life of material mediocrity or some vow of poverty. I assure you I'm not. Wonderful riches and comforts await those who are patient and earnest in their yearning for what is right in the spiritually inspired human heart. However, the willful chase of favorable outcomes, even praying to influence events, is the mark of an egocentric personality who's not yet broken free from a lifelong pattern of trying to become God. Even if you achieve prosperity, you will only have succeeded in becoming a willfully rich failure.

Futile attempts to manifest goodwill, happiness, and abundance out of a universe that only He controls becomes a selfish preoccupation. There is, of course, security in material wealth. When possessions are acquired free from fantasy or avarice, the quality of life is far superior to any type of lifestyle that's attained through ambitious energy.

If you're already affluent, then this should not be too difficult for you to see. If you aren't, it won't be long before this makes perfect sense to you too, once you practice the dissolution of ambition as I suggest and experience a quality of life you'd never have otherwise devised for yourself.

While we must exist in a world filled with diversion, we can't just quiet the noise by placing ourselves into seclusion. It is dangerous to willfully silence the certain thought-traffic running through our heads. That would evade our life's purpose. Instead, by facing the constant barrage of thinking from a position of conscious awareness, we find courage within. We express faith in patience so that we'll be saved from the inner din of chatter. Then lo and behold, we are!

***

Struggling with problems only precipitates failure. Anytime we impart willfulness we also withdraw trust from the Creator, placing faith in our *Selves* instead. His protective care instantly falls away and we stand *Godless*. Even during those times when we believe that we are succeeding at life, there is an ultimate price to pay for the faithless breach of this simple spiritual principle. To the extent that we're moved by inspired reasoning, we will no longer struggle with decision making. *The next right* thing becomes apparent and effortless.

You may remember from childhood a paper novelty toy called the *Chinese Finger Trap*. Essentially, it's a paper helix braided into a hollow tube. Once both fingers are inserted, the harder you pull to extricate out of the trap, the more the circumference of the tube shrinks, the tighter the hold. The only way to forcefully get free is to rip and destroy the entire apparatus. Meanwhile, letting go of will, patiently allowing the fingers to slip easily through would take only another instant. These Chinese *handcuffs* as they are also known, have become a common metaphor representing triumph over impatience. Accessing the power of self-will to extricate out of one's problems is like struggling to get free from the finger trap, while actually, our problems seem to resolve all by themselves once we stand back and surrender willfulness.

I know you want to get rid of some of your more objectionable traits. The idea is strong, that if you could just lose that excess weight, give up that filthy nicotine habit, be free from drugs and excessive drinking, find true love, solve economic hardship, whatever it is—then you'll have found the way to peace and joy. I also know that I may not have yet persuaded you that to experience these, you'll first have to stop trying. Surely you find it an intriguing idea at least, even if it's a large pill to swallow right away. It's still early in the book. You may not have yet begun the meditation technique I present with a sense of real commitment. I hope you'll begin the meditation exercise as you go along. The sooner you do, the sooner you'll see results.

So, where does this *not trying* get us, and why should you be interested? Why should you listen to me? I'm not a preacher or minister. I've no degrees from a Divinity School. I'm not a guru or spiritual guide speaking from a hilltop of superiority. I've no impressive teacher or mentor to point to. I do not live in a palace to brag of. I am simply a person who's been down the same road as many other people, and I've suffered similarly along the way. Having survived, I am just a common man carrying some uncommon ideas.

Admittedly, these have produced some extraordinarily deluxe conditions in my life—but shouldn't it be so with all our lives? Why can't the extraordinary become more ordinary? Freedom from worry, fear, anxiety, physical, and mental handicap should be commonplace. Families filled with love, order, and harmonious achievement should be the norm, not so much the exception—and it can be.

Perhaps this will help convince you. If I may be personal for a moment, without trying, I lost a lifelong addiction to sugar. The obsession to overeating automatically fell away and I lost 60 pounds. Without trying, the need for nicotine simply vanished and I gave up smoking effortlessly. Without trying, I was cured of major depression, anxiety, and Attention Deficit Disorder. Consciousness, *without trying*, has separated me from the desire for alcohol and prevented any sort of drug abuse. *I'll go into these in greater detail in the next chapter.*

Of course, there's much more to the metaphysical world than noticeable recoveries such as these. For now, I just want you to consider that these problems were not true culprits at all, each being but a symptom of a single underlying cause founded in a curable spiritual dysfunction. To ever *try and fix* any of them only serves a lower ego-nature. That never comes to a real solution because willful effort always booby traps true success.

When we stop *trying* to fix what is broken in our lives, we aren't surrendering to our problems. We are sidestepping deeply ingrained willfulness, automatically encouraging change in our lives that we could never expect.

Some claim the Non-Contemplative consciousness technique I use has resulted in their being cured of terminal cancer, neurological disorders, and other baffling diseases.[54] What are these but miracles of physical and emotional healing?

Notice I didn't say that *I cured* them, or that *consciousness* and meditation cured them. I am saying that God has done the work. These are real miracles of healing, but they come from God alone, once a person awakens to how and where He is found. I'm merely pointing the way toward that discovery. He issued cures for these problems, made possible only through *conscious contact* with Him. In each case, all a suffering person need do is discover how to become themselves once again. *I am keen on this point and careful about how I phrase it, lest detractors mash my words on this matter.*

Non-Contemplative Meditation is merely the tool bringing you to the mindful state of being where this metaphysical magic happens. In the following Chapters, you'll see how that's possible. Once we stop *trying*, self-will is moved out of the way. True healing, propitious success, and the answers to all our problems begin to unfold for us.

This requires committing to a lifestyle devoted to God's will alone. *Conscious contact* with Him maintained each day, ensures our dedication. The next Point will help explain more and bring you closer to discovering an infilling of inspired reasoning that cannot happen by any other means.

Stop Wearing Yourself Out *Trying*

How do you sleep at night? Ambitiously wresting happiness out of the world is a distracting struggle. It dulls the awareness needed to become truly successful. It runs you ragged, depletes your energy. It breaks down the body and mind. You have within a special Presence of mind carrying the power and energy to do what you could never do by self-will. Become still. Allow inspired reasoning to show how to easily access everything you need in this life, without willing, chasing or trying to make it happen. Then it does, spontaneously.

Point Three

The Third Chapter

By which you are encouraged to begin a very special kind of meditation and to begin practicing it as if the preservation of your life and all progress depends on coming to consciousness and remaining mindfully aware—because it sure does.

It has long been recognized that pressure in the stream of life results in emotional discomfort. But it is only in recent years that stress has become such a hot topic. Magazine articles, TV shows, Talk Radio counselors and psychologists are all discussing the negative kinds of stress we all encounter every day. The more people learn about stress and the deleterious effects it places on the body and mind, the more interested they become in doing something about it.

Worldly burden will always be around. It's easy to blame others, the world, bad luck or even God for the stressful situations in our lives. But in truth, it's you who's been the chief conspirator in setting up the negative consequences of stress.[55]

You became resentful.

Negativity stirs the pot of emotional stew, fomenting a line of force between you and a stressor. Immediately you become bizarrely linked to your tormentor and subject to whatever and whoever you hate.

A spirit rises behind the emotional energy generated. It projects negativity, regardless of whether a situation is imagined or real. Until freed from anger, others will have sway and you will never be your true self.

A negative field of ill will doesn't need fact or truth to form. All it needs is imagination. Confrontations with cruelty that are fabricated to serve the intellect's need for drama work just as well as the real-life encounters with genuine unfairness.[56] A flip, "Oh well. It's my fault," may momentarily help smooth over an unpleasant encounter, but the relief won't last.

Unless you see how stress is never a one-sided affair and learn how to neutralize it from your side, you will remain locked into a lifetime of repeated aggravation. The wear and tear of daily living will slowly chip away at you, in time breaking you down completely.

This is avoidable. Protection is available. But first, you should know just what you're dealing with. At this very moment, your sensibilities of mind and integrity of body are each being taxed by seen and unseen pressure in the surrounding world. There is a bitter exchange of energy between a *stressor* and you, the *stressee*, stemming out of unwholesome emotional ties we all have with one another. By itself, this stress energy doesn't cause all that much trouble. It is inadequately meeting these stressful situations that becomes the problem. If you could just meet with the pressure of stressful conditions properly, no matter what they are, there would be no trouble or problem that could not be conquered.

Notice I did not suggest that you should strive to eliminate stress in your life. That would be a grave mistake. We must be stressed to grow. We shouldn't dodge all difficulty. But we can instead develop a graceful attitude protecting against the harmful effects. A right attitude is activated by character and inner resilience. Then, life goes much easier.

To help develop these features, realize the nature and origin of stress:

There are only two human conditions of existence.[57] First, there's a plane experienced by awakened individuals. Then

40

there's a different existence for those who are *not awake*. These are the only two existential paradigms of reality available to us in this lifetime. The difference between these two modes is relative to either heaven and hell. This simplicity is all that the essence of our existence comes down to.

What comprises all of existence modifies constantly, as it always has since the beginning of creation. The makeup of the universe flows in dynamic fields of ever-changing energies containing everything we can know and cannot know. There is light, gravity, time, matter, positive and negative electrical force, even energies ultimately coalescing into hate and love. These are what exist and there is not a mind or demand so authoritative as to alter or affect this truth—except God's. His Heaven is the default state of all existence. The original. Continuously the first, and the last.

You've heard before that the Kingdom is found within you.[58] It's true. It exists *now*, in *the present moment*, inside, anytime that you are conscious. In the moment, with illusions removed, there remains one, true paradigm. It is God's Kingdom—the heavenly plane where there is no fantasy. This is the realm within that I'm proposing for you to discover. It's real. For that to happen it's now necessary to reawaken, but just as importantly, to stay that way. Wake up this moment to the objective, conscious state and become placed into the one, singular paradigm called *now*.

First become conscious. Then the Kingdom comes, manifesting within. Your life becomes a living projection of Heaven, onto earth just as it is in the Kingdom of Heaven inside. This is existing in the Presence, in the present—the realm from where there is clarity of thought and unparalleled confidence. You live in the Light.

Whenever you aren't conscious you exist in the dark. This is an inevitable discovery once you begin practicing consciousness through regular, non-contemplative meditation. You'll also find that even now, you've lost your bearing in the past and have fallen to the unconscious side. It happens to everyone.

Once this realization comes, don't be frightened. The situation isn't hopeless. Be glad for the conscious awareness revealing this terrible truth. Everyone experiencing hell on earth escapes it once they allow consciousness to unfold in each moment. In that instant, and for all time going consciously forward, you become *saved*.

There are moments all throughout life when you'll exist in the awakened, conscious realm and other times in the dull realm of unconsciousness. Perfection doesn't come all at once. It begins in minute increments, gradually unfolding into a state of continuous awareness. If you will just allow this simple principle into the center of all you do, the journey will be marvelously interesting and fruitful as you grow toward your perfection—toward your perfect Creator.

Once accustomed to reality, you'll develop the ability to practice this experience from an increasingly aware perspective. As humans, it is our job to grasp reality, not to invent it. Meditate properly, non-contemplatively, and you'll awaken into the established heavenly paradigm. You'll become responsive to true life, now, and as each moment comes to pass, leaving fantasy aside. Equally important, if you continue to practice, you'll remain awake. People have come to know this as *the fourth dimension of human spiritual existence*. There is such a place. It is not a man-made fabrication or illusion.

If you search, you'll discover there are many techniques termed as *meditation*. Depending on origin, they're designed to induce certain effects.[59] There's meditation intended to help you relax. If you're a stressed out, nervous type, then those methods will offer obvious relief. There's also meditation that will help induce feelings of bliss.[60] If you're depressed and anxious, anything to counter the discomfort will seem appealing. But neither of these self-serving objectives is behind the meditation I propose.

Don't worry. What I'm suggesting will surely result in your coming to lead a relaxed, contented life. Even so, a life lived freely isn't a selfish quest for bliss, happiness or enlightenment. It is coming into conscious contact with your Creator so you'll do His will, whatever that is, no matter what. For now, put all selfish benefits aside.

Once taking our rightful place in the Family of Humanity, we come under His direction and discipline. We stop expending energy wastefully. The futile struggle to re-create a new and improved world of our own design and for our comfort ceases. We know peace at last. We can understand and experience real joy.

First and foremost, meditation is a metaphysical tool that permits you to handle resentment-affiliated stress, through God-consciousness. This is the one, true protection we have against worldly pressure.

To safeguard grace, do not treat meditation as though it were some optional leisure pursuit. It must become a working part of your existence, a facet of daily life that you practice every single day and in the measures prescribed without fail. This is a lifetime commitment. It's every bit as vital to human survival as food and water. Meditate properly, and everything about your life will change incredibly, even if you never finish so much as one more page in this book.

***

Try to avoid identifying as a *Meditator*.[61] Become a child of God instead. Don't be enamored with the process or get hung up on a routine. Meditation mustn't become a basis for any kind of religion or cult.[62] Meditation is merely a tool. It opens a passage to your psyche so God's will can enter and fill you. You will stand at the threshold to the Kingdom, wherein lies the magic. This endowment was passed onto humanity long ago as an extraordinary gift we ordinary people can, in turn, pass on to each other—that I pass on to you. If you accept this gift you will know security, contentment, and affluence beyond your expectations.

The object of this meditation isn't to train you. It isn't to indoctrinate you. It isn't to stimulate your pleasure centers while I feed you principles hypnotically altering your beliefs. Non-Contemplative Meditation™ leads you within to simple consciousness—nothing more. It is a metaphysical device getting to the heart of matters. It gently pries open the psyche, allowing God to step in to rectify everything that has been internally broken and in need of His care. You awaken to discover God's truth. I don't tell you what that is. You see it for yourself.

By waking up, life will set onto the course for which you were born. Once this happens, emotions become regulated. Life becomes easy. You know peace—not because you are ignoring your problems but because they are all answered and the symptoms simply melt away. It's so effortless and simple that it will be hard to believe but once you commit your life to your Creator in this manner, it'll be impossible to deny.

Airplane designer Kelly Johnson, chief engineer at Lockheed Skunk Works, Lockheed Martin's advanced aircraft develop-ment program, became famous during the Cold War for getting top notched results, "cheaper, sooner and better," than anyone else. Famous for his brusque but efficient style, Johnson is credited with first coining the acronym KISS, "Keep it simple stupid" as a constant reminder to his staff to keep paperwork to a minimum. This simple wisdom is easy to appreciate and today the popular cultural idiom can be heard everywhere from Twelve Step programs and in group therapy to education and software design firms.

Nowhere else is this minimalist concept more important than when it comes to *conscious contact* with God. It's essential in effective meditation practice. The moment *how and where* to discover God becomes complicated, efficacy isn't merely diminished, but it is lost entirely. Minimalism is why the meditation I'm offering you is so unique and effective. It's devoid of religious trappings and hypnotic platitudes. There's no spellbinding dogma attached.

This meditation is a *non-contemplative*, stand-alone technique. You dare not modify or supplement it in any way. It is the simplest means humankind has to discover God.[63] It is the ancient practice of backing out of the stream of thought inside your head, allowing a separation from those thoughts so consciousness can return from where thought has taken it. Practicing *this meditation* raises consciousness from the dark recess in your being, activating the spiritual eye at the fore of your mind. At once, you are brought into an aware state and released from a sleep-like trance you don't know you're in, where forces like resentment enter.

When you are conscious there can be no negative emotional incursion into the psyche. You're placed out of harm's way. It's that simple. You can keep it that way too. You don't need to learn philosophies or to follow rules. You need no rituals or affectations of any kind, no prayer cloths, circles or candles, no beads or bells. There's no culture to adopt. In fact, any of these things are likely to block understanding—never improve it. Once you begin meditating, you are free to be you, because once conscious, it is revealed exactly who you are. And here is the shocker: *It probably isn't who you thought.*

Use *this meditation* and only this one.[64] Don't combine techniques. Some people try to blend *this meditation* and with practices and philosophies they've learned elsewhere. They follow the directions to a point but then ruin it, introducing devices common to other techniques, but having entirely different objectives. Don't attempt to incorporate any gimmicks other meditations teach, like paced breathing or visualizing images in the head. Positive affirmations, chanting and memorized prayers, no matter how well intentioned, will spoil this meditation. It is perilous to entertain even one of these. We are not trying to stimulate the senses during meditation. Any such stimuli will counteract progress.[65] Here, less is best.

Sometimes people are tempted to incorporate sound into meditation by playing music or ringing bells in the background. This is also an artificial stimulus having a mesmerizing effect. It defeats vital aspects of this exercise. Don't use it. Music, tones, and background ambient sound effects are powerful tools, but they are frequently used to create a suggestible condition, inducing mild euphoria. Many guided meditation recordings encourage blissfully seductive feelings for this reason. Inserting soothing audio effects into this exercise, advocates of spiritual mischief encourage psychotic states. Dangerous, hypnotic side effects are possible.

Any sound resonating inside the head, real or imagined, can be as mesmerizing as those outside. For this reason, don't ever use mantras with meditation. Like music, mantras will countermand the benefits of the awakening experience. They prompt a spellbinding effect, making you defenseless to the psychic manipulation of a spiritual guide. They are to be avoided always. You don't want to become hypnotized and controlled by the will of a hypnotist. You want to be awake, subject only to the will of your Creator, no one else.

The Non-Contemplative Meditation™ in this book is anti-hypnotic. It does not exploit suggestible human nature, which virtually every hypnotic technique will surely do. There aren't any audio tricks of any kind used in the production of any of my meditation recordings.

While breathing exercise incorporated into meditation is a common practice among some well-meaning but misguided meditation teachers, you need to know that this is merely a physiological ploy. Deliberated breathing creates a physical phenomenon producing a temporary state of well-being, that mimics spiritual serenity.[66] This false sense of well-being acts as a drug. It becomes an addictive narcotic. Once indulged, we must keep returning to whatever or whoever induces the feeling of well-being and peace. We become a slave to that source.[67]

This isn't a truly inspired spiritual state. It's a trick, comparable to taking a mild *happy pill*, later associating the resulting euphoria with the meditation. Or worse, with the teacher providing guidance. Fall for this, and whatever is already troubling you will only increase.

Do not insert physical exertion that accelerates ventilation into meditation. The combination of the two will mimic a *false* euphoria and only mask your problems, leaving them unanswered. While believing you are doing something wonderful for your body, mind, and spirit, you're getting worse, not better. Even if you weren't so bad off prior, you will be after. I'm not suggesting you must abandon activities that emphasize stretching or help develop physical stamina. These can be beneficial of course, but there is a right way and a wrong way to engage in physical exercise. During meditation is not the right way.[68]

True serenity doesn't feel like anything. It is experienced from a position of neutrality that's 100% free of seductive emotional energy and the addictive qualities anything or anyone can hold over us.

It is possible to be meditative[69] while active and physical, say when working out, walking etc. The ability to live all of life in the awakened, aware state is, after all, an outcome of this exercise. But do not deliberately merge physical exertion with meditation. Mingling their individual purposes is extraordinarily risky.

If you've been classically trained to combine spirituality with physicality, then you're going to have to cease that immediately for *this meditation* to work properly. I know this may be the opposite of what you've been told before now, but remain amenable to this idea and you'll be glad you did.

If you're unable to get past this, then I'm sorry to say that this technique isn't for you. I wish there were a less harsh way to say this and for some of you, this is going to be a deal killer. So be it. If your objective is to anesthetize, numbing your consciousness to escape inner pain, then you would do better to leave this meditation alone completely for now. Perhaps read further into this book, investigate me little more, considering my life and background.

Then, come back to Non-Contemplative Meditation once you're less ambitious or are at least willing to consider abandoning self-willfulness. But if you're ready to awaken, confront your inner pain and experience forgiveness, then heed these words, and proceed on to a life you could never have fathomed possible.

When meditating, take care not to meditate on ideas, wishes, questions, or thoughts of any kind, especially written or memorized words. Problems created while under the narcotic influence of intellect will not be solved by the same intellect. So, don't deliberately focus or contemplate at all. Contemplation is *anti-intuition*. It is the Ego entity's replacement of faith in God with opinion and only diverts attention away from unwelcome thoughts by refocusing on pleasurable ones.

Although this is easily done and widely practiced, it's plunging further into intellect, making you worse off than before, not better as you might have supposed. Through rumination, escapist meditation, mental recitals, and concentration, the Ego identity within plays God, placing faith in Self instead of Him. Even thoughts that are about God, which endorse heady spiritual philosophies, are still merely decoys the Ego uses to bait seekers into a sense of false piety.

Contemplatives, people who believe they are becoming enlightened through thoughtful reflection, are deliberately getting lost in the din of their thinking mind. Bursting with wondrous, profound ideas, thoughts become a relieving departure from the reality of God's *now*. The Ego identity relishes a certain kind of consciousness that does not involve God. That is Self-consciousness where instead of remaining asleep you awaken inside a new dream, the fantasy of self-empowerment. It is tantamount to waking up to discover that you are God. You're not. It is an illusion.

Placing faith in Self by fanaticizing you are God is just imaginary contrived by the Ego entity to elevate Its stature in God's universe. It uses intellect and emotionally uplifting language to convey faux-supremacy It doesn't deserve and will never truly attain.

In God-consciousness there are no words, while in Self-consciousness there are only words. They excite and instigate emotional response. In stillness, there is no emotion. Observe without reacting while self-proclaimed spiritual people deteriorate in physical and mental health over time. Observe without resenting their suffering or error lest you also fall to the same maladies. We always become what we hate. It has happened to them and it will happen to you if you allow anger inside to feed a rapacious Dark Self.

Whether they're *happy thoughts* or *stinking thinking*, every thought is still *thinking*. Any time contemplation calls for deliberately focusing on ideas or words holding beauty and meaning, it becomes an especially odious practice. You could blissfully imagine your own enlightenment, but you'll also fall deeper into a dark abyss. It's a trap. All immersion into the thought stream creates a distraction out of consciousness, pulling you away from God.

Be very wary of pleasurable thoughts filled with positive projections for future happiness. They may seem the opposite of *worry* and, therefore, desirable. But even optimistic fantasizing is a departure away from the consciousness in the reality of *now*. Thoughts like these will always rival conscious-ness. They compete with your awareness and scoff at the *present*. If they prevail, they'll ultimately rob you of intuitive-ness to manifest a negative outcome.

Instead, separate from *all* thoughts, regardless of whether they are *happy* or *stinking*, breaking your dependency upon them. Place reliance on inflowing intuition. This is how God conveys His vision and will for every individual—never through thoughts. Safely placing your faith in the *wordless knowing* makes clear the proper application of your thinking mind.

I am showing you how to practice the exact opposite of contemplation. Rather than focusing on thoughts, I want you to allow consciousness to rise above the stream of thinking. Non-Contemplative Meditation restores God-consciousness without the use of thought and concentration. It liberates us from the effects of anger-energy, preventing those inevitable, pesky negative emotions cropping up through everyday events from penetrating and causing harm. This is freedom from the bondage of the thinking Self.

Once *thinking* loses the gripping influence it has over us, we gain insightfulness. Wisdom adds to observation and clear discernment automatically alters the journey on our life's path. What we think of as the future, modifies and emerges, seemingly out of nothing, to become a new *now*—a *present* that never would have otherwise been.

There's a heavenly flow of energy that fuels our life's progress without much planning. For access, we have only to step back from thinking and watch. In each watchful moment, we become the spectator to thought and right then, everything changes—not only for us but for each life we touch. Our mere presence in the stream of life alters the course of events in ways we are unable to know in advance. We cease repeating old mistakes. Uncommon thinking replaces common thinking. We become inspired beings, deriving energy and encouragement from a positive Source. Time pushes past us while we remain more in the present, less dragged along into the uncertainty of a future that doesn't yet exist.

Subsequently, our fears melt away. Aging slows. We develop a sense that Something Great is in charge. It isn't us. It's an exceptional guiding force, originating with God, intuitively emanating into the world from within us—if we let it.

This intuitiveness is the sixth sense you've heard about. It is far superior to whatever information the thinking brain provides. With this prescience, you can't make wrong decisions because there aren't any to make. You live in a decision-free realm with the natural capacity for forgiveness and true clairvoyance. You always seem to be at the right place at the right time and find just the right words at the right moment.[70]

No doubt, you've been tempted in the past to believe that if thinking causes problems, then the way to solve them must be to modify your thinking. This isn't true in the least. It has been your abject reliance on thoughts *at all* that has ever caused any of your difficulties in the first place. It is dangerous to place faith in that same process with hopes of rectifying your errors in the second place.

It sure is tempting to try and outsmart problems, but please realize that you have no control over the source of information emanating out of intellect. All thinking is a distraction away from understanding and only feeds into erroneous thought. The idea that you are the originator of your own thoughts and, therefore, have control over thinking has got to be shattered. You may have thought of this as being self-reliant. That it is, but self-reliance isn't the noble, desirable trait you've been taught it is.

The Self upon which you've placed your trust in the past is an imposter. It isn't you. It's intentions are not to your benefit. Self hates God and all mankind, including you. In placing reliance on It, instead of attaining the freedom envisioned, you become enslaved. This is the ultimate oppression that destroys lives, elevating self-centeredness to the max. Surely, you've heard the term, "Bondage of self."[71] This is precisely that—psychic slavery to a wicked entity within.

With its high potential for abuse, thinking, without inspired reasoning, *in other words, pure intelligence,* is your own worst enemy. Intellect obstructs inspired reasoning, inhibiting the flow of intuitive grace.

To contemplate is to fixate to ideas and words. It comes at the expense of wordless, clear communication with flawless conscience. Therefore, for meditation to be effective, it's got to be *non-contemplative,* releasing the meditator from his thinking and on to the objective state.

Once rising above thoughts, you'll be free to observe as they appear without them motivating you. You'll be safe from whatever nefarious forces are hiding in the never-ending loops of thinking. Grace then enters unimpeded.

Consciousness grants psychic release from intellectual bondage. It annuls an unwholesome affection with the thinking mind, liberating the human spirit from the choking control of the lower Self. God gave us a brain to use, not to abuse, and now we can. In each moment that you are conscious, your psyche opens to receive God's will. Allow it inside and He will never let you down.

Contemplation shuts the psyche to God's will, replacing His vision for us with self-will. It'll always disappoint.

The meditation shown in this book maintains a *non-contemplative* element of *consciousness* that should be characterized as true *mindfulness*. Take caution here. I specify *true* because there are two conditions that can be described as *mindful*. One leads to life and the other leads to death. Chose incorrectly and move closer to death. Choose correctly and move toward living forever.

This presents a rather ominous warning, I know. Nevertheless, these are serious matters and so I am obligated to be forthright and make the point. Please understand what I mean when speaking of *mindfulness*. Ask this question, "When the mind is full, what is it filled with?" Some have surmised that "mindfulness" suggests a head packed with pleasing thoughts and mental projections for a happy future. Here, the idea is that by replacing objectionable thinking with desirable, happy thoughts, you will also live happily. If this were true, contentment would require a pre-load of your brain with happy ideas, reinforcing the programming each time your optimism fell in danger of lapse.

Live this way and you'll become reliant upon affirmations, memes, and *positive thinking*. Daily life will become a fantasyland of happy words and ideas, pretending all is well, even when it is not.

In this mild yet dangerous trance, the only semblance of joy you can ever know is the artificial happiness you've been programmed to feel. You become trapped inside a real-life version of *The Matrix*[72] with your existence tied to willful instructions emanating out of a lower self. You come under a hypnotic spell, susceptible not only to a nature of Something inside that isn't you, but you could also connect with the same Darkness residing inside someone else. Then happiness would hinge on another individual to create void, refilling and overwriting the original understanding of your conscience with the *happy* elements in their brand of programming. This is a primitive form of brainwashing and precisely how cults, gurus, and self-proclaimed spiritual guides cultivate followers. Do you see how dangerous this kind of *mindfulness* is? It's a trap to avoid.

Wholesome *mindfulness* is altogether different. It is nothing like the store-bought, pop-mindfulness you'll find touted in dharmic yoga classes or by modern-day gurus on New Age websites. For our purposes, *mindful* means that your mind is filled with *substance* superior to mere thought—not those inside your head or out of anyone else's head either. The substance is not physical material. It is metaphysical material. It's called *consciousness*.

When we are unconscious there is a void in the psyche. It instantly fills with whatever the ego-intellect would like. Intellectual sensibilities begin to rule thinking and behavior without regard for wisdom. Alternately, when we are conscious, there is no void within the psyche. There is an infilling of awareness or what some religions might call *grace*. This isn't a disassociation of perception. Rather, there is a clear *re-association* with the original conscience. It's a wordless reunion, and it restores intuitive sensibility, driving out all doubt. Willful decisiveness melts away and what seems to be indecisiveness is really the revolution of humbly inspired energy that accomplishes wonderful things. It is the inspiration to do God's will automatically. When awake and aware, separated from thought, you are *mindful* in a spiritually healthy way. You're able to live the expression of spirit, not of thinking.

Allow no one to fill your mind with their ideas. Even when sounding pleasurable and right, realize how their ideas are not *really* their ideas. They are thoughts from other people who came before them, whose ideas weren't theirs either, and so on. Their words are designed to seduce, not enlighten. A mind filled with understanding from within will always trump a brain filled with the language of thinking. You can't *think* yourself into happiness, awareness, or enlightenment.

Hopefully, I've persuaded you that there's an unhealthy *mindfulness* and a healthy *mindfulness*. Beware of the former at the risk of spiritual life and ultimately your physical life. If you've been taught to ruminate in your thoughts or to focus on concepts while meditating, please discontinue. This has been an incorrect and extraordinarily dangerous practice. By placing you in a position where your own thinking pulls you into a whirlpool of ideas, the slippery and seductive nature of words will sidetrack you away from awareness.

You might *awaken* into a new dream, discovering you've been convinced that *you are God*. This *oneness* is a fantasy that will supply immediate elation but could also mark the end of your ability to ever again distinguish dream from reality.

When engaged in contemplative meditation and reflective, self-centered prayer, you are no longer living in the *present moment*. Instead, you exist inside thinking, where inferior, intellectual rationalization occurs. This is why these do not work. Most of you have been taught to pray this way. Sorry.

Here, a well-nourished Ego will excuse selfish behavior. It will rationalize unsound emotional energy, such as anger. It will tell you, "You're all right. Resentment is normal. Anger is only human." Then It will offer futile recommendations for how to manage anger. Believe It and suppression will come easy, while It continues to feed on the destructive, negative energy pooling within. To the *happy thinker*, it might appear that his *stinking thinking* has been mitigated. Nothing is further from the truth. A jolly façade conceals a deadly cache of bitterness.

The first realization, that you've been living in a hypnotic, sleep-like trance for nearly all your life is one the most shocking revelations you'll experience from this meditation. Don't fret too much, because just beyond the shock is understanding that is liberating. *This meditation* will free you from the pre-existing unconscious state. It'll reactivate lost consciousness. This is redemption.

The adage, "Meditate, don't medicate," is deceptive. Meditation should never be considered a substitute for drugs. *This meditation* isn't some ersatz anesthetic, as this stale idiom implies. Treating it as a drug abuses meditation and instead of becoming mindfully God-conscious you'll likely desensitize to guilt without ever finding the resolution to its cause. However, if you follow the meditation directions presented here without altering them, you'll be safe.

Whatever you do, don't treat *this meditation* exercise as though it were an experiment or some *feel better* option to pick up occasionally for spot treating bouts of personal distress. This is a lifetime commitment. You might as well know it now. It'll do little good to just go through the non-contemplative exercise, wake up to experience the benefits of consciousness, and then not allow that graceful state to go forth into your life and milieu.

The world around us and the lives of others await. Conscious contact isn't designed for a bedside experience. It should endure, carried forward into each day, the days turning into years and the passing of decades to come. Commitment to conscious contact with God is a daily dedication, not a spiritual fad. A wonderfully prolific lifestyle is given once you proceed on this path. Its enormity and universal importance are staggering.

Having been born into a cruel, unfair world, you were touched by some of the injustice you first saw and experienced as a child, that had leaked into your immediate environment. Everyone has his or her own personal story in this regard. You had nothing to do with that, but you became intimidated nevertheless.

By the trauma of becoming upset with what you saw, something concealing Itself inside the nature of the defective, cruel world gained access to your psyche. It entered. You became as flawed as the world you hated, contaminated by a dangerous nature from which no one can escape on their own. A lower Self took up residence inside and from the pit of your belly, began to feed on a universal negative energy called *resentment.*

Prideful and emboldened, It judged people for their wrongs, *playing God.* The more nourishment It received in this manner, the larger It became until you could no longer see where It began and where you ended.[73] As It thought, it was as though It's thoughts were your own. When It acted foolishly you blamed yourself, developing into a boorish narcissist to compensate for the pain of it all.

Disoriented and awkward, desperately trying to maintain self-importance, you retreated into the velvety reassurance supplied by the thoughts inside your head. Once there, you were kept in a psychic slumber, unconsciously devoted to judging others. You became an emotional prisoner trapped inside your own skull. Somewhere on life's journey, you were deceived into a cycle of thinking, judging, and *playing God.* Proceeding unwittingly down that road a lost being, you refused to see what you had become: A self-centered, comfort seeking bore.[74]

Awaken to realize that for all your life, what's transpired has been part of a cruel nightmare you didn't know you were having. This can be a heady experience. There will be some shock, some awe, and perhaps some tears as well. Weeping isn't uncommon during this time. But after you go through it, you'll experience mental, physical and emotional security as never before.

As grateful as you may personally feel, the impact of the experience should not remain entirely a private affair. Once becoming mindfully aware, that consciousness is easily carried forward into a life where you, directly and indirectly, affect others.[75]

Are you getting a clear picture here? Can you see why at the beginning of this book I say that this is not like anything you've ever seen or experienced before?[76]

In committing to living in the Presence, you are set on an incredible course of discovery. Your newly heightened sense of intuitive awareness will bring understanding that will challenge all that you've been told about everything. A new perspective will impact you in ways you cannot imagine until the time comes, and then won't need to imagine. You will have emerged from the Matrix into the real world.

Consciousness doesn't only affect mental and emotional position. Just being awake and aware, your newfound resilience to stress moves beyond the mind to your body too. It directly touches physical health. To many of you suffering from emotionally induced illnesses and conditions, this will be nothing short of miraculous.[77]

Unless met with properly, emotional pressure increases your chances of illnesses like heart disease and nearly all forms of cancer. That's because worldly stress lowers immune system response. However, consciousness protects and maintains well-being. Once you begin meeting stress properly, your immune system normalizes. Your body develops an increasing resistance to daily trauma, preventing future incidences of disease, disability, and premature death. You'll evade encounters with life-threatening maladies you never knew were looming. What a blessing!

An increased energy level means your immune system will be charged, *in full*, with the energy it needs to fight off antigens. This is as it's designed to do. It means you'll be less susceptible to infections like colds or flu as well as most forms of cancer and inflammation. Your body will produce less cortisol, the *anger hormone*. This chemical secretion is harmful at prolonged, high levels.

As if the preventive feature weren't enough, *mindful consciousness* is also a restorative agent. If you're already ill, an improved immune system will help you too. Just as improperly reacting to stress will cause disease, physical aberrations already present can be reversed. Diseases triggered by the improperly met pressures of daily living can be resolved simply by neutralizing the negative energy inherent in all stressful situations. Your own immune system will heal you, once you let it.

Mental tension caused by anger will inflame the vascular system, resulting in heart disease. When you *get mad*, your heart beats rapidly. Over sustained periods, say years, the heart becomes so affected, the arteries so damaged that coronary artery disease (CAD) develops. Sudden death is not out of the question. Suppressing or repressing negative emotions also leads to aneurysm, arrhythmia, blood clots and massive failure.

When brain biochemistry is continually subjected to out of control emotions, energetic abnormalities develop in both the brain and the spinal cord. Aberrant electrical impulses induce a range of neurological disorders. Their symptoms affect the neural network and can trigger deterioration or malfunctioning anywhere in the body.

A body can become riddled with hate and rebel at the cellular level. The immune system overreacts, causing anomalous growth. If you suffer from heart disease or certain types of cancer stemming from emotional pressures, then please consider this. Also, bear in mind that as pressures are dealt with properly, emotionality no longer rules. The body can get back to doing its job without interference.

Over the years, I've been involved with helping people suffering from some heinous conditions. I don't tell them how to treat their diseases. That isn't my domain, I am not a doctor. Physicians deal within the physical realm. Instead, I speak to the metaphysical nature of spiritual illness that precedes nearly all diseases. I tell of my own travails and rescues from disease and conditions stemming from periods of lost and then found consciousness. I've been down the road to emotional, mental and physical dissipation.

I know what it is to hear a voice within saying, "Kill yourself. It's the answer," and other vile things. But, thanks to the gift of consciousness I also have ample, personal experience with healing. Not only have I fully recovered from alcoholism and drug abuse, but through the mindful, God-conscious prescription I propose, I've also experienced physical and mental healing from major depression, anxiety, smoking, ADD, pre-diabetes (Type II), obesity, high cholesterol, sugar addiction, colitis, diverticulitis, and other dysfunctions.

While these healing experiences are well founded, I do not advise anyone to stop taking medications prescribed for these maladies without adequate medical support. Withdrawal from intrusive medications can be unpleasant, and in some cases, dangerous. It was my doctors who *un-prescribed* virtually all the prescriptions they had given me. These include Lipitor for cholesterol, TriCore for Triglycerides, and ADD medications like Adderall as well as the antidepressant drugs Effexor, Wellbutrin, and Lexapro.

My wife Nancy has been taken off both Paxil and Lipitor, for anxiety and cholesterol. Her immune system, weakened by emotions she'd bottled-up and repressed deeply since childhood, were breaking down her body. It worsened as she got older, eventually revealing in Shingles and Celiac Disease. After several exorcisms and re-establishing consciousness, she is doing fine now.[78] Since beginning meditation in earnest a little over two years ago, both diseases are in remission. She is now protected from impious forces that she never knew tormented her.

With rare and brief exceptions, our children have never required prescription medications. There's been the occasional antibiotic or decongestant when they were much younger or a skin cream since becoming teenagers.

Many of you reading this right now will be shocked to learn how powers you don't understand can cause so much pain and suffering within the home. When anger is not present in the home, there's a naturally occurring peace, good will, and health that permeates family life.

I've also been blessed to have been a party to hundreds of people all over the world who have had even more profound healings than I've had—experiences regarding narcotic painkillers and powerful, anti-psychotic medications. They've been able to fire doctors refusing to help them taper and wean off conscience numbing medications, finding open-minded professionals willing to assist. They've been taken off the drugs they no longer need. All it took to lose the need was learning how to become themselves and to get back to God.

Pill popping while hoping and praying for wellness always fails. All it does is help cultivate faithless, spiritual catalepsy and support the negative energy at the cause of all mental and physical problems. Most medications formulated to treat serious psychosis are still only experimental drugs. Those who can safely get off them and get back to God cease playing the guinea pigs to reclaim health of body and mind.

***

We humans are special beings. We're of a different order than other creatures. We can enjoy the company of our species and thrive spiritually having them in our lives. Either we live and grow through interaction with people, or we wither and die by it. Whichever depends on how we meet the stress others inevitably raise. This will hold true with complete strangers but also the people we deal with regularly. It makes little difference. It isn't the *well* people who enrich us most, but the *sick and suffering* from whom we learn to live free, without bitterness for the faults we discern in them. Once we're able to give up anger, the coarse brokenness in people sharpens our ability to forgive.

A deceitful politician on cable-news or a lying lover in bed, either can hold the power to upset and test our resolve. The most constant temptation to become upset comes from those with whom we spend the most time every day—family, spouses, work associates, children, and siblings. We find a steady supply of frustration at home and work. The absence of anger allows for spontaneous forgiveness, despite what anyone says or does against you. This is an expression of real love for them. Once you allow it, life goes much smoother. We remain tolerant and patient under otherwise frustrating circumstances. It's a positive force entering through you to the benefit of us all.

Why then, can it sometimes be such a challenge to get along well with others? That's simple to answer.

Some *thing* inside people wants to upset you, just as there is a thing already inside you looking to become upset. It craves the challenge of emotional response so It can feed off the negative energy that passions stimulate. It uses your eyes, ears, and senses. It hijacks your personal experiences in the stream of life, running all It encounters into the ground with judgment. Your life becomes Its primary means of contact with God's earth, and you become the unwary host to a most unholy parasite.

It has replicated Itself throughout all mankind. Each person carries the infection within and each time this Thing encounters Itself in others, unless at least one party is conscious, then all Hell breaks loose.[79] Then, the willful nature of darkness projects *onto earth as it is in Hell.*

The crucial element in escaping this nightmare is to find a way to deal with people a little differently—from a position where you are disengaged from the busy stream of thought. It will be necessary to become more mindfully conscious, more of the time. The more time you are conscious, the less likely it is that any given encounter will catch you vulnerable. If you're not used to dealing with people from the conscious side of existence, then this will feel a little uncomfortable at first. Don't worry, you'll soon notice positive changes in your attitude toward people and in your behavior. These changes can be either drastic or subtle depending on circumstances, but they always happen quite naturally. There is no effort on your part required but to simply remain awake and aware as much of the time as you can.

Spiritual progression is accompanied by freedom like no other. It's a pleasant, inner liberation that isn't *bliss* but a more secure sense of ease and peacefulness. There is confidence that projects outward onto others. When you lose your need for approval and the false love of others, your dependency on people for a sense of worth becomes negligible. Be careful. They are likely to take notice.

There could be rebellion. They will experience anxiety arising out of their own pandering for your supportive love as well as your holding back, no longer seeking theirs.[80] Real friends will appreciate the new independent you while those who've never been your true friends will find fault.[81] You could find that you are suddenly uncomfortable around people from whom you may have previously sought out company or guidance, and vice versa. Their counsel and presence no longer seem as attractive or appropriate as it once did. The reason for this is that as you disconnect from your lower self, selfish needs begin to disappear.

Simply observe how others object to your new way of life without resenting their lack of respect or courtesy and frankly, love. Overlook the name calling that may occur. Observe any rising annoyance or temptation toward bitterness in retaliation.

Regardless of how old you are, now you are finally growing up.

Living from the conscious state brings a refreshing perspective to how you treat others and how they treat you. Now you'll look at the past to recognize how unhealthy alliances have been at the root of tense ties to wrong people, as well as a repellant to the right ones. Many relationships will now be reset. It may seem as though you're starting over with them. That's because you are. It is very much like rebooting a computer with a fresh operating system. Old corrupted files get replaced with fresh, working ones.

Deep remorse at this phase is natural.

Notice it. Experience it. Feel the pain you deserve for judging others. Then calmly watch as bitterness for people over unfortunate events simply goes away. When you are in the proper frame of mind, regret and sorrow over the past fall away on their own. You are not stuffing memories. On the contrary, you can recall them vividly and as necessary, offering suitable restitution to those harmed.

An awakened individual can never be as they once were if they remain conscious. They are free to amend their past without regret or scrapping for the lost approval of those whose lives they've damaged. Watch the pull toward indulging in self-pity. Realize that no human being erases the past and that a loving Father within has already forgiven you, long before you were ever born. He has never *not* loved you.

How you conduct yourself among friends, in professional circles, and with family goes smoothly when you're awake and aware. With unhealthy dynamics removed, people can no longer serve self-centered purposes, and relationships endure as never before.

Even intimate relations will be greatly affected by your mindful attitude. A new morality in your sexual conduct naturally emerges, greatly affecting male-female relationships. In what had previously seemed normal behavior, you'll now see your own selfishness and how it perverts the fundamental purpose of human interaction. Look the other way at great risk to your sanity and the well-being of those to whom you suppose great love.

Don't be surprised when romantic dalliances you once saw as loving unions crumble unexpectedly. You haven't lost anything worth keeping. If it were, it'd strengthen under the lighted lens of awareness, not disintegrate by the burning truth.

Once awakening to truth, you'll begin to see clearly where you have used others, and where you've been used too. There will be no doubt in your mind how sick exchanges between you and others only serve to turn you and them into dehumanized slaves to each other's selfishness.

Petty squabbling, mistrust, and irritation become a thing of the past once there's a shield of consciousness to protect against resentment. True love between individuals can flourish as the clouds of suppressed negative emotionality have been cleared away.

Consciousness affects the dynamics of dealing with children in powerfully positive ways too. As you share awareness with your immediate family, life becomes indescribably harmonious. A forgiving spirit passes from you onto your children. There's security, stability, and peace in the home. Family members prosper without you pressuring them to succeed. Learning to live unaffected by anger is the greatest gift a father can give his family. If there's no father in the family, then a mother can too.

When you're right within yourself you gain authority. You hold a credible strength to positively influence your children like you never have before. It's as though your word becomes rule. Not because you're some infallible family ogre. Not because you're special or superior. It is because you are becoming the conduit for a powerful, positive charge of benevolent righteousness. It's a confident force standing wordlessly behind your every word.

You'll demonstrate purity to your kids, projecting genuine integrity they will sense and see. Virtue is contagious. It molds them, supplying with security and confidence they need to meet the world squarely. This isn't some specious morality you are acting out. It's an unseen force emanating from within. It projects truth and positive influence, with no effort on your part.

You'll see how natural and simple parenting becomes once you stop injecting self-will into your children and instead allow God's will to disciple them. Your existence in the Presence makes it so. How so? Simply put, a home stripped of anger cannot become charged by underlying resentment. There is no longer an overwhelming need for each other's approval. An environment conducive to easygoing cooperation with each other evolves. Family members thrive individually by also coexisting in true love. There comes an ease of living. Natural joy emerges through you, passing onto them as your *fruits* grow physically, emotionally and mentally fit.

Your family will become well adjusted. Members of the household mature into a cohesive entity, not pitted with anger. You enjoy a heavenly harmony across all domestic affairs. Disputes turn into shared learning experiences. The relentless temptations to bicker, find fault and error help strengthen family ties instead of tearing them apart. There's no betrayal, dishonesty or deceitfulness among one another.[82]

Divorce is hardly a viable choice anymore because it becomes pointless. The same for infidelity. Ditto unmarried sex and the tragedy of uncommitted parents. Each of these unfortunate consequences disintegrates into the realm of absurdity. They are never an issue. They just don't occur and if they ever did, they're amended. Good conscience comes to oversee.

Under such auspices, there can be no behavioral problems, no learning disorders, and no physical sickness. There's joy, peace, patience, kindness, and faithfulness, in the home all the time. As with the ancient metaphor, when it comes to family you are a tree, and your children are the *fruit* you bear. It's good fruit.[83]

Nancy, our two children and I live the *meditative* lifestyle just described. We experience these things in our family life. Don't let anyone tell you it isn't possible. Don't let the chattering voice inside your head convince you that this is some sort of

Pollyanna thinking. My family is exactly this way and so can yours be. It's no fantasy. It is *real*.

Now with *Non-Contemplative Meditation* in your life, here is how I suggest you begin each day. When you wake up in the morning, avoid going back to sleep. Even if you feel a bit short of sleep, stay up. Unless you have some physical ailment requiring you to immediately rush to the bathroom, don't rise out of bed right away. Instead, think briefly about the new day, the whole new day, from this moment until the next time you wake up tomorrow morning. Don't plan details of how to do your chores, pondering what hurdles await or what you'll say to people. See and drop the temptation to do all that. Acknowledge the reality of pending obstacles, of course, but don't scheme or fixate on any of them.

Observe the temptation to worry, without suppressing fear-based thoughts. Mentally but briefly, borrow a tiny bit of intellect in the *present moment*. Gently acknowledge each task you know needs to get done today, one at a time. Allow a timetable of activities to form on its own. *Schedule, but don't plan.* Then move on. If you forget and become pulled into the stream of thought, scheming and planning again, don't fret. Just see that you have and move on once again. You're now using your thinking brain as intended, as a tool to exploit and then keep aside.

Then meditate. Don't allow yourself to become predictable or rhythmic. Avoid focusing on breathing or the beating of your heart. These will modify all on their own as your consciousness allows for a New Force to resume rightful stewardship of your body. There's nothing more to do than simply noticing changes as they occur. Do not make them happen. Focusing on anything, especially rhythmic body functions like breathing may seem pure and close to your humanity, but they are still physical manifestations. Any concentration on these now only encourages a disrupting intrusion. Mental concentration removes you from consciousness, distorting the flow of energy and placing you into an unavoidable trance. All trance states are undesirable and very dangerous.[84]

Just follow the straightforward direction in the recording, and you'll be safe. Keeping it as simple as possible, use only your hand and head. Energy will enter, flood your head and splash the pineal gland with light, moving as if in a circuit—first down through the hands and eventually through your entire body. Notice this without *trying* to induce it. Be wary of the temptation to analyze as you read, because as you *practice,* it'll become plain. Analysis is impossible.

Allow this to become something you do each day as if each time is the first you've ever experienced it. Then, get on with your day, clear minded, conscious and awakened. This seems ultra-simple, I know, but there's enormous peace and efficiency in meeting each day exactly as I have just outlined. Worry and fear will soon be a thing of the past. If you lost this book even before completing the first chapter but did just this, you'd never miss it. If you read this entire book and don't do this simple thing, your reading will have been for naught. It's *that* powerful. So, do it.

The longer you live this meditative life, the less negative effect stress will have on you. At first, the contrast between your formerly *contemplative,* now *non-contemplative,* existence can be stunning. That depends on how deeply and for how long one has been asleep. But after a while, it won't seem so drastic anymore. You'll become more used to the mindfully awakened state. You'll shake off some bad spirit. You'll notice how physical health and mental outlook improves. Old illnesses and obsessions will begin to fall away and life will go on the way it was meant to be.

Now, with consciousness, you'll be able to do something you could never do before. That is, maintain a watchful eye, vigilant to adversity and stress, noticing these negative forces prior to their arrival, before they can harm you. You are protected through vigilance.

Exercise Consciousness Every Day. *Really*

How's your day going? By regularly committing to awareness, spirit dominates and builds inner virtue, protecting you from adversity all day long. In remaining awakened to reality, you can easily distinguish true from false, without eliciting judgment. Meditating non-contemplatively is true prayer. It is the silent, daily regimen we all need to remain free of the dream world dramas into which we'd otherwise be drawn by stress. Grasp reality by giving up the struggle to invent it. Intuitive prescience awaits, ensuring you'll never lust for anything. You will already have whatever you need.

Point Four

The Fourth Chapter

By which you discover how error and the flawed nature in us all ultimately work toward good and that once becoming still, courage rises to vanquish all fear.

There are two ways to view the world. First, there's the perspective that sees and recognizes a cruel, brutal planet through emotionally prejudiced eyes. From there, reality becomes filtered. Facts are rearranged and distorted. Truth seems false and false seems true.

It's a twisted outlook that permits people to play on our emotions. React, and you become sensitized, vulnerable, easily manipulated by anyone who's learned how to access those emotions. Friends, family, media, business people have a field day. Their collective *wills* become your motivation and life flies out of control.

Then there's another view of the world that is free from this kind of biased, emotional contamination. Here reality is naked and exposed in all its crude nature. Facts are clear and no matter how unpleasant, truth remains readily distinguishable from lies. From this perspective, you view reality without falling victim to controlling, manipulative people. You can regulate your behavior and are never obsessive about anything. You keep your cool, and no one can use you to serve their selfish need.

When we're mindfully awake, we see people as they truly are. We aren't easily upset by them, no matter what they do. We cannot be teased into emotionally vulnerable states. We can't be provoked to anger. We perceive while simultaneously comprehending truth in our affairs. It's an imperfect and unfair world, but all it takes to maintain dignity is awareness—calmly watching. Then in the stillness, stepping back, experiencing tolerance for the error in others.[85]

Tolerance is an asset that conveys loving forgiveness. It's a dispassionate carriage of grace that is steady, even under the most emotionally charged circumstances. Compassion, often mistaken for love, is really a sordid fusion of emotional energy between us and others. It's an unwholesome liability, setting us up for co-dependency and obsessive approval seeking. The need to feel compassion, a swapping of emotional narcotic aid with others, becomes a crippling liability.[86]

If you want to be truly helpful to others, you won't do it by becoming emotionally entwined with them. First watch people through clear eyes so that from your inner-being you can discern in safety. Then you can understand and assist without the ravening influence of emotionality tugging on your heart strings. This is clarity that will keep you free of sentiment, preserving the ability to watch and assess without bias affecting your actions.

Whether you're to give time, advice, or even money to any individual or to withhold it, will become abundantly clear in each moment, as required. You cannot err from this perspective, nor can you assuredly second guess actions inspired in the *present moment*.[87] They'll always be right. No matter what.

Reading people by looking into their eyes is legend. For some, peering deeply into the core of others is a reliable way to foretell intentions, secrets. It can help bare their foibles.

When I was in high school the principal, Brother Andrew O'Gara was reputed for an enviable ability to know when a person was lying simply by looking at them. It was like there was some magical lie detector built into his brain. He'd gaze fixedly into the eyes of his uneasy subject and ask a question. Like, "Did you tell Brother Aurelian you were late for chemistry class *just because you felt like it?*"[88]

This was psychic water boarding. The truth was inescapable. *How did he know? What mystical powers are at work here? Is Brother telepathic? Is he divinely connected to the heavens, Jesus whispering into his ear? Or is this phenomenon merely a matter of grand deduction gained from years of working with scores of adolescent scoundrels?*

Andrew was undoubtedly well versed in the moral psychology of adolescent malfeasance. His innate understanding of teenagers, males especially, was legendary. By many accounts, mostly surmised by the other Christian Brothers at the school, this gift was virtually infallible. But couldn't there have been something more practical at work here too?

Whatever it was, Brother Andrew always seemed to have an instant bead on the truth. Later as an adult, I came to better appreciate the good Brother's technique.

"When you can't look at me in the eye and tell me the story, that means you're lying," TV's Judge Judy tells the defendant. Police and court officers routinely observe eye movement and pupil dilation in assessing a suspect's sincerity. When someone recalls truth they generally look up and to their left. But when they are constructing stories, they instead look up and to their right. When they lie, the pupils will dilate. No wonder Judy constantly reminds witnesses to, "Look at me," during questioning. No wonder Brother Andrew was so perceptive with his glare.

Poets and prophets have long held that our eyes are windows to the soul. Believe it. But, if the soul of a man can be viewed looking in from the outside, isn't it then also possible for the spirit of the individual within to peer outward—*from the inside out*? Can he observe and watch all that surrounds him with discerning purpose? Windows are, after all, *two-way*.

Think of your brain as a computer. We constantly receive images through the visual portals we call eyes. They are magnificent peripheral devices gathering and inputting data to the brain from the surrounding environment. The physical gift of vision occurs at this ocular junction where information enters, becoming absorbed for processing through the mind. What a marvel of human physiology, and yet merely a starting point for our human perception.

Beyond the optics, there's another kind of seeing called *insight*. Along with our capacity for intellect, we also possess the God-given ability to intuitively interpret all that we observe into discerning perception. Here, *seeing* is much more than just gathering visual data. It becomes *watching*. Animals can see, but they are unable to *watch*. They can think but they cannot discern. We humans are different. We're special and much more than just highly evolved masses of neural networking and flesh. We have also been given the extra ability to decide whether we become conscious, communicating directly with our Creator. It's a gift given no other creature on earth.[89]

By living in the conscious state, more of what you see and experience begins to pass under the lens of awareness than when you are unconscious. In that awakened condition, you observe the environment and people with discernment rather than through emotionally infected eyes that otherwise rarely fail to judge. You experience life without becoming carried away into emotionally charged thinking where morbid influences lie in wait, ready to ambush.

Once we become free from emotional engagement, we automatically revert to the original human condition that existed for Adam, the first man. We cease playing God and begin to enjoy a nonjudgmental presence of mind—or *Presence* of mind, to be more accurate. This becomes our personal slice of Paradise.

There are times and places for human emotion, depending on the source of the stress initiating it. There is a time to grieve, to express joy, to share empathy. But be careful. Don't become absorbed into events. These will dull consciousness, making you immediately defenseless against those who know how to get under your skin. As Something unholy in people senses your vulnerability, It plays on your weakness in order to manipulate.[90] True contentment is void of emotionality. There's no ecstasy or bliss in true happiness—just joyous neutrality.

It is possible to experience feelings, without basking in emotions and having them control you. One can eat, drink and be merry, without becoming fat, drunk and gratuitous or ruled by appetite. We can love others, work hard and prosper without becoming emotionalized, shallow slaves to power and people. Just by watching, humbly seeing and observing you'll find peace and ease even under the most stressful conditions. It's simple to move about at home, in the workplace, school or anywhere comfortably once you awaken to become the real you. Through unemotional observation, you'll no longer be overly sensitive.

Notice stimulating emotional sensations that wrap around you—especially seductive, pleasurable feelings. Simply allow consciousness to separate your true self from emotional involvement, and you become immune to the negative force packed into the sentiment others use to take advantage of you. You'll remain free, without reacting to how people make you feel. Peace and joy will no longer hinge on others. This is a liberation of spirit you don't want to miss.

Let the eye properly serve as the input device to your brain-processing unit, free of emotional corruption. Then you'll respond appropriately without the sway of energies that have no legitimate place in motivating you through life.

Once freed from the emotional ties of ambition, we'll properly employ a *will* in a manner so empowering, it changes the course ahead without our effort. We become confident beings living from faith, no longer propelled through time by self-will. Armed with the realization that what once seemed a frightening future doesn't actually exist, we discover courage. Now we proceed fearlessly. You may have heard it said that God's plan is better than anything we could ever come up with for ourselves. It's true.

Time continually forms as experienced in the *present moment*. We are in its flow, *now*. When we exist *now* we discover a Superseding Jurisprudence that directs all code of human ethics and morality. It is heavenly programming. Access it anytime and you'll carry vision forward into everything you touch, positively influencing others. All that's required is to remain attentive to your existence and what is going on around you. Your commitment is rewarded with an uncanny protection against the inevitable emotions that might intervene and distract from consciousness.

This doesn't mean you ignore the good and evil of the world. That would be a denial of reality as both certainly exist. Never turn a blind eye to injustice or error. Simply allow clear vision to reveal all that's around, both the good and the bad. Unthinking, selfish people will always create negative flotsam and jetsam in the stream of life. Through discerning objectivity, fearlessly watch the debris of their actions as it floats by. Objectivity alone, not suppression, will protect you from becoming overwhelmed by the hidden negative force contained in events and within people.

Negative, resentment-inducing pressure exists for a purpose. It's to upset, inviting more negative energy. It is intentional.

Something *does* want to destroy you. Never think, *Oh they didn't mean it.* That is merely a mind trick to help you suppress anger. Perhaps they didn't mean it. But Something in them *did.* People are programmed through emotions to compulsively inflict onto others the same harms that have been imposed on them. Face the emotional response to injustice. See that people *know not what they do.*

No human being has the power to pardon others for their errors. That is judgment of the kind properly reserved for God alone. Instead, forgive as we humanly can by not hating people for their shortcomings. Notice injustice, then freely move on, leaving anger behind. This is a "righteous judgment" of which you've surely heard. It has a far-reaching effect on our lives. We find that we can remain vigilant of the imperfect behavior in others without becoming bitter toward them.

Once liberated from the emotional binding of Self, we'll discern right from wrong, good from bad and true from false without acting the offensive arbiter of people's conduct. With emotional energy no longer contaminating our perception, loving jurisprudence triumphs. It supersedes the awful invitation to *play God.* We remain at peace, free of anger.

When we stop judging, we no longer waste valuable time squandering life-force, depleting the body and mind of its restorative energy. Without the complication of playing God, we're able to discern rather than judge. The velocity of emotional stress dragging us toward the end of our days slows down and time begins to lose meaning. Our body parts don't wear out as quickly. Our vascular system, brain circuitry, and joints last longer. Even the loss of hair and muscle is deferred.

There's a certain judicial economy within us to encourage the health of mind and body. It becomes activated with a forgiving spirit. What were once incapacitating issues eating away at our mental and physical integrity, now become contributors to overall wellness. We live long.

Let the buck stop with you. There's no difficulty or problem you can't endure safely once you've become immunized against emotional pressures. Invulnerability through watchfulness offers automatic mastery over all resentment.

***

You have read in this book about the dangers of an ambitious nature. Ambition establishes a resistance to God's will. It reinforces the wills of other people as well as the will of the Self, already in residence. Self-will cuts you off from God's vision, instantly disenfranchising you from the role you might otherwise play in service to Him. For this reason, you can spend a lifetime pandering to an excessive desire to secure earthly possessions—wealth, power, respect, and recognition. But does acquisition ultimately result in a better life? A better world?[91]

Surely you can recall Wall Street's greedy tycoon, Gordon Gecko. Or Mr. Potter from the 1940s movie *It's a Wonderful Life*—classic robber barons who plunder and sneer at corporations and society, taking their share, unwholesomely at the expense of others. This type of pillaging is iconic. But avarice and covetousness aren't limited to the canyons of Wall Street or Bedford Falls. It happens more in the less obvious niches of culture, among all of us.

Manipulation, greed and the chase of self-importance are firmly in place on Main Street and all the side streets too. Narcissistic, controllers abound at PTA meetings, on supermarket checkout lines, in police departments, at Girl Scout campouts, and most tragically in households—where emotionally greedy family members unwittingly feed on each other's life-force, depleting health and happiness. There are forces operating within which cannot be seen but need to be acknowledged and faced if we're to live wholly and in peace. You never know when or where the opportunity to either face and be rid of, or accept and embrace temptation will be presented.

See if you can identify with this scenario. Several years ago, I was standing at a convenience store counter paying for a loaf of bread. The clerk handed me my change and I decided to spend it on the spot so I wouldn't have to carry the cash around in my pocket. There I stood with two singles and some coins in hand. My eyes drew over to a colorful sign promoting the State Lottery. It advertised a $2.00 ticket for a chance to win $100,000. *Wow. That would be nice.* I compulsively bought it.

In that single deciding moment, something happened. First, there was a sense of exhilaration. My mind toyed with tantalizing thoughts. A vision of material comforts appeared in my head like a banner ad or one of those invasive pop-up videos everyone detests, the kind that starts even though you haven't *clicked play.*

I was instantly propelled into a happy future, experiencing a level of financial security well beyond what $100,000 could ever provide. It was as though I'd taken a mild stimulant, similar to cocaine or caffeine. Anyone observing wouldn't have caught it. I wasn't drunk. It was pleasurable, a little intoxicating really, a mild surge energizing my entire body.

Then in an instant, the mood soured. Artificial bliss drained from my solar plexus and was gone. I felt cheap, now stunned not with the fantasy but by a keen sense of guilt. I had artificially elevated my stature, playing God in my head. Now I hurt. The emotion hangover lasted hours.

Everyone experiences fantasy. But the guiltier you become the more fantasy you'll need to fill the void where virtue is missing. You'll find dreams and support for self-centered desire anywhere you can. It can be by volunteer work, business success, bank robbing, telemarketing fraud or drug dealing. Yes, it can even be found through State Lotteries.

By the way, I did win that lottery. My ticket paid off with two more dollars. With those, I could have purchased yet one more ticket for still another chance at even greater wealth. It would have launched me into one more guilt-inducing exploit.

I tossed the winning ticket into the garbage, breaking the cycle. *No thanks*, I thought.[92]

Just like all those who hit big in lottery drawings, had my winning been more substantial, life would not have become better. The ensuing loss of consciousness would have ultimately contributed toward a diminished existence. There are people for whom lottery gaming and casino gambling becomes an obsession. Whatever preoccupies the mind becomes a diversion from a consciously lived life, blinding and preventing us from seeing our errors.

We all start out as inquisitive, brilliant children. But then willfully fall to pursuing the mundane. Something as trite as a lottery ticket purchase can dull the soulfulness of the brightest individual. Once we begin to view creature comforts and wealth as the cure for emotional discontentment it becomes extremely difficult to face the world again. Money and ambitiously obtained comforts never deliver the enduring freedom from fear or anxiety we need to live truly well.

There is a proper way to access and maintain material possessions. But unless motives are in check and free from ambition, they can never bring true joy. Not because you're punished for avarice, but because of the self-centered person you've become to chase them in the first place. The slightest bit of greed clouds our ability to prioritize. We lose the advantage of intuitively knowing what needs to be done in each new moment. Schedules turn into schemes. Organizers become connivers.

Ambitious overreach for material comfort booby traps the labor toward it, eventually turning work into resentment filled drudgery. Self-willfulness destroys all hope for ever attaining what we believe we're working toward. It sucks the joy out of enterprise, career, and profession. How ironic it is to be blocked from truly enjoying the pleasures we've so determinedly wrested out of the world.

Don't think for a second that I'm suggesting complacency. I am saying nothing of the sort. The inability to execute is as draining of vitality as being wrongly motivated. It too is failure. A passive attitude in business and commerce is an invitation to be overrun by predators and outmaneuvered by competitors. Hard work, developing skill sets, getting tough, durable and excellent in every way possible, in all endeavors, are vital.

There will always be moments to act. Sometimes, elements of competitiveness and even outright aggression are appropriate. Ambition-free savvy is, by far, more effective than conniving. In abandoning willfulness, you'll know when to apply energy and when to reserve. You'll rise above the fray of those who seem to have so many good ideas, yet little initiative to execute them. Your creativity will activate and you'll have the energy to carry innovative ideas to fruition more often. Physical and mental integrity is preserved for proper use without worldly stress draining you of life-force.

Your business and workplace environments will become enhanced naturally because you'll surround yourself with productive people. These people will love working with you and for you.[93] No one can conduct business for long or work well beside a nervous Nellie or Ned. Emotionally charged anxiousness not only wears down the body and mind, but it upsets everyone else too. There's a much better will. It isn't your will. It isn't the will of any other human being. But it's readily available anytime for you to borrow. It's God's will.

Becoming conscious even for a moment opens the psyche, allowing God's will to enter. A smidgeon will do. The moment you let it in the flow begins, and you are drawn in His direction. God graciously gifts us with a shard of His own so that we become God-conscious. Then we discover Him within.

In activating *conscious contact* with Him, the first thing you'll notice is increased patience. Oversensitivity to negative, emotional energy like anger, diminishes. You'll also notice an infusion of energy. You will properly meet each moment going forward with just the right measure of force. Think of this as "Daily bread"—*strength* fueling the mind and body, gently nudging you toward Him. This is God's call, supplying the means for the journey. It's an unmerited gift. A minuscule but potent chip of this power keeps us moving toward improving our *conscious contact* with Him.

So abandon the idea it is your will that contains the power to accomplish anything worthwhile. See how what you've always thought of as your *will* isn't yours at all. It has been the will of a lower nature. Through your unconsciousness, the dark will of something sinister has expressed through you. This Ego must diminish for the sake of your well-being, that goodness might come through you. Now starve your Self. Allow God to supply you *Daily Bread.* In awareness, there's food the Self detests. It supplies the fuel that strengthens the spirit.

In accepting God's will, His vision and positive flow of energy overwhelm and weaken the baleful will of your lower Self. While It chokes on God's vision and goes hungry for hate, you become nourished by His power—love flowing in and through you. Now you become incompatible with anger.

By now you've noticed some rather surprising proposals in this book. It's only natural that you might approach these with at least *some* skepticism. This is healthy and to be expected. Until one has embraced and lived the conscious state doubts can remain. But please don't close your mind to the spiritual principles and practical understanding found here. Elsewhere in this book is a chapter on meditation. Please read and use it. Once illuminated, doubt does not survive the Truth.

There is a struggle between good and evil. It goes on in the minds of us all. If you meditate properly you'll experience *mindful consciousness* as the *Spirit of Doubt* meets It's Superior—the *Spirit of Truth*. In becoming conscious you'll become a witness to the battle for your sanity, your serenity— for your life.

As long as you don't reject consciousness, your experience will parallel those I write about in this book. If you reject consciousness, then much of the wondrous predictions you'll read about won't happen. But a beginning should be made. Meditate as directed, or you may never know.

For most, the initial experience with the *non-contemplative consciousness exercise* is too remarkable for words. But allow me to describe some of what to expect at the outset. The first thing you'll notice are light emissions inside the forehead, followed by a transfer of energy from the head into the hands. This is all that's necessary. If you've never meditated properly before, please don't be alarmed by the simple physics here. It is easily explained.

Your body is an intricate electrical machine. Your cellular construction, the protein in muscle and tissue, is composed of electrically charged amino acids. Each molecule carries a perceptible charge. You are constantly absorbing electronic energy which the body pulsates throughout its structure, making you *abuzz* with tiny currents. We all literally run on this electricity.

When you meditate as shown you'll see and feel some of the positive force the exercise stimulates to flow. This energy comes from God. Soon, as more is absorbed, even more Light will become noticeable. It'll illuminate the darkness within—a displacement of negativity. The Light increases. Darkness decreases. You are becoming a child of Light.

Be sure to follow the recording exactly. Then after just a few moments of practice, you'll learn precisely how to extend Light from your head into your hands. As a circuit within completes, a new code of living is switched on. With continued practice, you'll notice this energy charging first through the torso and then the entire body. I liken it to a *warm chill*, not unlike what it feels like following a gulp of alcohol or the rush from a snort of cocaine. In this case, however, there is a low voltage pulse or *shiver* that moves downward through your body.

No need for alarm. The electric surge sensation is only mildly stimulating. Its delicate current is barely detectable in the beginning. But don't let that subtleness fool you. What may at first seem flimsy will not be for long. It is comparable to small drops of water collecting into a trickle, then eventually sufficient to prime a powerful pump, activating a free-flowing torrent. Just one tiny glint of energetic will—His will, is enough to nudge you in His direction.

Some of this physiology may seem extraordinary. Rest assured, you'll become used to it quickly. But do not get hung up with these effects. They are simply a few of the physical reactions to metaphysical infusion. The real magic is yet to come.

As you are drawn nearer, God comes to meet save you.[94] But you'll need to make the first move. He's set up this seemingly bizarre existence so that rescue from all the hellish harm it contains could become possible. Go toward God as He draws nearer to you or else move away, giving up your freedom. Make the decision to commit both life and will to your Creator. You'll experience daily clarity, one moment at a time. The power of awareness will affect you, me and everyone in ways never imagined.

Just one single moment of clarity within one single person can change the world forever.

Take Bill Wilson, 1930s New York Investment Banker, for example. You may have heard of him as the first co-founder of "Alcoholics Anonymous." I use him as an example because I have an affinity for the people in "Alcoholics Anonymous," having once had a problem with liquor in my own life. His fall from grace is so classic that nearly everyone can identify at some level, alcoholic or not.

Wilson was an ambitious man, driven by an egoistic obsession for success. But he was also prone to promiscuity, depression, alcohol abuse and finally alcoholism. We know how he developed these obsessions. It happened the same way it does to all alcoholics and addicts. He was betrayed by unloving parents. There was nothing he could have done at the time to stop it.

Before Bill had reached his teen years, his philandering father ran off, leaving both he and his younger sister with his mother, Emily. She was an impatient, overbearing woman who resented motherhood. She hated her own children. So, within a few short years, she abandoned them too, leaving for Boston to pursue a medical career. It was a terrible one-two punch for any kid. A self-centered couple like the Wilson's, having no love for their own children would have been terrible parents. Unfortunately for Bill, he was raised by them. He ended up living out his teens with his grandfather in Vermont.

Like many, Wilson's first big obsession came as a teenager. It was sex. He became emotionally reliant on the approving affections of a girl named Bertha Bamford, a dependency he later shifted onto the equally conscience-numbing effect of alcohol. Bill became increasingly fueled by resentments and fear, those negative emotions hampering his ability to reach the heights of success he craved. He developed an absurdly oversized self-will, the kind that takes control of the thinking in all obsessive people.

Under the strain of this scenario, Bill never had a chance for a normal life. His parents betrayed him and he was instantly infected with hatred toward them.[95] This is the classic setup. Weak parenting, brokenness, rising resentment, pursuing relief through sex and foods like alcohol or sugar, until one of these makes life so corrupt, either one recovers or else takes the debauched lifestyle to the bitter end.

Bad parenting didn't directly create Bill Wilson's alcoholism. He managed to do that all on his own. Wilson became an alcoholic the same way that all alcoholics and problem drinkers develop an obsession with alcohol. It was fueled by resentment projected onto him by a selfish mother and father. Betrayed, anger drove him to seek obsessive solutions to his internalized heartbreak.

Bills case leaned toward the drastic side—a complete rejection. This is not so with everyone. Some people cry, "Oh, not me. I come from a loving family." They are appalled at the possibility that there has been little or no love in their upbringing. What is sometimes construed as love has not been. Betrayal most often comes in subtle ways. Impatience, deceitfulness, infidelities and the absence of virtue in the slightest will cause a child to resent and to seek relief.[96]

The failure of a father, through weakness or absence, to teach his children how to forgive both real and imagined injustices, always sets off a lifetime of emotional grief. No one's immune.[97]

Bill's passions, especially anger, set him on a course where he became a lousy husband, physically and mentally ill, and unable to work effectively. Finally, there was what would be for him, a critical irony. Financial ruin.

But we also know that he found a way out of the predicament, co-founding "Alcoholics Anonymous," one of history's most significant spiritual movements. Bill Wilson went down a tragic path but then recovered, discovering God-consciousness.

The solution was not simply to stop drinking. That would have been treating an effect and not the cause. There had to be more. *There was.*

Newly sober from a stint in a hospital specializing in detoxification and recovery, Bill Wilson found himself dejected, standing in an Akron hotel lobby at the bad end of a failed business trip. He was already abstinent of alcohol, but he was also financially broke and full of emotional discontentment. Dry as a bone, Wilson had lost what he had back in the Big City. There he had enjoyed freedom from anger and a release from obsessive boozing.[98]

Now, antagonized by reemerging ambition, Bill's thinking sped him toward the kind of solutions with which he already had a disastrous familiarity. Ambitiousness, sex, and booze—three of Bill's longtime famous darlings. Not original as far as distractions go. Still, a tried and true trio of corruption whenever used this way—the way he was itching to. With these, he could prevail over self-pity and boost his esteem to a high place where pain could not reach.

It was a scheme, of course. *Have a couple of stiff drinks, find a willing sex partner and willfully roll up his sleeves to fix the problem.*

Boy, now that would have put his mind to rest for a spell. Pleasures do that.

In that moment, millions of certain lives were going to be lost to spiritual dereliction, disease, and alcoholism. Then something astounding happened. In a flash, in a twinkling of an eye, Bill has a special moment. It was as if something or

Someone had descended upon the hotel lobby, tapped him on the shoulder and said, "Psst! Billy. Wake up, pal. You have responsibilities, you know… to your family… to other alcoholics who will die unless you show them how not to."

Ah yes! He gets a sudden realization. This new idea enters the stockbroker's consciousness. And with that innovative attitude, before Bill can move so much as a single muscle, the future of the world is instantly altered. Suddenly, *all hell* is bound up, packaged and sealed into a box. The temptation to cheat on his wife Lois, to drink, then ambitiously play the hero with his busted business deal, are each likewise bust.

He's led away from temptation by an invisible force of protection he doesn't even realize is *Present*.

Instead, he'll seek out another alcoholic. He'll call a local clergyman to set it up. Now, Bill is going to meet Dr. Bob. The pair is going to find a whiny voiced attorney named Bill Dotson. They'll go find a fellow drunk named Clarence Snyder. AA is going to form a worldwide fellowship. I am going to include this narrative about the event in this book and you're going to read these words, *now*.

Bill is saved from his pessimistic thinking through *consciousness* and a new *now* can unfold for all of us—even non-alcoholics. He thanks God for his restored clarity and moves forward into a series of activities leading him to a certain mindful lifestyle. He maintains *conscious contact* with God. Later he would write all about it, saving millions of lives.

This awakening event, on the ground floor lobby of a busy, Midwestern hotel was the founding dawn of the granddaddy of all Twelve Step Fellowships, "Alcoholics Anonymous." A worldwide spiritual fellowship flowered out of a single spore of conscious awareness in the mind of one man, in one moment of one day in 1934.

Bill never did *close* on his investment banking deal. He never earned his prized commission or received a single share of stock from the deal. Yet a new future was created. The world was changed forever. And as for you dear reader, this change is so only because the story now exists to be told. Just like Wilson, your own circumstances are simply a torrent of events—new *nows* continuously streaming by.

The precise shape taken by that non-existent time we refer to as *the future* depends on how you meet each new now moment. By simply watching, remaining awake in the conscious state, you allow your personal role in the universe to disclose.

Worriers are rebels. For them, nothing ever goes right. However, the simple act of becoming aware brings us into contact with God and we find peace. Then, as we demonstrate the willingness to allow Him into us, He employs His will over any other. In those moments, life unfolds under His vision without the challenge of your rebellious nature against God. There can be no worry.

If you could travel in time back into the past, even with the knowledge of the future, you'd still make the exact same decisions again, including the mistakes. Whatever trouble your actions brought upon yourself and other people would be repeated. Unless your nature changes you can't help but duplicate error.

Fortunately, no one has to go back in time to reorder their current existence. By properly meeting new *present moments* as each instant becomes a new *now*, a non-existent future that could not have been predicted is perfectly revealed. In taking your place on life's journey, the *present* will simply unfold as you go along. Remain conscious and awake for life, *now*.

Sometimes you'll hear someone lament a pained life saying, "I don't want my past to become my future." This is the haunting voice of dread speaking. The stress on the body and mind of someone who lives in such fear is ultimately fatal.

Fear is an emotion—a brand of resentment energy spun out of imagined events yet to occur. When fear fails to take us out *of the present,* we remain here, *now,* and there isn't any future or past to affect us either negatively or positively. We stop worrying. Our bodies and minds ease, always prepared and useful. *Consciousness* is the only protection we have against fear, ensuring we remain ever watchful and living only in the present moment. It's the only time any of us has or will ever need.

During our lifetimes, we are regularly placed into high spots as well as low spots. The most efficient ride is down the center, experiencing events from a position of emotional neutrality. From this middle ground, we experience the good along with the bad without becoming overwhelmed by the emotional energies of either.

Unless understood, this principle is one that others can use against you. People who understand how you respond to conditions can control you by manipulating those conditions. Remaining centered and free, you will retain your integrity despite their efforts. No one can take advantage of you as long as you are objective. Just know in a general way that there will be trials from which to grow as well as triumphs to enjoy. Avoid fixating on a future that does not yet exist.

Impatience encourages a fearful attitude that is resentful of the unknown. There can be a great temptation to willfully struggle in the attempt to alter an imagined destiny, manifesting desirable outcomes, as god may. Seeking specific knowledge of events to come is dangerous. Even if you obtain it, you'll find yourself more frustrated than had you never known what to expect.

So, never deliberately try to know the future. To purpose your days trying to alter the imminent course of an imagined destiny will embroil you with struggle. Lost in the scheming mind, a lapse in consciousness guarantees approaching opportunities will be ill-fated. Perhaps not immediately, but ultimately.

In the dulling struggle to receive what It feels It deserves, the lower Egocentric Nature attempts to wrest control away from He who orchestrates all events in the stream of life. Life reduces to, "My will be done," instead of, "Thy will be done." This is the pitiful plight of all who become involved in the occult and the services of psychic mediums, egoistically trying to foretell and manipulate outcomes.

Forearmed with the knowledge of a sorry fate, we will still choose self-willed determination over faith in hopes of altering outcomes. We will develop a self-centered lifestyle, trusting our limited selves rather than placing reliance on an unlimited God.

Just as the best way to limit one's future is to ambitiously try to make it happen, the way to ensure misfortune is to center on evading every hardship. No alcoholic, addict, or obsessive individual, preoccupied with their own security and comfort, can ever develop into a sane, sound individual. How could they? They've never developed the necessary aptitude for meeting hardship properly—with patience and love.

Alternately, if you were to obtain prior knowledge of *good fortune*, your immersion in ecstatic thinking would quickly turn into an all-consuming preoccupation. Anxiety would soon be nipping at your heels and quickly sabotage any peace that might otherwise have been. The reason psychic fortune telling ultimately renders participants worse off than before isn't necessarily because mediums and soothsayers are charlatans. It's true that some are. But many are not.[99]

Still, failure is inevitable, because even when information about the future proves to be accurate, intellectual foreknowledge subverts the goodness of natural prescience. The ambitiousness of a selfish desire to know eclipses what you would otherwise realize intuitively. It introduces a strange mysticism, placing an arrogant reliance on outmaneuvering fortune ahead of a humble faith in God.

Rejecting intuitive precognition in favor of rote knowledge is a refusal of redemption. It places intellectualism before spirituality, blocking out God. For this reason, occultists who encourage divination and predict outcomes harm more people than they pretend to help. Promoting ambition and worry, these predators play to the fears of those who long for relief from anxiety, but haven't yet mastered resentment.

The expression *worried sick* isn't a misnomer. It's a warning sign, that you've set aside humility. Living to foretell or learn the future results in struggle, manifesting in emotional and physical disorders.

Insight also offers forward-looking perception. But instead of encouraging fear, it lends a healthy preparedness for what is to come, supplying discerning, nonjudgmental vision. It is only born out of intuition.

Chronic worriers, please be advised.

When we are observant in each moment, we lose all proclivity toward fear. We cannot worry because there's no imaginary future to swallow up our attentiveness in the *present*. Life never feels foreboding. We receive an instant installation of faith. But this only happens as we become vigilant in the *present moment.*

The unspoken stillness in one single second of conscious awareness contains more Power in it than do all the positive affirmations ever muttered. Through the clear lens of objectivity, outlook automatically becomes positive. In that moment, all fear melts away and we exist now, not in the future. There's never a need to conjure artificial counterbal-ance through thinking.

Our deepest, darkest fear is that we might discover the truth, that we are not infinitely powerful, we are not God after all, and that only He is. There's Something residing deep inside each of us, that masquerades as us and is terrified to learn It is inadequate, not the Supreme Being and never will be.

It is a Phantom that desperately wants to be God, curses the notion that It is not, and It will cling to any hope for infinite power over the universe as if It were God. Unless we learn to detach and live free of this Dark Impostor and become our true selves, we will share It's fear of inferiority as if it was ours.

But, once we become unbound from It, we cease playing God. Light enters. We sense the flow of power that is not of us but of our Creator. Then we become empowered to do His will on earth as it flows out of a heaven within us and unto others.

No one can teach you peace, serenity, or security. You cannot install enlightenment or happiness in yourself, and it can't be lectured into you to by a preacher or guru. No one has the power to coach it into your behavioral system or your mind either. If you try to collect enlightenment out of reading, studying or absorb it like news, you will only become frustrated and ironically, unenlightened. Peace and goodwill through enlightened reasoning is a supernaturally intuitive gift. It is delivered simultaneously and automatically with becoming still, and realizing that you are not God.

Many people have had what they've come to know as *spiritual experiences or awakenings,* where they encounter changes in perception and attitude. These inaugurate a new era in their lives and are typically powerful experiences. You may have had one of these yourself. The difficulty comes in keeping this condition alive going forward. This will not be an issue once you commit to properly practicing awareness each day.

Just as cardio exercises like walking or running can boost metabolism for hours after each session, the benefits of exercising consciousness through meditation are carried with you all day long.

The stream of life is strong and persistent. It contains dangerous debris and temptation to get upset. Stress never ceases. Negative emotions arising out of resentment, such as anger, frustration, and fear are a constant threat. The temptation to judge is always just outside the entrance to our psyches. The fall of all mankind depends on human unconsciousness to enter, feed and nurture the ravenous Egos within each of us. We should be attentive, watching, always vigilant of its presence. Awareness keeps these harmful energies at bay. This is God-consciousness and it is our psychic shelter in the storm.

Without consciousness, we will be forever doomed to repeating old mistakes. Foolish decisions, retaliation, thoughtless errors in judgment will be the rule rather than the exception.

But exception can become the new rule, once we wake up. The lost discipline to always do the "next right thing" returns in the light of mindful awareness. A powerful force of consciousness activates attentive perspective from within. Ongoing watchfulness advances. A perpetual cycle of awareness and insight increases with each day of practice. We cultivate understanding and usefulness, automatically bringing forth goodwill from heaven within onto earth.

Through a neutral state of mind, strength, supplied by our *Daily Bread*[100] we stay awake and moving in God's direction. His clear vision remains alive within us. Otherwise, blurred vision is corrected. We come to appreciate values in seemingly negative events, each serving an ultimate good we may not see at first. We lose the nasty habit of indulging in resentful judgment. This is to say that *we cease playing God.*

Watch and Discern. Everything and Everyone.

What's happening right now? Observe without judging, never turning a blind eye to the injustice or cruelty you see. Discerning vision exposes both the good and bad. In the Light of Now, there can be no fear of the future. Through error observed, you overcome fear.

Unthinking, selfish people serve a great purpose.

Point Five

The Fifth Chapter

By which the nature and origin of resentment are revealed and you realize how crucial it is to get free from anger. In abandoning bitterness, you cease the lifelong struggle with irritating people. Inner peace is possible in this lifetime.

Whether in secret or out in the open, becoming upset is the cause of every trouble you've ever had or will have. Nothing else in life will have more vital an impact on you and your loved ones than discovering how to exist without resentment energy leeching into your psyche.

If you would develop mastery over the scourge of resentment during your lifetime, how different life would become. Along the way, you'd evade imminent diseases and nearly all pre-existing conditions would heal. You wouldn't harbor vices, bad habits or addictions.

Balanced and healthy, you could not suffer from any mental disorders or emotionally caused physical illnesses. Your body and mind would auto-correct against any aberration because you could no longer become upset. You'd be immune to literally all the so-called *lifestyle diseases.*[101]

Even environmentally caused diseases from natural and man-made origins would have a hard time doing you in. You couldn't develop any addictions to substances or behaviors like food, alcohol or sex because the need for the relief these obsessions supply would be non-existent. Obsessions for anything could never arise and those which have previously been a problem would simply drop away. You would not become subject to emotionally induced conditions that warp and kill off the body by morbid energetic force.

Then, at the natural conclusion of your lifespan, your body parts would just stop working—the result of normal wear and tear. Instead of dying from heart disease, or immune system malfunction, you would peacefully pass away from old age.

By *peacefully*, I mean without a body or mind that's been shot through with resentment. This horrible, life destroying force is at the core of all your problems whether they be physical, mental, financial, or having to do with relationships. Discovering how to remain unaffected is essential. If it were as easy as saying, "Okay, I just won't be resentful anymore," everyone who could recognize this would do it. They would simply wish their hostile emotions away.[102]

Although it is simple, getting free from resentment isn't possible by sheer will. Resentment is as pervasive as it is ubiquitous. There is no psychology that can manage it. Intellectual analysis can't. You would become reliant on the people supplying those devices if you used them. It would do little good to try and arrange your life as though you could dodge resentments. Even if you seclude yourself alone in a cave, you'd soon be tempted to get angry with the cave walls. To remain free of negative emotions and clear of anger we must have Supernatural help.

Or, let's say you were to eliminate all sensory inputs and attempted to exist in an isolation tank. Your mind will taunt you with manufactured illusions. Before long, you'd spin resentment into a hatred for imagined enemies, succumbing to bitter loathing—first for yourself and then God. Finally, you would go mad.

If you could create a long-term environment for yourself, free of stress, surrounded only by tranquility and quiet where no one could upset you, one of two things would happen. You'd either go mad in the "perfect" world or you would compulsively bring ruin to your mock paradise. Whichever, eventual chaos would prevail, making your effort to escape the pressures of the world a futile farce.

Even if you moved to another country to escape the source of irritation, an inner appetite for destruction would follow, projecting bitterness into the new environment. Resentment is everywhere. There's no way you're going to avoid the threat of universal negativity. There's imperfection in the world and we all must live with it. They are essential temptations, each cruelty and unfair episode another opportunity to meet stress with a forgiving spirit. No matter how traumatic, every incident strengthens us when met with dispassionate awareness. This becomes vital to growth.

Conversely, with each failure to meet upsetting pressures gracefully, we become weaker and subject to even more of the same.

People in your life who upset you are setting you up to do their bidding, not only now but also in the future. In responding with bitterness, you become their slave. Since life isn't flawless, welcome other's imperfections. Their shortcomings are opportunities to overcome the temptation to hate by loving.

Consciousness ensures that even the most horrific event or the most contentious behavior of people in your life will work toward eventual good that you can leverage into benefit. There is safety in simply rising above the temptation to resent them, no matter what the circumstance. Each time that consciousness masters a resentment the will of a lower Self automatically becomes subject to God's will. Now you can observe injustice from a neutral vantage point. Whatever your actions, though flawed, they will eventually serve to fulfill the Creator's vision for you rather than Self's will. It won't like this. *Too bad for It.*

What is resentment made of and why are its effects so fatal? If you only knew the magnitude of this universal energy you might cry out to your Maker to be saved from it. But the truth is too horrible. And so every human being on the face of the earth who cannot bear to look must turn away, remaining defenseless in a world filled with cruelty and many unfair tempters toward anger.

Many people can tell you what resentment is from an etymological perspective. Derived from Latin, the word resentment simply means *to feel again*. This is good to know. But just knowing the origins and meanings of words provides little understanding of just what those words embody.

Intellectual knowledge isn't the same as understanding and is no match for the wordless revelation of truth. Without truth, the sheer knowledge of words leaves the yearning soul unsatisfied, always on the intellectual prowl for more meaning. When unrequited metaphysical questions remain, uncertainty leaves the seeker at risk of repeating error. Life becomes a hollow, fruitless journey of lessons never learned—a never-ending succession of distractions purposely designed to keep truth from as many ears as possible. It's to keep every affected person willfully fighting against a power they have no hope of ever conquering on their own. The struggle is in vain.

You can no more save yourself from the immense force of resentment than you can escape the power of gravity. Any distress you may have had in the past or may now experience falls immutable under this principle. This is part of a terrifying secret that's been reserved and kept hidden throughout the centuries. And so, unnecessary suffering continues. It is on purpose. However, by the time you've completed this chapter, this will change for you. Once truth is revealed, the education from within activates. Your life will never be the same.

Please come to grips with the startling truth that resentment doesn't originate inside you, but it does *get inside* you. It is one essential element in an inexhaustible field of negative energy originating with darkness. It radiates as an endlessly wicked force throughout the galaxies of the universe. By the time this unholy energy finds us, depending on our spiritual fitness, we're either primed and ready to receive it or else we are protected from it by inner Light—the infilling of positive energy.

The Source of Light is the only Power in the universe capable of displacing and saving us from resentment. We can't save ourselves.[103] For this reason, we yearn for our Creator, that He will "Lead us away from temptation, delivering us from the Evil One." Darkness cannot coexist in the same place as Light. To be filled with Light is to experience protection.[104]

Human beings are conductors of positive or negative energy, not generators. We're mere carriers of either depending on our attitude, entirely unable to manufacture or self-manage our own emotions. We don't create love or hate, but in moments of temptation, we'll take sides with either. Whichever will depend on our inner condition, and whether we have become still and conscious, allowing Light inside.

When we are conscious that Light enters and we are instantly rescued from all bitterness.[105]

If not, we remain in darkness, suffused in hostility. Anytime we are preoccupied and unconscious, we also remain attached to Self. This is when we're most likely to become upset.

In the subsequent emotionality, we unwittingly allow an Ego identity to feed on the negative energy It craves in order to judge. These are the moments where bitterness overwhelms. We regress into ugly, emotional creatures of the darkness. It is not we who have become dark, but a shadowy personality, the malicious entity within to which we unwittingly pledge our allegiance.

Please don't be upset by this. I know how shocking some may find this idea at first. It can be disconcerting to discover that God isn't the only powerful Force in the universe. There is ominous Darkness as well. But be comforted to know that there is protection available too. To access it, simply observe the Dark Thing that rises to feed. Once illuminated by the Light within, It shrinks, unable to nourish It's unholy nature. The appetite for hate goes unsatisfied. It cowers and shakes in fear. Remain awake and God's grace will protect, never letting you down.

The lower Self craves resentment energy. Every one of us has our daily run-ins with this terrible force. There is no escape in this lifetime. Unless you learn to live in a conscious, mindful state you'll continually become frustrated by anger and negative emotions. Emotionalized threats to serenity and conscious awareness appear during the times you are unaware. As they well up inside, it will seem as though you are the source of poisonous feelings. You may react unfairly by projecting anger and judgment on yourself. *Who but the most horrible person could enjoy such rancor,* you may think.[106] Each bitter occurrence reinforces the mind with thoughts of what an awful person you must be.

Without consciousness, the only resolution for self-loathing is to use whatever emotional counterbalances are available. You'll be inexplicably drawn to outward pleasures that deaden the inner pain of conscience. For most of us, this means to eat more, smoke more, please people more, seek more approval, drink more—the only way to keep up is to develop new vices or step up the ones we already have. Soon we will have become a despicable humanoid collection of bad habits, a disheartening condition that frustrates us even further.

Resentment is the food on which Ego feeds and grows. Without hate, It would starve. The more resentment It receives the more selfish nature[107] is nurtured. A vicious hunger for control of the universe evolves through you, whenever you hate. First, It takes you over, then It moves to control others. You've felt this unsettling force radiating from people. It has likely made you uncomfortable around them.

When it has been in you, others have become likewise suspicious. Until you are freed from the *bondage of Self*, they'll continue to feel this uneasiness with you. Relationships become hellish exchanges that instigate discord. The sooner you starve Ego of Its life-force the sooner and better you'll get along with others, and they with you. Learning to recognize the temptation to resent, *prior to* indulging, is key.

Please realize that negative thoughts are always out on the doorstep of your thinking mind. Placed there by a cunning Self, these take several predictable forms. They could be resentful opinions expressing doubt or frustration. They may be internal dialogues waiting for a suitable episode to judge a child or a stranger. They could appear as a voice in the head, angrily condemning you for some expired failing out of the past. They might even appear disguised as positive thought, manifesting a pleasant voice in the head, perhaps your own. These try to convince you how wonderful and superior to others you are.

To recognize them you must remain aware. For as long as we breathe, bedeviling forces beyond our doing will surface. Despite the ever-threatening potential for these to cause us great harm, it remains our legacy as humans to learn patience. Ignore, suppress or struggle to control these temptations at great peril. Sanity is at stake.

So, if what I claim is true, you may wonder, *If we can't avoid resentment and if it is indeed everywhere, is there any hope for protection?* "Yes, there is," I say. Some of us have discovered a powerful defense. Most haven't, but since you're already reading this book, then you've come to the right place to discover it for yourself. Within. This should be encouraging news to you.

To access protection, first realize the nature of anger.

You see, in truth, you never really *get angry*. It's more accurate to see how *anger gets you*. It can be seen rearing out of the universal miasma. Since anger originates as a foreign energetic force, it can be detected as it approaches, before it reaches you. But only when you're awake and conscious. Watchfulness, through the lens of mindful consciousness, affords resilience from all negativity in the stream of life.

There is spiritual hardiness available if you'll stop struggling in the attempt to install happiness through knowledge and deeds. Mindfully exercise the virtuous inclination of your heart while the protective shield of grace prevails. Simply allow yourself to become still for it. Be aware in the Light of consciousness and the Invisible Defender appears. Redemption is in that instant. You're saved from harm, led away from the temptation to hate. Too simple for busy, complicated minds, and ultra-simple for the willing.

Have you ever noticed how in the past, whenever you've gotten upset it wasn't until you were overwhelmed with the emotion that you felt the sting? By then it was too late. Resentment had breached your psyche while you were unaware. You never saw it coming. That's because the negative energy contained in resentment reaches our lower Self surreptitiously by means of our own thinking.[108] It needs the intellectual processing of ideas to gain access to the psyche. It will generate thoughts to make it so.

When conscious, we are placed into an extraordinary dimension of being, separated from thinking. It is a position from where we can spot emotional energies prior to them striking. As we observe, we naturally detach from the stream of thought. The simple state of mind where we are *aware* prevents resentful, psychic violation. We gain impartiality and foresight, neutralizing the approaching force of negativity pushing in our direction.

Now, thoughts pass harmlessly outside the psyche, failing to enter us where they might otherwise feed a dark Thing inside. We're spared. This is the *forgiveness* experience. It happens each time we overlook the error in whoever and whatever has tempted us to indulge in anger. Until each of us learns to live consciously, apart from the stream of thinking, not only will we never know what this is but we may never even know that we don't know.It's only when our attention falters, allowing emotions to crop up within, that we become susceptible. Then we are likely to get upset at any moment. Anger enters. The invasion wreaks unspeakable havoc in our bodies and minds. Self-centered behavior spreads our misery unto those around. We *foul the nest*, so to speak.

Often it is loved ones we do not wish to harm who suffer the most from our selfish lack of vigilance. What has been done to us, we do to them. In turn, they pass our cruelty onto others. Surely you can you see what a pandemic scourge negative emotion is and how *spiritual disease* can run in families— passed on from generation to generation.

For your part, for the sake of generations to come, let it stop with you. And it will. But only once you get free of anger. That will be the moment you become God-conscious and begin improving that state of being through daily practice.

Meeting resentment calmly, watching the world without becoming emotionally caught up, delivers the perfect protection. Then even though you may feel its sting, resentment won't overtake you. It is impossible. You'll bounce back from all threats unscathed, stronger and more resilient for the experience. The Ego will have been deprived of the vile, emotion-laced food it craves, and your true spirit will remain, now nourished by the Light of God's grace.

But be genuine about it. Spiritual composure cannot be forced or artificial in any way. If there's the slightest pretense, anger will continue to prevail over sanity and growth toward Him will regress. As the spirit degenerates so does the body and mind.

Like many drugs, anger is a stimulant. It arouses organic compounds in the body directing blood pressure and glucose levels, heart functions and neurological responses to the stress. For this reason, it's important to not gloss over irritations no matter how small. Smiling, pretending you are happy, joyous and free of the bitter emotional surge only allows an indulgent Self to feast in secret. Sooner or later the nourished beast will rise in It's cave to destroy your life. Then it will take you.

The fight-or-flight response directs how we respond to all the aggravating events we encounter in our personal life stream. Ultimately, the wear and tear of emotional stimuli will break the body down. Unrecognized resentments kept in secret cause your heart to beat rapidly. Over time, it loses its ability to pump properly. Sticky plaque buildup develops inside coronary arteries. The cardiovascular system becomes diseased. Strokes and other coronary tragedies are the consequences of long-standing emotions.

Over time, suppressed anger nurtures a ravenous ego-self. Heart attacks and aneurysms, where fragile aortic plumbing just pops, are too common. If you've ever wondered why the most physically fit, peaceful, even "spiritual" person is so often the one to drop dead suddenly, this is the reason. It is this simple connection between animal physiology and spiritual meta-physiology.

With a doctor's warning, you could be motivated to accept a clinical treatment of symptoms, perhaps even staving off disaster through medications, compensatory dieting or exercise regimens.

Even so, if you remain subject to emotions, illness and sudden death remain an imminent risk. The way to live long and well, free of these health risks is to conquer resentment. Become resilient to emotional upset. Through the right kind of mindful awareness, the kind placing you into *conscious contact* with God, you'll endure all threats to your health and well-being.

Unrecognized emotions like anger and fear are often masked by a mantel of phony goodness or outward displays of healthful or pious living. These are just external compensations. Internally, negatively charged emotional energy still feeds a lower self, that in turn will dominate. As It grows, the human physique continues to weaken under worldly pressures. No human being can long survive suppressed emotional energy.

Doctors have much of this information already, but they have no idea what to do with it. That's because all disease, with rare exception, has spiritual origins. This is not in any way meant to disparage hard-working, well-meaning men and women in the medical communities. There are many doctors who are incredibly gifted and well trained. Despite their many physiologic skills and wondrous abilities, work within the spiritual realm remains beyond the capabilities of clinicians and medical practitioners.

Fortunately, we do not need them for all that much.[109] We can experience the healing of an ailing body or mind once we go within, where we receive the means for anger free living.

Living off the energy of *fight-flight* response is fine for animals. They're built for that kind of existence. We humans aren't. We are much more than meager biological units. We are created as spiritual beings, superior to animal creatures. It is right that we live and breathe, deriving physical substance as biological organisms. It's right for us to learn how to live from spiritual food too. This is nourishment animals cannot access. In forgoing instinctual animal motivators, and instead, turning to spiritual intuitiveness, we allow our Creator to nourish us. He directs our lives and runs the show while we live long and we know peace. To live off instincts, as the animals do, causes us to become animal-like and subject to an early grave.

While we're still young, it can seem that we're getting away with *playing God* for a while. In time however, spiritual brokenness and disconnection from the benevolent Source of life-energy cause the walls of our lives to crumble around us. We fall apart—physically, emotionally and mentally unless we learn how to overlook the error in people.

Overlooking doesn't mean looking the other way or ignoring those who cause us distress. It means we encounter cruel or unthinking people without becoming upset by their actions. Struggling with personalities who deliver stressful negative energy only results in distraction. It pulls you out of God-consciousness.

Why battle with careless, flawed people? Better to remain conscious. Receive them with eyes opened wide. Stand firm with grace by observing the temptation to become irritated with their errors. Watch resentment rise while you fill with the power to stand up to them with dignity. Acknowledge the temptation, keeping it within your view. You'll be amazed at the results of this before long.

Unless you get free from anger, you might never come to appreciate just how unmanageable your emotions are. You'll squander a life bound as a slave to Self, preserving the sick nature deep inside holding you hostage to thoughts, feelings, and whatever bliss or excitement you can scrape out of the world. Then, becoming addicted to those emotional states, you'll find yourself constantly edged toward death by stress, strangely drawn to substances and behaviors that make you sick and miserable. What a weird mess of life this is.

Despite the apparent show of piety, many religious or so-called, "spiritual," people continue to suffer unnecessarily. Even those who appear enlightened struggle with stubborn obsessions you would think they'd have been thrown clear of. Food, sex and chemical addictions to drugs like nicotine and other psychoactive medications are common. Behind-the-scenes suppression of emotions permits unfortunate lifestyles to continue, allowing the projection of phony goodness. You wouldn't want what those who lead secret lives have.

Beleaguered by self-centeredness, broken relationships, issues with wild children or maladies like cancer and heart disease, tragedies begin to surface. Their suffering seems as though it were some cruel, divine oversight. It can be tempting to ask, "How could God allow such things happen to these nice people?" But we don't know what goes on under a projected facade of goodness. Hypocrisy exists to tempt judgment. Discerning love without emotionally playing God is crucial.

Every so often we might come across certain good-natured people, who recognize how harmful resentment and anger is. You may encounter them in a variety of settings like self-help groups, group therapy, Twelve Step fellowships, Bible classes, and churches. They seem to intuitively sense that negative emotions aren't proper for humans. They want to be rid of it, but rather than allowing themselves to be saved from it, they remain caught in a struggle to become spiritually well.

Often, these are egoistic folks who, despite the profound acknowledgment that something is wrong, remain enslaved to a malevolent energy within. They just can't seem to shake it. It's a heck of a rut in which they find themselves.

These aren't evil people. They are simply folks who struggle because they don't realize that resentment doesn't stem from spiritual illness. No one has ever explained to them how it's the other way around. They don't realize that spiritual illness is the result of resentment. It alone is the divisive metaphysical energy that first separates us from our Creator. You must not be angry or become judgmental with these people.

Seeing wrong in others does no good when you're still wrong yourself. In self-righteousness, there's an exchange of justified, negative energy, between you and your "guilty" target. Although you dominate in the narrative imagined, you also self-authorize to become sicker and even more corrupt than those you condemn. A cycle of error remains. Eventually, you become those you've hated, your own defectiveness of character surpassing the flaws in others.

If you've been self-righteous in the past, and you recognize yourself here, it is crucial that you do not become upset by this description. Solve the problem you have with resentment. First, get freed from anger and become immediately well. This isn't hyperbole. I mean right then, in that moment. Unless we get free from anger, we won't ever have a life worth much. Perhaps this is your time. *Right now.*

Doubt is an especially strange phenomenon. It's the Instigator of Despair. Once accustomed to living mindfully, you'll awaken to the emotional dangers waiting on the doorstep of your being. A doubtful spirit will likely be offended and fearful of your conscious state. It won't want you to see what you see. It will challenge your new attitude. It'll project conflicted ideas into your thinking, condemning your consciousness, as if your awareness were the cause of your struggle.

Then in a final insult, It will judge you. You could become caught up in a loop of angry, critical thoughts directed at you.

Yes, the accusing spirit of old resides in us all. It waves a bony finger of condemnation. If you've ever suffered from any form of gloom, this is the simple cause. This isn't so difficult to defeat. The solution is to allow the emotional ties to break so that Light can defeat It. You cannot cure yourself of depression. The source of despair can't be medicated away with chemicals, wished away or psychologically outmaneuvered. All these do is masque the gloomy effects and delay some of the physical manifestations of anger. But you can still recover, simply by stepping outside of the thinking machinery that foments bitter, self-loathing. Once the cycle of emotion disintegrates, the thought-connection delivering judgment also severs and depression falls away.

If you'll objectively watch negative emotional force as it approaches without resenting what you see,[110] you'll become filled with the Power that conquers all resentment. This is how to discover the peace of mind. It is the spiritual liberty that comes once you realize how the judgment you feel within isn't yours at all. It belongs to Something sinister inside you that *plays God*.[111]

Several years ago, someone wrote a popular book titled *Don't Sweat the Small Stuff.* I never read it but at the time the title struck me. I felt that it spoke to an important concept, that the sum of the *small stuff* adds up to as much or more trouble for us as the *large stuff*.[112]

The now banned Chinese execution method, *Lingchi* loosely translates into English meaning, *Death by a thousand cuts.* In this barbaric form of punishment, death doesn't come all at once. Instead, many small wounds, none of which are alone fatal, add up to a slow and torturous demise.

This is also true of resentment. The pettiest annoyance or irritation counts. It could be a gesture, a glib remark or something as simple as a glance. It may be unpleasant news stories heard in passing, minor disagreements or just inconsiderate rumors lodged in the recesses of the mind. These all provoke unrecognized irritation—some are obvious but many are unrecognized. These are the niggling *sticks, stones, and cuts* of everyday life. Each can indeed break the bones and bleed to death anyone unprotected by God-consciousness.

"You almost crashed into me," or "That umbrella just missed poking my eye," suggest events with the potential to inflict even more harm than had the *poke* or *crash* actually happened. The countless *near misses* in life come packed with the silent but powerful metaphysical influence to cause real damage. Combined, these inconvenient encounters prove to be more significant than the most blatant injustices, since over time we develop a callousness toward them. Indifference easily conceals the suppression of emotion without us even realizing it.

On the surface, it appears we aren't *sweating the small stuff.* We might project a stoic stance in the face of little adversities, while the opposite is true. It isn't only the obvious disturbances in life that cause difficulty. There are many unrecognized *flavors* of resentment, just as potent. These are carried through the subtle unfair events passing by in the flotsam and jetsam of life's stream. It's easy to let down your guard So as best as you can, expect the unexpected. There's no need to become paranoid. Just stay alert and conscious as much of the time as possible.

***

Have you ever been prone to feelings of loneliness and boredom? These two emotions are so alike we should look at them together. If you've ever been guilty of using relationships as a distraction, then you've become a *people user.*[113] In self-centered relationships, people begin to serve the same purpose as consciousness-dampening drugs.

Once having developed a serious people-habit, the absence of others can produce symptoms paralleling physical and emotional withdrawal from an addictive chemical substance.

The longer you've been *using*, the more intense and unpleasant the effect.

Derive self-worth and approving "love" others supply, and people-connections quickly become an addiction. Loneliness is simply one more of the many flavors of resentment—a hollow, irritating sense cropping up through resenting the absence of others. Unless you detoxify and get free, then your need for people will always supersede the true altruism essential for getting along well with them. Until then, you can only use and be used. Cultivating wholesome relationships will be impossible.

A close relative to loneliness is *boredom*. We *miss* the constant stimulation of interaction with others because we've *used* it to distract ourselves. Once the diversion in consciousness is removed, the emptied time forces us to either face or run from the anxiety of conscience. In resenting emptiness, we experience *boredom*. Stillness becomes painful.

We face an unnatural compulsion toward distractive motion. This is the same pressure someone feels once they first begin to meditate properly[114]. Something inside compels them to stop and think about something else, even to run out of the room and begin some mundane activity—anything but be left alone with an impugning conscience. As seventeenth-century French Philosopher Blasé Pascal once observed, "All men's miseries derive from not being able to sit in a quiet room alone."

Each instant away from the *present moment,* where the Presence exists, separates us from God. We become fearful of ordinary life. The void of distraction compels us to seek excitement and intrigue. We could become a thrill-seeking adrenaline junkie,[115] running away from the stillness of a peaceful existence to over stimulated extremes where the awareness of inner pain cannot surface.

All real or imagined intrigue and excitement creates diversion.[116] So don't be so quick to be rid of loneliness or boredom. Emotional upsets, feelings of anxiety or even panic are telling you something. Embrace the hollow moments and perhaps allow them to reveal an underlying need for diversion.

If you could never resent, you could never feel bored. For this reason, you also need to remain alert for it. Not to sidestep boredom, but just as with loneliness, perhaps learn an appreciation for solitude and yes, even tedium. You can acquire much understanding just by being still and alone with your Creator. He will show you where resentment has crept in. It isn't you who fears the quiet. It is a dark nature that has taken up residence inside and trembles at the idea of *stillness*.

It wants to avoid the *now moment*, hating the Light of consciousness-illuminating truth in the *present*. It's resentful of silence. It knows The Presence It so despises is discovered in the quiet. Through thoughts of events past and future, It'll often seek to carry your attention as far from *now* as It possibly can. It wants you in a mesmerized state where you become vulnerable to negative ideas, It's judging and bitterness toward others. This is the danger of worry, fear, and dull, meaningless rumination.

Be wary of the tendency to escape monotony or solitude by ruminating. The musing mind serves the Ego once life becomes uneventful. Contemplating in bitterness is especially addictive. It appeals to the lower nature deep inside every human being that savors judging. Once the bait is taken it can be difficult if not impossible to break free from It's beguiling grip.

The more you ruminate in the past or future the more of life you aren't living now. As you become lost in fantasies the imagination becomes fertile ground for worry to grow. Anytime you allow thoughts of future events to take precedence over awareness of the *present* you become overwhelmed by fear.

Whether they're pleasing or objectionable thoughts, ruminating in memories of the past evokes emotion out of events that have already occurred. Either way, past or future, we aren't dealing with what is real and happening *now*. The longer the anthology of pensive moments accumulate, the more self-bound and rudderless life becomes. So stay awake.

When we're living in the present we cannot become world-weary with resentment. Take joy in any quiet time that comes your way. It's an occasion to set aside personal moments for advancing toward your Creator. Each second going by without passing under the lens of consciousness is an agnostic moment. But the closer you come to Him, the more it becomes clear that you aren't Him. This is a humbling realization, one the Ego hates with an unholy passion.

Having no life of Its own, the only hope this lower Self has to ascend and rule the universe comes through you—your eyes, your ears, your senses. This can be a disturbing thought. Nevertheless, it's true. Without you unwittingly serving as It's host, this unholy parasite loses access to the food it craves.

Each time you become angry or upset, the Thing is fed. It inflates and grows within, nurturing Its existence on bitter judgment. You're as It is. It's as you are. United, you become increasingly unruly. Eventually, you can only be categorized as a subhuman godless creature in fleshy human form. Unable to regulate behavior and thinking, now you center on pleasing It to numb the subsequent guilt. This is how all obsessive behavior and thinking develops. Your smoking. Your drinking. Your pornographic rituals. Even your overeating.

Once you dedicate your existence to serving Self, you've already lost your true identity. The subsequent dullness will prevent you from reaching your full potential in a career. It could keep you forever making poor relationship choices. These bring further insecurities and judgments, sending people toward substance addictions, seeking food, sex or drugs for refuge. It will send you to them too. Perhaps it already has, to some extent. The manifestations of a self-centered lifestyle can vary. They might even seem manageable for a while. But eventually, you'll find that you're in emotional chaos. Those emotions may be expressed or they may be repressed and hidden away from view, even from your own awareness.

It is imperative to recognize the terrible impact negative emotions have on us all and how judgment arises out of feelings. See how raw resentment coalesces into annoyance, irritation, frustration, fear and a restless dissatisfaction with life. These are but a few of the many names that fall under the bitter umbrella of resentment.

Since all spiritual disorder stem out of resentment, the solution to all difficulties always lies in allowing natural resilience to the deadly energy to be your redemption. It's that simple. You'll find safety in consciousness. There is nothing more to do than this.

Give Up Resenting

Who's upset you? Why do you ever get pissed off? By giving up all struggle with irritating circumstance you develop an increasing ability to overlook the error in people. The flaws in others, the cruelties in an unfair world become a source of strength instead of frustration. You stop judging and begin to get along with others in a wholesome manner. People will always remain emissaries of either negative or positive energy. But neither force can overwhelm you when you look others in the eye with un-distracted confidence. Not getting upset, outwardly or in secret, is the mark of grace and spiritual growth.

Point Six

The Sixth Chapter

By which it becomes abundantly clear just how magical and life-altering is the power of forgiveness. As you emotionlessly observe defectiveness in others, you begin to experience tolerance, right now, in each new moment.

Whether it happened a minute ago, an hour ago or in years past, it is essential to forgive those who've offended at any time. Seconds count. Experiencing forgiveness in real-time, rather than after the fact, averts the damaging effects that anger inflicts on the body and mind. Putting it off only feeds judgment energy to the Ego entity within.

Dynamic, on-the-spot tolerance of others ensures that we don't cultivate self-centeredness. It also extends the length and quality of life.

When I was a young man and first met my future mother in law, she gave me a bit of advice I found to be remarkable. It came at a time when I was struggling with stresses common in the life of a typical American teenager. There was schoolwork and homework. Graduation was pending. I sought the approval of my peers, my girlfriend, my mother, and my teachers. I was getting it too.

After-school, I was running a small office cleaning business I'd started at night. With my own little company, I was making more money and taking more responsibility than any other kid I knew. I was learning about hiring and managing employees, finding clients, billing, collections, marketing—everything typical to any small business.

I was fulfilling my fantasy of becoming a successful entrepreneur and even persuaded some of my friends to come work for me. I know this sounds wonderful. Every kid should develop strong work ethic and be as enterprising. But while everyone applauded my initiative and industriousness, I was also getting hooked on their approval. It was narcotic. Pride swelled secretly within.

Good business is tough. Facing unpleasant people and hostile situations is a skill that every young adult needs to learn, even those who aren't building a company. You would have thought that in my circumstances I'd be hardening to the business world, developing resilience to adversity and honing toughness. I was, but it wasn't in a healthy way. Instead of success building true confidence, I was becoming cocky.

Though absolutely *cash register honest*, I sensed as a terrible streak of disingenuousness rotting deep inside that nagged me to no end. One day I feared it would surface and I'd be found out to be a phony—not the young, innovative business visionary that I and so many others had made me out to be, but an extension of something awful inside.

A home is supposed to have a father to exemplify strength and resilience to the tension of daily living. At seventeen and having grown up in a fatherless environment, I was not equipped to handle even the mundane stresses of running a small company. Like many kids, I had a resentful, guilt tormented mother who'd been given a raw deal in life. Without a moral man to assume his husbandly role, my poor mom struggled with passing patience on to her own children. The chops to lead a family by example just wasn't there.[117]

No one ever showed me a practical way to deal with those whom I found bothersome. For as long as I could remember, whenever anyone upset me, instinct would win over valor. The urge to run was strong and I'd choose flight over fight way too many times. Without correction, this became a habitual, progressive weakness and continued into my professional and social life.[118]

As I became an adult, fearfully running away from irksome people and situations became less of an option. Coping with difficulties this way started to taste sour. A sense of weakness began to curdle inside. It dawned on me that no matter what, life is to be lived and not evaded. My own ambitious nature aptly pointed out how any the fear of confrontation, unless conquered would be a debilitating handicap in business. It became a nagging thorn. Yet, I compulsively dodged intimidating circumstances. Feeling like a coward while walking a braggart's strut is the height of cockiness. It would be a contradiction preventing me from getting what I felt I deserved. Namely, *lots of money*. I was smart. I had good ideas. I worked hard. *God dammit, I should be rewarded for it!*

Doubtfulness in business or occupation can be a weakness. To be successful, it's got to be resolved. However, in recognizing my own hesitancy, rather than rise above it I began to resent myself. My confidence was threatened. I needed a solution, and Nancy's mom had developed one that worked for her. She fancied herself something of a good manager and was eager to reveal her secret to me.

It worked like this: Whenever she encountered wrong people in everyday life, she'd rationalize their behavior. She would look at the person who'd upset her, probably by some inconsiderate behavior or rudeness, and simply surmise that, "They must just be having a bad day." She'd feel sorry for them. In her mind, her life was superior to their life. That's it. Simple.

In effect, Nancy's mother discovered that instead of choking on bitterness she could repack emotional irritations into easy to swallow capsules. In her lifetime, she had scarfed down a lot of these pills.

I thought it was brilliant.[119] The justification had a soothing effect. To me, *reasoning* felt like *forgiveness*. I tried it and for a while felt much better. Certainly, this was an improvement over fuming and later hating myself for it. What I didn't know was that this was not so much forgiveness of others as it was the suppression of anger.

When we rationalize this way, we imagine that we've become bigger and better than those who oppose us. A lower Self feeds on an original irritation, feeling It is above the *sinners*. It tells us we're superior to them, secretly belittling others. Exhilarated by imagined Supremacy, it appears we've beaten bitterness. But it's too late. Bitterness has already entered.

Now, we no longer notice how upset we've become and for the time being, we feel fine. But the negative energy packed into the original resentment hasn't truly mitigated. Anger has overwhelmed us, fed to the inflated Ego creature and we unwittingly continue to nurture a vicious, dark nature within. Like some deranged, self-appointed Emperor, It puffs up to claim undeserved authority over all It perceives. This is how self-righteousness manifests. Instead of safely handling negative emotions, you allow a monstrous tyrant inside to flourish. It is Pride and It is not about to forgive anyone or anything.

The mistake that preachers and spiritual pundits make with their followers is telling them they must forgive, but then not showing them exactly *how* to do it. That's because they don't know. It is truly a phenomenon, how someone can talk for hours or write tomes about a subject like forgiveness, and in the end, not know the first thing about how to experience it.

We humans cannot willfully decide to forgive whenever we want to, or even because we are told that we must. Forgiveness is not some good deed to do to keep peace or capture lost approval. It isn't a manageable commodity, a skill or art that can be learned and practiced like philosophy or an academic discipline. There's no course of study or spiritual training that can transform an impatient, judgmental lout into a tolerant, loving person.

Forgiveness is a state of being. It's when we become freed from anger and stop playing God through resentful judgment. Once liberated from emotional energy we stand back from thoughts to observe the lower Self shrinking in the Light of consciousness. Then we become incompatible with hate, and in that moment forgiving others becomes spontaneous. It isn't a willful action. It's an attainable condition of human existence. No one can teach you to forgive any more than they can teach you to remove anger. What they can do is set an example for how to be, but only if they are first themselves truly forgiving. Anger is contagious among humans, and so is love.[120]

Concurrent forgiveness between Creator and man happens spontaneously as we give up anger toward people. As we no longer hate we are promptly rescued from resentment to discover His compassion arising inside us.

There's no need to listen to religious lectures or to study metaphysical principles like *forgiveness* to experience them. In fact, while ambitiously trying to gain knowledge of mystical truths, you're likely to come away more confused than ever. Trying to learn how to tolerate people will slowly drive one mad. You'll ironically place yourself even further from experiencing the ease and comfort of true forgiveness.

You could chase what you think of as *forgiveness* for all your life, but without consciousness, you will never catch it. Everyone who attempts it gets lost in the pursuit. That's because while you're caught up in figuring out how to forgive, you're also distracted from living now, in the present. In the present is where true forgiveness exists.

The forgiving Spirit is not as elusive as you may think. There is no effort to its discovery. The more you contemplate finding forgiveness, the more mysterious and inaccessible it will become.

If you want to experience forgiveness, discover consciousness first. Become still, go to the Kingdom within and everything else, including forgiveness, follows. The stillness found through conscious awareness allows God's forgiving spirit to first enter us, and then the world *through* us. There's a spontaneous projection of heavenly forbearance and love. It's yours if you'll just stop trying to find it.

The essence of sanity is in love. An inborn facility to understand right from wrong activates the moment we stop hating. Moral character and a healthy concern for justice return. Childlike innocence restores, tempered by a growing spiritual maturity. The natural capacity to regulate behavior arises from within and we begin to carry what is right[121] into the world—not as crusaders or militant do-gooders, but as spiritually civil beings, peaceably going about our productive lives.

The mean-spirited develop kindliness. The selfish become generous. The fearful discover bravery. Integrity replaces deceitfulness. Honesty will do wonders to safeguard emotional and mental stability. As it calms erratic thinking and unmanageable behavior, we find we're no longer stepping on the toes of our fellows. We stop causing harms to people requiring endless amends making. Sanity returns.

The further one moves from inspired, critical thought the closer they come to insanity. An absence of forgiving spirit encourages *unsane* thinking and eventually complete madness.

Many of the insane, even those afflicted with grave mental disorders, would immediately experience soundness of mind, if only they could come to this forgiving dimension of presence.

Not many can do that. For some reason, the willingness just isn't there. But of those people who are willing, stability and soundness of mind return, without even trying. When this happens it's a miracle. Existing in the *now*, rather than in the prison built in the bitter mind, is the answer to all mental illness.

Let this automated feature of forgiveness serve as personal evidence that you are forgiving others as you're also forgiven. A clear conscience and the unshakable courage to do what is right at any cost will be yours. You'll become an independent, *critical thinker.*

No one can rightfully arbitrate fairness or decide what is true or false for you. Knowing right from wrong in your life is for you alone to see as revealed under the clarifying lens of conscious awareness. It can never be properly defined by another's prejudiced concept of fairness. All they can do is rob you of the gift of discovery, making you weak and dependent on others for direction.

Everyone who's consciously awakened and maintains a mindful state becomes infused with a forgiving Spirit. In allowing consciousness to rise above thinking, the anxiety of a poorly lived past meets up with awareness in the present moment. We see our error illuminated by the Light of Truth. Right then, just as anxious humiliation rises, the discomfort immediately begins to recede and then dissolve away. We're left with reassuring gratitude for the revelation. We go about our everyday lives optimistically looking forward to each moment, now illuminated by the sunlight of the Spirit.

This is the most humbling experience known to mankind, one the Ego fears. Please know it isn't you who fears. It is that Dark Thing lurking inside you. It resists stillness and trembles in the presence of Truth revealed in quiet. It knows that in the absence of tangled thinking and intellectual reasoning there is understanding. It's painfully aware that once you are in the awakened state, you'll realize what It already knows and hates for you to know—that you aren't It, and that neither It or you are God. It trembles and hates this very idea. You may even notice this as you read these very words.[122]

In these instances, do not believe for one-second that it's your fear that you feel. Simply observe the impulse to run, to seek relief through distractions. The forgiving spirit will fill and surge through you. Positive energy will drive away any doubt, pain, or guilt. The Dark Self will shrink down to a manageable size and the sensation of dread will diminish.[123]

Until now, your only answer to anxiety has been to ambitiously rearrange life in the attempt to produce a comforting environment. In the quest for relief, you developed a fascination with control, power or money. If successful in obtaining any, these fast-become addictions. The hunger for *more* can never be satisfied. If you've ever been addicted to these or drugs, alcohol, food, and sex, it has only been your failure to successfully cope with resentment that has attracted you in the first place. Abuse out of use, becomes unavoidable in the second place.

The same holds true for avarice and greed. Once emotionality enters, *more* is never enough. Say, a man owns a rowboat. He may feel lifted by the peace and serenity of a leisurely row or fishing excursion. He might enjoy working on his boat, maintaining its hull, sanding, painting and preserving the beautiful wood.

But, enter ambition and before long the simple enjoyment of his small boat turns to lust. Now he feels he must have a motorized skiff to be happy. Once obtaining the skiff, he soon begins to crave a luxurious cabin cruiser and the prestige *that* brings him. The self-induced seduction of pain and reward is underway. His ambition has catalyzed a disquieting agony he chases but can never be truly subdued.

After a while, only an ocean-going vessel will do. Then, a superyacht. Then a bigger superyacht. Finally, in a secret contest with other boat owners, he must continually have the newest, the biggest and best of the best, even after it is no longer a practical endeavor.

Does this mean all that boat enthusiasts and superyacht owners are materialistic, depraved and morally corrupt? *Ridiculous.* Each situation has its own nature. A superyacht owner can be perfectly content and secure, not fueled by ambition, while a rowboat owner can be an emotional train wreck if driven by the quest for personal pleasures—and visa-versa. The point is that it all depends on how each has obtained their possession, along with the attitude and treatment of either.[124] It could be boats, cars, homes or cowboy boots.

The allure of the world never ceases. Sometimes it may seem that a willful rearrangement of life is the only way to escape the discomfort of anxiety. Visions abound of having a secure family, story-book relationships, a successful career or wealth and material assets. We might see people living lifestyles we would want for ourselves. We imagine the comfort and well-being their possessions might provide. This flight of the imagination plays with our brain chemistry issuing fleeting feelings of well-being and intoxicating relief from the pain of guilt. Meanwhile, underlying resentment continues to coalesce into envy. We could watch people with a jealous eye.

We may even develop secret resentments for those who already have what we want. If we fail to realize our desires we feel left out and abandoned, perhaps even punished by God. Blaming *His will* or the lack of *good luck* for a life unfulfilled we'll expend all our physical and mental energy striving to establish a life we feel is rightly ours. This is energy our bodies and minds need to remain healthy in cogent service to the Creator and His children, our fellows. Now it is wasted.

An ambitious pursuit of bliss leads to a sense of entitlement. The compulsion to selfishly attain happiness can become so strong, we might risk ethics and morals to get ahead. We may even place those we secretly envy on pedestals. This is how admiration societies for TV personalities, business leaders, sports celebrities and movie stars develop. Through artificial admiration, feigned respect turns into a sick exchange of allegiance, contaminated by self-centered greed.[125]

Under this system, even if we do manage to accumulate wealth and comfort, we'll still never feel truly contented. Like the millionaire lottery winner who did not earn his prosperity, or the oversexed, drug and alcohol addled trust fund baby, we shall continue to spoil. As we degrade from within we'll ruin our lives accumulating depravities, abusing our earnings to serve a dark need for still more happiness. The vain chase for egotistic joy never ends as long as we live.

If you're a business or academic leader who's attained celebrity or social prominence at any level, you have a moral responsibility broader than most. It is essential you learn to safely assume your leadership role. There must be conscious compassion for other people but without psychically accepting emotional devotion. Accepting even the slightest approval from *loving* admirers presents great risk to your well-being as well as to those who look up to you. Simply recognize the potential for any sick service you may unwittingly provide. It is inevitable, but just see it. This is enough to break the spell. Consciousness prevents unwholesome attachments.

When conscious, a new attitude fortifies and improves your connection with people, making it wholesome. Great leadership qualities will emerge. You'll become an astonishingly more effective communicator whether approaching people in groups or individually.[126] There's no one more influential for the good of others than a humbly enlightened leader serving as a virtuous model of success. This holds true in business, entertainment, and family life, as well as politics— anywhere authority and a benevolent commanding presence is required to lead.

If you're the one doing the *looking up to*, then please know how your need to create a God and the self-worth you receive by placing another human being on a pedestal is slowly destroying your potential for peace and serenity.

No matter what our lifestyle or the conditions in our environment, a self-centered lust for comfort can never be satisfied once and for all. Whether we're rich or poor, drunk or sober, fat or skinny, alone or surrounded by loved ones, without mastery over resentment we simply do not survive well in this world, with or without our possessions.

A king can die surrounded by the splendor of his grand palace, yet still feel tortured and miserable from the harms that an unforgiving spirit wreaks on the body and mind. His problem is the anger he's concealed for all his life. While steeped in financial security he still stews, although anesthetized by pride for his numerous accomplishments. Riches can delay the inevitable moment of truth for one who's never truly mastered negativity. But it won't stave it off forever.

***

If you never became angry you would never feel the need for forgiveness. You would have already forgiven others and *been forgiven* before the need for either ever arose. Anger is a negative force and thinking is the carrier of the resentment signal. Anytime you allow awareness to raise consciousness above thought, your psyche comes to a place where anger has no effect. Right then, you experience the inner neutrality

127

necessary to discover judgment free, critical thinking. Intuitive guidance triggers, ensuring that you always do the *next right thing*. There's no more struggling to make right decisions. You become clear thinking and certain.[127]

Though anger may approach, it is unable to penetrate. Emotionally charged thinking loses power over you. You find you are the observer of thoughts rather than a subject to them. Subtle separation from the think-stream is enough to place you out of reach of anger—out of danger.

Without the contamination of angry emotional energy, you'll forgive automatically. There will be no need to willfully try to issue *absolution* as though you were God. You'll simply find *forgiveness* is already so—that is has become part of the fabric of your personality. This is because you cannot judge without anger. The two always go hand in hand. Judgment needs the emotional catalyst of hate. But now, as you forgive on the spot, in real-time, you'll live free of anger and all its deleterious effects.

Each day in the stream of life you face approaching emotional force. Cruel people and the injustices of the world are a constant threat. They arouse emotions. These are the little temptations to become angry and upset, to resent and judge, and they are not by chance. The imperfections of human existence exist with a purpose.

They're deliberately projected through others to feed a dark nature inside you, allowing a vile Thing to nurture as Pride. It is the Ego identity and It swells in judgment of others. However, It's hunger for resentment and craving to become God are frustrated in each moment of consciousness. In that instant, when negatively charged emotions fail to penetrate, It starves and love fills. You become truly forgiving, *right then*.

Forgiveness and not resentfully judging are one and the same. Therefore, it is so important to learn how to live consciously, for while awakened are you immune to the toxic emotional effect of resentment energy.

Love, tolerance, and patience require steady vigilance. But these come easily once you develop a watchful attitude—the more you practice consciousness in your daily life. When conscious you cannot judge, and to not judge is to express forgiveness. Then, you will have forestalled the infectious nature of hate. Allow awareness to dissolve those forces in the Light of consciousness within. They're unable to overtake you if you remain observant. Watch them.

As you observe, you'll see reality in the Light of Truth, in the present, but that's not all. Recollections of those who you've judged in the past will also come up for review. Perhaps unexpectedly. Don't shield consciousness from these memories. You are being shown what you need to see. As you heal, you also see whether and how to repair what's been broken by your past indiscretions.[128] It could be essential to make amends by straightforwardly repairing the damages done.

Approaching someone we may have harmed in the past by selfish behavior can have either a positive effect or a negative effect depending on attitude. A begrudging apology to smooth over a relationship can look good on the surface. But an amend is worthless unless it's fueled by the supernatural energy evoked through a forgiving spirit. If we go to someone filled with love, free of the slightest rancor, the event takes on a metaphysical elegance. There's a transfer of positive energy. Kindness becomes contagious and there is an exchange of true love.

See that forgiving others and being forgiven does not need to be a complex matter. It's a simple, automated element of consciousness exquisitely built into mindful living. When we're conscious, we are in a state of psychic detachment. Inherent objectivity keeps us safe and protected from negative emotion. In the absence of hate, both love and tolerance from within emerge. Then we experience forgiveness, without even trying. It's a spiritual reflex for anyone who's gained mastery over resentment.

***

Obsessions are compulsory behaviors. They serve to relieve internal agony triggered through shame and guilt. Seemingly innocent activities quickly convert into chronic, futile efforts to relieve a pained conscience. For this reason, substances like food and drugs so easily lend themselves to abuse. A nourishing food becomes a narcotic drug, turning a person into an obese diabetic. An opioid medication properly prescribed to relieve the pain of a surgical procedure does its job, but then use escalates, turning the person into a drug abusing fiend.

This isn't the foods fault. It's not the drugs fault either. Nor is it the fault of the companies producing these substances. Casting blame on corporate executives, shareholders or free enterprise ignores causes, focusing only on effects. The real cause of abuse goes to the spiritual dereliction of the individual consumer.[129]

There's no denying that McDonald's and Pfizer benefit financially from the physical dependencies people develop to the ingredients in their products. If it'll increase consumption, companies will naturally seek to step up the addictive fixings. They'll promote sugar and run advertising campaigns designed to expand distribution. Whatever it takes. This is America, a still somewhat free society where we are at liberty to make choices in what we produce, how we market our products. But we are also meant to be free to choose how we consume them. So realize that it is the individual's powerlessness to regulate his own obsessions that companies exploit.

A spiritually fit person, conscious and secure in human spiritual existence can certainly notice the allure of a greasy Whopper, dripping with mayonnaise and ketchup. They could experience the feeling of well-being supplied by a fat dose of hydrocodone after a medical procedure.

But unless that same person is afflicted by the pain of guilt, they simply won't become addicted to either of these. They are not powerless, and will naturally marshal the mental resources necessary to snap the attraction and regulate behavior. Even once having developed physical tolerance, they will cease using—no matter how unpleasant the effects of cessation or intense the withdrawal.

Prolonged addiction always comes back to spiritual dereliction, not physiology. The role ordinary physical tolerance and dependency play in substance abuse and addiction is simple to conquer. All it takes is conscious awareness. With it comes the power to regulate. Consciousness triggers a release from the resentment at the base of all addictive behavior and substance abuse.

To lay the weight of blame for an addiction problem on corporations, parents, society or anyone else, is excuse making. All human obsession originates with a metaphysical phenomenon, that occurs within. Allow the power of Supernatural correction to enter and all addictions fall away, effortlessly.

This is why spiritual awakening works to free addicts from their addictions where other methods fail.[130]

Self-willed restraint of inner pain warps both the body and mind, eventually expressing in morbid physical consequences. Nearly all sickness and diseases originate with the bitter suppression of resentment energy—anger and hatred in all its aliases.

When these emotions strike, don't cry and plead to your Creator. Don't try to negotiate a deal with God. No matter how polite, who are you to suggest to Him what ought to be? Instead of struggling or begging for relief from infirmities, humbly long for their removal. Quietly allow your true spirit to yearn for peace. Become still in faithfulness. *This is prayer.*

The moment our vision comes into agreement with God's will, guilt and shame dissolve. Serenity comes, catalyzing an inner protection against invading negative emotion. *This is prayer answered.*

Without the pain of guilt, the need for relief disappears. Addictions vanish without effort. The body and mind begin to heal. You can watch in safety as errors and shame begin melting away. You'll begin to see how anger, leading to obsessions, has ruined your life. You'll also begin to identify the same affliction in others, without judging. Now, as people offend, see how it isn't they who are doing it. You can realize that you are no better than they are and they, no better than you. We've all become subject to the same external forces that have somehow gotten inside. What a thought! This is a great secret, kept from mankind. Exactly how this has happened is important to know too.

Please now understand the etiology of *spiritual disease.*

The first cruelty to which you were ever subjected came at the hands of a parent.[131] When recalling the past, see that no matter how harsh or traumatic an offense, even the cruelest, most wickedly abusive mother or father was not acting on their own accord. It was Something horrible that had gotten into them. Realize how Something thinks and acts through them.

Just as you hope others would realize it has never truly been you who's harmed them, now extend the same spiritual genteelness you'd provide for yourself, especially to your parents. Recognize how out of control people are and you can also see the folly of hating them for their wayward conduct. More than human personalities, we are dealing with supernatural forces, inhuman sub-personalities that exist inside every living human being.

There is a vile, alien entity that lives for hate. It's an unholy creature, craving death and destruction for all of God's creation. It will do anything to ensure that Its existence endures unopposed while remaking God's handiwork into Its own design, so It can reign forever over the universe as God.

To some extent, It's nature has invaded and gained control over every human being you've ever met. Recognizing this horrifying truth is the secret to forgiveness. Just as you had once lost control of your thinking and behavior, it isn't people who've upset you. It's been a Dark Occupant inside them to which they've unwittingly relinquished control.

Now, armed with this forethought, you can maintain prudence before each temptation to become angry as judgment arises. Give people the benefit of your understanding even before they offend. Nothing they do, no matter how cruel, is *really* them doing it—just as the harms you may have done others in the past has been due to Something inside of you. It has been a *not you*, that you've mistakenly identified as *you*.

Like you, these people may have had good intentions at one time. They could have wanted to do right, but just couldn't. Operating under an internalized misidentification system, they do not realize they've become the extension of whatever they hate. Even when they may have known that what they do is wrong, they could not help themselves. Some horrible entity has taken control of their thoughts and behaviors.

If someone was hypnotized to hit you over the head and rob you, would you not cut them some slack, knowing they had been involuntarily forced to commit the misdeed? Of course you would. Then make allowances for others. They are under a hypnotic spell, trapped in a stream of thinking that keeps them imprisoned through mindlessness.[132] They don't know it. But now you do. This understanding makes forgiveness possible.

Not hating someone who's wronged you does not mean you endorse their actions. It also doesn't mean you've become blind to their errors. Instead, it means that while observing people's shortcoming, you do you do not project emotionally charged judgment onto them for those flaws. This is true forgiveness—living in the realm of a magnanimous life-force emanating from within.

"You spot it you got it," is a lie. Like other similarly hackneyed adages, it's often heard in pseudo-spiritual circles, posing as a self-analytic tool. It is meant to discourage you from seeing the error in others. This is nothing more than sneaky, psychological sleight of hand. It encourages unawareness, allowing something dark within to flip the wrongs of the world onto you. So clever.[133]

If you heap groundless blame on yourself, you consent to the Ego's egregious condemnation of the consciousness that might guide and discipline you correctly. Self revels in a gloomy outlook because as we look the other way, laden with indignant judgment, we also fail to calmly recognize the error in the world. The opportunity to defeat wrong through love passes us by. Disregarding evil entirely isn't tolerance. It's allowing wickedness to foster—a kind of deliberate ignorance that activates bitterness within. We never experience patience as long as we remain attached to a lower Self.

Sometimes people can be too quick to give us their approval. Giving approval to others loosely tends to grant undeserved esteem. We can do it to them and in a parasitic exchange, they reciprocate. It's an easy way to generate adoring admirers who become addicted to flattery. Smitten by adulation, they'll bask in what is perceived as your *positive aura*, while you help them gloss over their own inadequacies.

Provide others with the psychic anesthetic of approval aggravates their fallen condition. It allows the uncomfortable emptiness they already feel to become filled with your saccharine endorsement of their error. Helping to suppress the shame naturally stemming out of their own issues is harmful to them. Remember that forgiveness for another's shortcomings isn't the same as giving approval. One is the expression of inner strength and love. The other is feeble, self-centered appeasement.[134]

Begin each morning consciously and your psyche will more easily remain receptive to intuitive understanding all day long. Then, in each moment you'll be able to distinguish the true from the false. There's no need to be concerned with making it so. In extending awareness throughout the day, you'll find that you're forgiving *on the spot*, whenever forbearance is appropriate. Simply be awake and aware and it will be so. The ability to forgive in real-time is a vital asset in life.

As you go through your regular routines with clear perception you'll observe people differently. Some will sense the clarity you possess and become alarmed by it.[135] That's their problem, not yours. No one is beneath you and you are beneath no one. We're all in the same stream of life, encountering the same seductions and occasions to become upset. In becoming mindfully aware, an inner Energy gently guides you away from these temptations. It is a protective spiritual Force on which you'll soon come to rely.

Forgiving yourself is a misnomer. Judgmentally indulging the spirit of hate when observing your own defective nature is just as harmful as becoming angry with others. The force that Ego accesses as It plays God and judges other's wrongs is the same negativity It directs at your behavior. If you are depressed, you will never stop hating yourself until you've first discovered the secret to giving up all anger. It's *consciousness*, the permanent cure for depression.

What is clinically termed as *Depression* isn't really a disease with physiological origins. It is only the word we use to describe a certain state of mind originating out of metaphysical phenomenon. Biochemical indicators and other aberrations symptomatic to the "disorder" are merely the visible effects of an underlying cause.

Subsequently, even pharmaceutical and psychological treatments are not true solutions since they only masque the cause. And so, despite the development of many theories and after decades of clinical investigation, *Depression* remains mysterious, the cure hidden from scientific discovery. This is no accident.

The Accusing Spirit within relies on stealth. Once exposed, It loses influence. As you observe from a position of neutrality, It curses you for seeing the truth about yourself. But now with clarity, you see It is a Dark Imposter *playing God* through judging you. It isn't you.

You cannot *forgive* yourself as God forgives. However, you can realize you have already been forgiven by not hating others even when they are wrong, as God has also not hated you despite your error. In not hating your own faults, you experience the love of the Creator.

Looking for forgiveness from others is seeking their love. When we're lacking love within, we'll try to fill the hole with the assuaging approval of people. So, be careful about making apologies. Seeking forgiveness from other people is an attempt to reclaim lost approval. It is infinitely better to make things right.

Judgment cannot form in the mind of the individual who's consciously connected with the Creator. Without judgment and the ensuing guilt from *playing God*, you remain free to move about the world inspired, and with confidence. Once consciousness has freed you from anger, intolerance no longer has a place inside you. You walk with God, not acting as though you are Him. You're a living example to others.

All the obsessive behavior that has ever plagued you, every bad habit you've ever had, is nothing more than the egoistic attempt to dull the pain of concealed guilt. Conversely, once guilt truly resolves, you will effortlessly exemplify good living. No longer burdened by the pain of a tormented conscience, you become helpful to those who sense and appreciate the truth conveyed through your behavior.

Then there's no need to ever willfully motivate anyone to be *good* or *right*. Not even your own children. Parenting skills turn powerful once our *help* is void of anger. Family members respond positively to the patience and tolerance you exemplify without even trying. They see you in a light that earns their respect and they'll be encouraged by your upright lifestyle.

Once you begin each day cultivating God-consciousness, seeing people in a different light, you'll also notice a certain peacefulness inside. Through consciousness, the human psyche opens for a divine transition. Patience begins to flow naturally. You may have judged every angle of your behavior along with the actions of others, but now it becomes a simple matter to meet each new encounter graciously.

Whereas previously you were so caught up with life that you wore yourself weary, now you're able to take pause during the day, watching negative emotional energies as they inevitably crop up, but then fall away without overwhelming.

Through awakened consciousness, you are being *led away from temptation. Delivered from Evil.*[136] Instead of pretending to be

God, trying to control the world and outcomes, you find that you're no longer going about the world like you own the place, as though you were a co-founder in Creation, Inc. *Now* you can humbly accept your role as a part of the created, not part *Creator*. In this realm, as a child of the Father, you can never die. There is no death in the *now*. There's only life.

When people can no longer affect you negatively or positively, they lose the power to upset. God-consciousness replaces Self-consciousness and a new energy dominates. Infilling love tempers overreactions to people places and things. Life becomes more active and less reactive. People will not have changed right away, but you will have. Over time, your new attitude will impact and change them too. They will certainly respond to the loving energy unfolding from within you as it spills into the surrounding world.

You're effecting change in your environment even as you are also transformed. Behavior gradually regulates, seemingly all by itself. Certain ethics, personal qualities you once possessed but lost, will reinstate. A latent capacity for honesty shall re-emerge. You are becoming the genuinely nice person you once were a long time ago. This is personal growth directed by conscious awareness, not by the collective wills of other individuals. Not by self-will either.

Your progress during this lifetime is important and change is certain. I can't tell you specifically what those changes will be. No one should know the details of the future. I can only broadly predict that there will be a return to lost virtue, perhaps not experienced since you were young. With your eyes opened, the pain of guilt for your own past errors arises. As the pain begins to melt away a bright, new *now* emerges out of humility. Many religions call this *repentance*. Now you are experiencing it.

Hold on. This gets even better.

You'll see the same terrors that upset you, also active in others and not hate them for it. Now you can realize how they have no more control over their own lives than you are in control of yours. We've all become subject to the same external force that has somehow crawled inside and set up shop. You're no better than they are and they, no better than you. How can you hate people for the things they do? They're unable to stop themselves. Unconscious people do what they do compulsively and are not in control of their actions.

Once given to realize how people are compelled to act outside of their own volition, it is a simple matter to let go of bitterness toward them. To be forewarned on this matter is to be forearmed. That's why it's called *for*-giveness and not *aft*-giveness.

The mystery of addictions to substances like nicotine, heroin, cannabis and other consciousness-dulling drugs has baffled our best scientists for years. Yet, through conscious realization, a spiritually awakened individual can easily realize what science has never been able to explain to him:

How unrecognized resentment has led the charge to his obsessive abuse of substances.

Drugs and foods like sugar or alcohol are implicated here. Compulsory, self-centered behavior too. There's also gambling, porn, promiscuity—any of the anti-social misconduct which has seduced and then degenerated civilized societies for centuries. All addiction and obsessive pleasure seeking, common among those guilty of playing God, are symptomatic of *spiritual disease*. Having metaphysical origin, such abuses are nothing more than the indication of underlying moral dereliction.

These destructive activities are not so mysterious after all, are they? The need to exploit any substance or behavior beyond wholesome purpose stems out of unconsciousness, for without consciousness there's no human defense from the ravages of resentfulness. No one who remains mesmerized by the world, mindlessly meandering through their days will ever escape the consequences of anger.

The ensuing dullness of mind will bring categorical ruin, trapping all who fail to wake up into a lifetime of illness, disorder and an unhappy existence. Depression, anxiety, heart disease, cancer, bone and neurological disorders that none of us are ever meant to experience await unless we get free from emotional states.

Once you awaken and exercise mindful consciousness, you'll automatically break free from a reprehensible way of life. You'll even look back to wonder why it took you so long to wake up. With practice, the state of objectivity will become increasingly familiar and little by slowly you'll begin to extend the watchful state of existence into your daily affairs, especially when dealing with people.

As others continue to test your patience, rather than becoming upset by them you'll see how it is something *in* them that tempts you to judge. They may appear transparent, unspoken motives becoming clear. You'll realize how irksome, frustrating people do irritating things for this purpose. Something inhuman resides inside them, existing as if It were human. It waits for the opportunity to project venomous seed, replicating Its nature inside you when you become upset.

Watch them do it. Observe your watching them do it. If you get involved in the dramas, the barbs, and shocking irritation that people throw your way, just notice you have. Then, in noticing, the effects of emotional bitterness will slip away, leaving you unharmed.

You won't have to wait for pressure from people. Allow consciousness to supply a spiritual tap on the shoulder, bringing you to reality at any time. It's as though a loving poke from a parallel dimension comes reminding you of who you really are.[137] You'll find you can practice patience moment by moment anytime as you go along. In taking a moment every now and then throughout the day to pause and become aware, you'll soon find you can come back to consciousness anytime you remember. Even just a few seconds at a time will be helpful. A little goes a long way.

At first, you may forget. In fact, you probably will. You'll react much as you have in the past, with emotion or even an impulsive urge for vengeance. Even so, now there will be a difference. It won't be the same as before. Instead of basking is self-righteous indignation you'll now become increasingly uncomfortable in your judgment of others. Allow the discomfort to be your wake-up call. It has a purpose, a good one. You're being saved through mindful God-consciousness.

Living each day awakened, you can now realize how inconsiderate and mean people are really just as undisciplined as you have been. Like you, they've been wronged. Their emotions have rendered them unable to manage their lives. The trauma of betrayal has encouraged a force inside them they'd rather not know. It has cost them the human spiritual connection they once had with their Creator—the same painful severance that all human beings suffer while playing God.

Many continue to struggle. Others seem to have abandoned themselves entirely to Something they cannot see as horrible. But literally everyone, at some time, is affected by forces within of which they have no awareness. Most are currently under this spell. Shaded from the Light of Truth, they've become blinded by the Dark and cannot see what they're doing. Even if they do, they are still unable to break free from the spell of emotional bondage gripping them. Ripping them. Tearing apart their sanity and destroying their usefulness to God and man. They've been pre-programmed prior to your ever meeting them, long before you even knew of them, their selfishness, or their cruelty. Therefore, how dare any of us blame others!

As you become increasingly aware you can clearly see this phenomenon in action. Now as each event in your life streams under the lens of conscious awareness, you can forgive others. Not by decree. Not by pronouncement. You forgive the only way a human being can, by simply not hating.

But be careful of rationalizing. Just as justifying the wrong in ourselves nurtures our own defects, it is equally damaging to excuse the errors we observe in others. Either will only keep anger and judgment active, inhibiting spiritual growth.

Stepping back from thinking, you can observe hate without it seizing and taking you for an emotional sleigh ride. You'll do well to bear in mind that this isn't your hate. It is resentful energy belonging to Something residing inside. It only seems as though it's yours to the extent that you've identified with It, joined in the contempt It holds for truth. You only thought It was you.

This may be a shocking truth to hear. Know that it isn't you who takes offense, scoffs at these words, and tries to drive you away from this book and the discovery of consciousness proposed. It is It that fears. Remain calm. Keep an opened mind, taking care not to blindly accept or reject this appalling exposé. Allow consciousness to rise and discern what is true or false while observing the intellectual inclination toward judgment. If you've been meditating using the mindful-consciousness exercise I propose, then in a short while this will become simple to do.

As the shock value of awakening fades, you'll see the wisdom of remaining conscious as much of the time as you can. Practicing consciousness through meditation each morning will prevent you from straying too far into mindless territories during the day.

Anytime you find that you've been pulled into a dream state, the recent recollection of awareness, still fresh from morning meditation, will enable you to quickly find your way back to sanity. It becomes second nature after a while and some people take longer than others before this mode of living is fully integrated. But if you are sincere in pursuing the purpose of all human life, then eventually it will be, for sure.

Be patient. Be persistent. I cannot overstress these two words.

The vision to clearly discern without judging is immediately available once you're awake and aware. The awful tendency to bite into the apple of anger is revealed. Conscious discovery arms us with the power to let temptation pass. We discover the Regulating Authority within.

Keep it up. The moment you stop practicing is when you'll regress backward as the Spirit of a cruel world repossesses your mind, having Its way with you once again. Knowing the wondrous life that consciousness brings, you'll pay a dear price for the lack of vigilance. Deep regret, but then joy if at once you come back to awareness.

In the present moment, where time past and future do not exist, you will see what is true, *now*. Information leaking out of memories past or from the imagined future no longer weigh so heavily on the life choices you make. True, accurate and current information ignites the intuitive fuel required to make effective, emotionless choices.

There is no speculation for the truly informed individual. There is no luck. There's no rumor or gossip that can seduce or sway. To him, choices are always just the next thing to do on an obvious path unfolding before him. He regularly buys at the right time and sells at the right time.

Allow me to present you with a parallel out of the business world. When I was in the Investment Banking business, I had a device called a Bloomberg terminal. It was a data feed computer for real-time news, stock and bond prices, as well as trading analytics and a host of information streaming across the financial newswires.

Access to information like this is an advantage the retail street investor doesn't have. It's why the average person competing in the financial markets can never win going up against the sharks unless he is willing to do the extraordinary amount of homework and research necessary for informed, stress-free investing. Some do. But only a few.

For this reason, most people lose money investing on Wall Street. Trying to get along with the ruthless big boys, pre-armed with real-time facts, mom and pop investors and wannabe day-traders who haven't the gumption to likewise obtain what makes for success in financial markets do not stand a chance.

Wall Street is no place for fearful amateurs. Spin and misinformation cultivate a feckless investor with little ability to compete in one of the most cutthroat marketplaces on earth. The more current information one has, the more courage naturally rises, and the more appropriate the investments that will be made. Subsequently, the more financial success one will enjoy. It takes guts.

Just as the canyons of Wall Street are no place for the insecure, life on Main Street is also too harrowing for the fainthearted to survive. There are those who if handed a million dollars would build value with it, multiplying the money many times over with apparent ease. Then there are those who could not help but lose every cent of it. Try as they might, they'd waste the money into self-serving oblivion without creating anything of durable value. This is not a matter of luck, brains or education. It is a matter of attitude.

A witless citizen cannot participate in a dangerous, evil world. A fearful individual will have too little faith to live peacefully and comfortably. Timidity is always a liability. Motives and means may vary, but people who invest or live based on relevant, up-to-date information are free to discard the inevitable emotional impulses that spoil objectivity. Fear never overwhelms them to make wrong decisions.

If you could come out of your head, and observe the stream of chattering inside your thinking mind, there would emerge an unseen, positive power. It's a quiet force that would overtake the babble and begin flowing through in ways you cannot see and much of the time need not be cognizant.

You'd become charitable in the present, exhibiting patience and tolerance for people even when they're wrong. This is the true expression of love. With real-time perception that is founded in current reality, one galvanizes the stamina to make tough decisions with intuitive confidence. This is a state of mind you can't make happen. Live *now*, and it just does.

Each action comes as naturally as breathing once you are no longer tied to decision making as much as simply following the clear, obvious path. Life in the stream unfolds before you. Then, no matter what, you don't hate others and you don't fear failure. This can only happen for sure once you become free from anger. Forgiving.

There's humility to be found in the hearts of truly successful people. Clarity neutralizes the emotions that would otherwise undermine success. It invokes an attitude that supplants cockiness. It supersedes greed. Clearheaded, conscious people brim with integrity and courage.

When you put your head down on the pillow at night after a day of real-time forgiving, you can do so with clear consciousness. You can sleep and dream in a healthy way without dragging the baggage collected from a dramatic day of improper, emotional dealings.

Once you've tried this for a while you may wonder how you ever got good a night sleep before now. Truthfully? You probably never really have. At least not since you were young, before you were corrupted by whoever or whatever betrayed your innocence.

Forgive Now. Don't Wait

Can you "Let go" . . . right now? The positive force of a forgiving spirit best expresses as love on the spot. Right in this moment, in the present, tolerance yields immunity from unseen energies that exchange between you and everyone you meet. Remaining spontaneous, clairvoyance flows. You become attractive to right people and repellant to wrong ones. Without judgment, right choices in romance, business, and friendship are automatic— every time. Become resilient to resentment so that a new unexpected life-path that cannot go wrong unfolds in each moment. Forgive now. It is magic.

Point Seven

The Seventh Chapter

By which you discover that anger isn't normal for human beings, that not everyone gets upset, and how simple it is to discover honesty, truth, and peace within, once freed from resentment. The psychic clockwork of dishonesty is exposed and you can never view the world as you once did.

What if the majority of a nation became so demoralized and dishonest they could no longer rely on the good-will of the people to live well?

Daily life for an entire country would become unmanageable. Morally, ethically and practically rudderless, society would have turned away from their intuitiveness in order to play God. Anger would fester within. The internal pain of a guilt-plagued conscience would be excruciating.[138]

Screwed up relationships, paralyzing fear and doubt affecting economies and family life would trouble so many people at one time that the whole country could slow to near paralysis, hardly able to function on its own resources.

The anguish of defeat inside each citizen would become intolerable as they compulsively surrendered liberty for reliance upon incompetent authorities. In desperation, those suffering people would turn to politicians, ministers, or counselors to tell them what to do about it.

The services of doctors, drug dealers, and bartenders would become solution providers to the ailing spirits of the masses. Medicated, mesmerized and intellectually brainwashed, what type of society do you suppose this would be? It would be a nation of feeble marks for victimization. A feast for bullies.

Once the spiritual, mental and emotional states of enough people are sufficiently corrupted, an entire nation can be completely taken over. It may not be a violent coupe or a single conquest. It would have to be a gradual invasion, perhaps over decades of election cycles. Thus, nearly undetectable, and seemingly civil.

First courage and patience would be smothered, replaced with fear and intolerance. Then the population would be overwhelmed by a scourge of self-centeredness. An epidemic corruption of individual spirits would multiply across the nation.

Finally, there would have to be potential tyrants in waiting, those who could nurture his or her sick need for control at the expense of the feeble. They'd be frauds, matching the weaknesses of the people, exploiting those they handily deceive. Authoritarian rise would parallel cultural decline and it'd be, for the most part, spontaneous. The public would not even know it was happening. Save for the change in nature by the citizenry, or else a miracle, a nation could sink to a level of demoralized depravity too low to peaceably salvage.

The decline of a civilization isn't rooted in faulty politics or economic mismanagement. It originates in the hearts of individuals who've lost their connection with the Source of all life from within and subsequently aren't free from mounting fear and anger. Emotionally ruled individuals will give away their freedom to an oppressor in exchange for relief. This is as true for personal relationships as it is on the societal scale.

In turn of the century Germany, a sizable lull in human virtue followed by ensuing guilt could be easily exploited by a madman. And so out of the toughened hearts of a corrupted people arose a vile and contagious spirit. Predicated on a clear perception of human vulnerability, Hitler's demoralization of those whose confidence and principles had been previously broken wasn't difficult.

Sick Hitler could mastermind his equally sick social theory out of the thoughts streaming through his brilliant but distorted brain. He honed and explained these philosophies through writing his book *Mein Kampf,* and was soon exploiting the collective inner sufferings of individuals who had no idea they were being taken over. He believed that if a lie were repeated often, then eventually enough people would come to believe it. Deception holds power over certain demoralized individuals. He knew it.

Like dutiful servants to a master, a nation of disheartened souls answered to a *savior's* promise of a reprieve from their grieving consciences. They elected a hero they thought would anesthetize their pain.

While the rise of Hitler's Germany is often studied from economic, political and social perspectives, the holocaust didn't spawn out of some perfect, socio-political storm. Modern cultures are constantly perfecting societies through political experimentation. Neither was it merely due to a decade of economic woes. Human virtue survives and thrives during financial hardships when they are gracefully met.

The rise of Hitler, his Nazis, and their holocaust was a metaphysical event—a convergence of wickedness linking programmed bullies with vulnerable victims. It was a supernatural cataclysm and can be duplicated anytime or anyplace if the germ of dishonesty is given license to root within the psyches of people. All it takes is their becoming upset. You may have experienced this in your own life through injurious relationships with lovers, business partners or family members who've been less than sincere. The dynamics are the same.

When we fall into unconsciousness, we become full of fear and are unable to tell the true from the false. It weakens our sensibilities altering personality, changing us into feeble, gullible people others can exploit to their advantage.

In 1933, the German people were *there*, and Hitler could recruit a legion of decrepit human beings ripe for hatred, and exploit the fears of an entire nation. It was like taking candy from babies. As a pre-conditioned collective of fearful, distracted souls, spiritually sick and detached from wisdom, they had become suggestible. They were ready to place faith in an oppressor's promise to help them remain dull and unaware of their miseries. Unconsciousness and a yearning for more of it had overtaken a debauched country. Through internal excuse making, they had become ready for conquest by evil incarnate.

At first, the excuses had been lies with which every individual could deceive himself. But now the German people were ready to believe bigger lies, those provided by a tyrannical dictator, no matter how extravagant or vile.

It's simple to get liars to accept lies. Through excuse making, something terrible easily undermines already diluted human virtue. Into their imperfect storm wandered Hitler to rescue the German people from the awareness of seeing what they had become.

A new generation's holocaust, making Hitler's Germany look like a picnic in the park, can coalesce anywhere people fall to the lower, dark nature residing within and seek a human savior to rescue them from the inevitable torment of conscience such corruption always delivers.

This is a hell of a way to begin a chapter in a book about spiritual metaphysics, I admit. But there is a point to this. We all have a mini, Nazi Germany going on inside. There is a tyrant within that degrades us with cruelty while sweetly promising to take away our difficulties. It supplies the hope to secure happiness sometime in the future, while secretly gratifying Itself through control in the present.

It will use lies, deceit and undeserved praise to rise to power. When playing *Minister of Propaganda* inside your own head, you manipulate the truth and serve this invisible evil potentate. You end up lying to yourself. There may be no *Big Lie.* Still, it's the many tiny deceits, repeated within your own intellect that create a false personal image of yourself.

Fabricating an embellished picture of yourself in your own mind is phony and treacherous. Unless your own view of you jibes with reality you'll begin living a lie, becoming an artificial vision conjured through the imagination. It'll feel wonderful at first. Fantasy is a powerful intoxicant. This is the reason that *positive thinking* and all the related philosophies that embrace visualization and spiritualized Pollyannaism are so attractive to guilty, shamed people.

Cults, spiritual course studies, and pseudo-mystical societies arise, delivering much-needed relief. Indulge in these and it won't be long before the fantasies will produce conflict within. You won't feel right. Eventually, you'll only feel wrong—more than ever before. Even when at first it works well, the internal conflict of *positive thinking* soon makes you miserable. Forced positive ideas are soon overwhelmed by negative thinking, raising higher anxiety. You'll never get ahead permanently.

What does personal pandering for approval, phony altruism and psychoactive medications like antidepressants[139] all have in common? They each make us feel right when we aren't. They enable us to feel as though we're getting better, when in fact, we are becoming much worse. Self-imparted valuations on ourselves are gratuitous and prone to dishonesty. They permit us to secretly become sicker while we pretend to be getting better.

Sane people intuitively differentiate the true from the false. No one has to tell us. We can see for ourselves. Unsane folks live inside fantasies fabricated in their heads—and from their unsound perspective, imagine how anything can become manifest out of their dreams as if they were God.

The only real answer to the pain of low self-esteem is to earn true esteem. That only comes through virtue.

One of the chief ways of lying to one's self is by excuse making for behavior and ill feelings toward other people and circumstances. Excuses are evidence of the Ego-Self attempting to validate Its existence. It wants to keep *playing God.* Rationalizing, self-serving attitude, and egocentric behavior all serve as powerful narcotics and are the biggest obstacles to personal peace.

To exist peacefully in this world, you're going to have to stop making excuses, even the seemingly insignificant justifications which until now, you may have never even realized you were making. They are not inconsequential. Even the smallest excuses become selfish aids that help suppress and hide resentment, the fundamental cause of all your problems. Once you stop, you break the cycle and everything changes. The problem is that while you're still unconscious you'll continue making excuses and not realize it.

Every time you find that you've erred, whether in judgment or through being upset, take responsibility. Always admit your wrongs. When overwrought by outrage or frustration don't say, "Doesn't everybody get angry?" No. Everyone does not get angry. There are a few of us who have been liberated from emotional slavery. We've discovered the secret to human redemption and have made a conscious decision to stop self-managing all aspects our human existence and turn all of it over to God.

Coming clean internalizes honesty. It silently acknowledges the temptation to judge, revoking its power over you. You become free from anger. Virtue comes through a spiritual unification between you and your Creator.

You are not a beast. You are partly comprised of a spiritual nature. Your total composition is a unique blend out of the physical and ethereal realms. In prioritizing your attitude, you can accommodate the true order of your human-spiritual construction. Deeply acknowledge your humanness, but, also recognize that you're much more than just an ordinary animal. See the significance in taking care not to place *spirit* in the back seat while on your journey through life.

Once we allow spiritual Discipline to become the preeminent guiding force in our lives, the Power to manage the mind and body arrives. This is a very special Authority that does a wonderful job at keeping order. Better than you ever could.

You may not be a saint. You may or may not ever become one. But don't allow your current shortcomings to deter you from aspiring toward perfection.[140] You just might become a saint, as long as you don't pretend to be one before it is your time.

It's one thing to be proven wrong in the presence of others. But as error reveals within one's self, it gets easier to give ourselves a pass to justify shortcomings. We all know what it's like to eat crow occasionally. Many of us have learned to endure certain embarrassments at least occasionally, even taking a perverse pride in enduring the brief sting of embarrassment for having been *outed*.

There is, however, another kind of embarrassment—a secret mortification felt only within. This is the private humiliation we experience before the Spirit of conscience. For those reckoning to have been placed on the spiritual path, disgrace of this order can be difficult to own up to.

Nevertheless, until we learn to smash false esteem and endure personal shame, no matter how slight, we will never develop a capacity for honesty. We should accept this responsibility or we'll never lose our fears.

Every day we experience thousands of secret moments where personal truths or consequences present opportunities either for honesty or self-deceit. Being new to *Non-Contemplative Meditation*™, in the beginning there are bound to be successes along with some failures. Remain patient. Humbly stick to your guns and in time, gains in virtue will begin to far outweigh the losses of immoral living.

By admitting current error immediately, you'll remain *present* to observe the inevitable temptation rising to judge *you*. Courage will then rise, overwhelming all fear. You'll find the strength to face and take responsibility for the "little things." It won't be because you read a concept in a book or were given outside counsel. It will be because you're becoming a virtuous human being. Your nature is changing. You're being transformed from within.

This will be the starting point. Soon thereafter, you will regularly find you are no longer making cowardly excuses for the bigger things either. The courage to be true, no matter what, has begun to build. Living honestly with yourself, you'll experience tiny *Aha* moments regularly. Soon you'll also notice a mitigation of fear. Dread and hopelessness and gloom you may have carried for a long time will diminish. The immediate freedom from these emotional stresses will be noticeable.

If you have a background in Christian Scripture, then you're probably already familiar with the following story. A man with two sons divides his estate between them. The younger of the two takes his inheritance off to a foreign land. There he squanders the money on prostitutes and a debauched lifestyle.

A famine strikes. Having exhausted his father's inheritance, he is forced to go hungry, living in poverty.

Through the pain of life's adversity, he finally becomes level headed. Coming to his senses, the wayward son admits shunning God and his earthly father. He sees his way clear to returning home, offering himself as a servant in his father's house. His sanity is restored. Now a contrite, transformed man, he heads back to his father house.[141]

Before he gets there, his father sees him approaching. Though still a long way off, dad eagerly runs to meet him, welcoming the rebellious son. There's no fear of the father's remonstrance. The son experiences his father's forgiveness. This isn't amnesty or a pardon. It is the father's love for his child—the absence of rancor for having rejected his protection in the first place. There is a metaphysical exchange of positive force we call *love*, between father and son. The two move closer to each other, finally reuniting in the father's house.[142]

Anytime we fail to take responsibility within ourselves, as in *The Prodigal Son* example, we unwittingly move away from God. Then in admitting our wrongs, we experience a personal moment of truth and the opportunity for realignment. The private confession of faults before our Father opens our being to Him, allowing His will to flow in. We are transformed into God-aligned individuals, no longer bound to Self. Sincere attitude emerges and we become energized with a power flowing through us containing supernatural inertia, reuniting us with the God.

Restored consciousness supplies strength. We're immediately redirected back in His direction, even as He draws nearer— exactly like the Father in the Prodigal Son story. Some religions observe this phenomenon as repentance and redemption.

A contrite human being can no longer do wrong because the wrong Self ceases to control him. God dispenses His discipline with the quiet inspiration to do the next right thing *no matter what.* Notice your failings as often as you can without excusing or justifying error. The earnest admission of fault builds virtue upon even the crumb of honesty, whereas justifying wrongs completely degrades all good character.

Watch out for even the slightest dishonesty. It will promote the corruption of honor and encourage fear. When a spirit of deceit develops within, it reconstitutes the original error. You'll be compelled to repeat the same mistakes over and over. So, acknowledge fault without delay, letting no opportunity to exercise courage slip away. The ensuing falling away of fear will astound you once you begin to live this way.

We often use the word *fear* to describe the gnawing, inner electric-like, anxious hum—sometimes escalating to a shudder, that we feel in response to certain thoughts. You can feel it from the solar plexus up through the thorax. It's the emotional evidence of lost awareness, that we've begun to resent and to judge, *playing God.* This means our original faith in Him has been switched out in favor of a belief in ourselves. Fear represents a lack of trust. Once we resent, we're immediately disposed to overwhelming worry and doubt.

Though you may never have thought of it this way, fear is a form of resentment energy. Like anger, contempt or frustration, we experience it as an unpleasant emotion, a flavor of upset we feel following each failure to trust the direction that conscience supplies.

Most fear is just irritability the thinking mind derives out of events that haven't happened yet. Doubting our inner discipline in *the present* results in aversion toward the future. It's an egocentric reach-ahead into time in order to suck and nourish on negative imagery fabricated by the intellect. In an attempt to merge future fantasy with present truth, It foments unnecessary discontent. We nervously agonize, while a lower Thing delights in the negative emotional flow of worry.

Once ruminating in past and future events has pulled you away from awareness, dread easily sets in. Anything that controls our thinking also holds the power to fill us with fear. Unconscious, you'll begin to trust your finite Self rather than the infinite God. It's an aimless existence, full of sorrows and regret. But those bedevilments are avoided by waking up and allowing consciousness to connect with a Higher Source of discipline. It's so simple.

When living in the moment, in the sunlight of the Spirit, we are never again overwhelmed by fear. We no longer get angry in the *present moment*, or in the future. Our fears fall away. We live in perfect peace and ease. We become wise. "When?" you ask. The moment we become conscious of His presence.[143]

The solution to fear is in returning to consciousness. Become unmoved by distracted thinking and return as a little child, awake and reconnected to the loving discipline of your conscience. You'll never be more confident in this lifetime as when you live this way, always intuitively knowing what *the next right thing* is without fretting or scheming to make anything happen. God-consciousness can be practiced using the *Non-Contemplative Meditation* exercise offered in this book. Try it and successfully face life with courage. It's immediate and fail-safe.

***

Everyone is familiar with what it is to become upset. It's likely you've been told it's normal to be angry. Doctors, counselors, and clerics tell us how *everyone gets angry* and there's nothing any of us can do about it except learn to manage our emotions. They offer an array of techniques and theoretic pronouncements on the subject. Some of what they propose could be helpful as these may help mitigate outright catastrophe in the short-term. But what these professionals and experts don't know about anger, will harm you in the long term.

Living resentfully from cradle-to-grave, repeatedly battling inner irritation is far from normal. We are meant to grow out of our harmful emotional responses as we spiritually mature. That nearly everyone experiences self-inflicted emotional ills is no good reason to resign ourselves to a resentful existence.

While anger energy is a perfectly natural, motivating force for animals It is not natural for humans at all. Unlike animals, we are made of both spirit and flesh. Anger for animals fills them with life. For human beings however, anger brings ultimate fatality. Each time you respond with emotion, stress brings you closer to the animal side of existence, further away from your spiritual connection.[144] Closer to death and further away from life.

The word *emotion* literally means, *to move*. If anyone can gain access to your psyche, they can also impart a certain energy, easily upsetting you, even further *moving* your thinking and behavior. They will have the power to *emote* you into action in accordance with their will, regardless of your wishes or needs. You are under their *spell*, so to speak.

This is the emotional energy others use to control. It could be wide ranging, affecting many people or up-close and personal, targeting us individually. Large-scale, it may be the empowered evil dictator who *moves* the somnambulant population of a nation, overtaxing, imposing unfair governmental rules or overtly engaging in acts of misconduct to purposefully upset his public. Shocked by cruelty but powered by resentment, they'll serve the will of a greedy national figurehead and work for the support of his regime.

Or, it might be the scheming woman who upsets her husband, furtively bullying him into working longer and harder. She may display irrational thinking, inciting his resentful nature, driving his devotion to her. She'll motivate him toward financial success so he can supply the material assets she craves to sustain her and her children's personal comfort. A sexually addicted man is an especially vulnerable target for this class of woman.

The examples are countless, but in each case, there's betrayal followed by the rise of a tyrant. This is how anyone who makes you angry can manipulate you. At some time in your life, you found you were being controlled or manipulated by an unreasonable boss, an over-demanding teacher, a best friend or lover, who wielded a spellbinding authority over you. It was emotional terrorism—the hostile bid for a disturbing takeover of your very being. An easily upset victim has no choice but to comply with their bullies and oppressors.

It isn't one hundred percent the bully's fault, though. Once a tormenter has tasted power, he's further tempted by a victim's disposition toward resentfulness. Are you a victim? If so, your persecutor is drawn to you by your weakness. He first projects his will by upsetting you. Then as you react with emotion, he moves in for the kill. Self-centered tyrants cannot resist responding to feebleness. Your own susceptibility for becoming upset draws the worst people into your life. In effect, you unwittingly seduce your own oppressor making him your master. He can't help it.

Recognize who the emotional terrorists are in your life. Then forgive them. The strength in true tolerance scares the hell out of them. You cannot change the past but you can stop baiting bullies with emotional weakness, keeping them out of your life. They'll go elsewhere to find weaker prey.

The key to regaining manageability isn't to defy the actions of your personal tyrants with emotional force or resistance. It's to neutralize the power they wield before being overwhelmed by their intimidation. You can develop personal immunity to all forms of resentment energy including anger, frustration, and fear.

First, see the order of the *takeover*. It has been anger, upset, irritation and annoyance in the first place that has placed power into the hands of the bully. The victim becomes as responsible as the bully.[145]

Second, consciously accept responsibly for your irritation. Don't revert to the excuse, "Doesn't everybody get mad?" No, everybody does not. Some have discovered the metaphysical secret in this book and committed their lives to it. Thus, they are free from anger. If you'd like to become one of us, then you'll also have to accept this before you can make much progress.

Do not justify negative thinking as though it were normal. Have a skeptical attitude about all negative thinking as it occurs. Be suspicious of your own emotions. When someone tells you, "Hey it's normal. We all get angry," realize that this person has bought into a common but hazardous misconception.

It's often true, that to recognize the lie we will first have to have engaged in the deception, suffering the bitter consequences of misguided reckoning. But we do learn from our past errors. Even a badly calibrated ship's compass that sets a wrong course receives that misdirection from some unseen deviant force. It sends an unknowing captain and crew into waters they have no intention or desire to navigate. They become lost. Likewise, when misguided by the deviant force of obstinacy, we are similarly cut off from Gods perfect direction. A force of erroneous discipline comes from somewhere, and life may appear to be ordered or it could seem blatantly reckless.

You've been designed with an unseen spiritual GPS to receive flawless direction from your Creator. Once cut off from it, you are no longer under His protection. You're placed in a vulnerable state and exist only on fate. This is an anxious, aimless way of life many people experience. It's full of nervousness and fear of indecision. They can hope their insecurities aren't real, that they can be simply wished away, but it will not simply go away by the power of wishful thinking.

Anxiety is real. It's no illusion. When you feel uneasiness, you haven't created it yourself. It's a metaphysical warning, designed to protect. It's telling you that something is wrong and will not go away just because you want it gone. It is symptomatic of the distressed human condition many have come to know as *Spiritual Sickness.*

Whatever it's called, suffering from metaphysical malady leads to nerve-wracking insecurity. Entering each day haunted by the feeling of dread, lacking confidence, without God in your life, you become the living definition of *agnostic.*[146] No one can make right choices under the emotional blade of worry. So beware, because even the strongest of human will cannot remedy the misfortunes of a misguided soul.

Now, living in a Self-disciplined realm, life becomes rudderless and subject to chance. You attract adversity, becoming increasingly subject to overwhelming negative emotion. Fear sets in. You feel like a bundle of nerves, haunted by doubt, projecting your anxieties into those around, confusing and upsetting others. Instability evolves because without God-consciousness you are short of discipline needed for security. Without the supernatural influence of Divine Correction, life is nothing more than an existential coin-toss.

Inevitable difficulties in the stream of life make us stronger if we remain God connected. *Not so* the self-disciplined person. If we continue to deal with our problems with willfulness, we become feebler, less connected with the Source of good guidance.

Unless we properly meet adversity, we undergo a dissolution of goodwill with each encounter. Moral character reverses and we become increasingly overwhelmed by the cruelties in the world. Whatever virtue we once had evaporates as our behavior distorts to fit into a cruel mold. We are reshaped into subservient zombies. The world beats us into a pulp, while we become subject to sickness and despair. Now serving people rather than God, the takeover by our tyrants is complete. Then, what a cruel world we shall live in.

There is a way out. We can get back on the path illuminated by Spiritual Sunlight. There you'll regain access to Gods loving, wordless correction. When we live under God, distress, even the relentless nudge of anxiety is no longer the threat it once was. Suffering helps hone character and virtue when each troubling issue is conquered by patience. Then instead of tearing us up, adversity becomes mental, moral training the likes of which does not exist except through God-consciousness.

Discipline and character development are essential for human progress. But it won't come from moral teaching or rote knowledge. It can only come from a loving Source while we are God-conscious. Allow Inner Light to enter and you will experience Leadership from within. You'll always see where, how and when to go. As you become more virtuous and morally sound, you'll pass good character onto your children and to people around. Once connected to our Creator we no longer need role models to follow—we *are* the role model.

To the extent that you fail in consciousness does your environment also regress. Family and children will revolt with the slightest indication of hypocrisy. *They know.* In the attempt to shield themselves from your infection, they'll become as fallen as you in the process. So be on guard, even for the little things. With vigilance, the tiny temptations awaken us to truth before they ever have the chance to harm us.

We're blessed in that we need not look far for protection. We can connect at any time, at any moment. As we do, He steps in to shield us from harm—to *deliver us from evil*. All it takes is allowing *conscious contact* with the Creator to become the most important thing in your life. Put this first, then everything we need to do the will of God follows.

Without *conscious contact* with God, the opposite is true. We will continue to succumb to the constant, harsh pressures in the inescapable torrent of life. Passing on poor examples of moral character, our children will hate what we're becoming. Mounting anger inside ensures that they'll become duplicates of us, making the exact same errors. A legacy of corruption continues and we become the matriarchs and patriarchs of generational misery.

Our lack of discipline projects into them and their lives become as unmanageable as ours. Then, they will hate themselves. Children living under this system become unruly. They turn promiscuous and dishonest. A gross, self-centered attitude develops. They become disillusioned, forced to abuse substances for relief and manipulate others for personal gain. In time, they'll do nearly anything to feel better.

Watching the excruciating existence of our own children we think, *What could have gone wrong?* The question to ask is, "Where have we failed to go right?" A self-absorbed existence guarantees the progressive inability to know God's will. Dullness and self-absorption inhibit the capacity to receive power and carry it out. By remaining unconscious, we are the ones who fail our own children.

***

Our nature is the blending of two modalities—the spiritual with the animal. Human beings are the only living creatures on earth that can cross these modes. When we're conscious, we maintain our connection with the spiritual realm, encouraged through life by the light of conscious understanding. We come to trust this otherworldly side of existence, receiving intuitiveness and inspiration moment by moment as we go.

As soon as we lose conscious contact, instead of relying on spiritual power we become sensually driven by self-centered instincts and nervous energy. We immediately begin a nasty descent into the animal realm. It feels empowering at first, even uplifting. Something base inside loves it. But as we blissfully relinquish the spiritual life we also transmogrify into altered beings, becoming increasingly more like animals in the wild than human.

The longer this goes on the greater the imbalance of conflicting natures and the further we degenerate. It's a fatal rejection of our divine heritage. Then in defense of our decline, we begin to eagerly embrace the obsessive pleasures of the world as if they were superior to our once virtuous life. We'll celebrate the animalized reconditioning of humanity as "normal" and justified, excusing our shape-shifting. We'll believe that we are evolving. Really, we're devolving from human beings into human beasts.

This is how morality breaks apart within a society. First, one by one, inside individuals, then as a cultural phenomenon. Finally, a conflicted civilization see's right as wrong and wrong as right and self-destructs, perversely excusing annihilation as some ascension into imagined paradise.

Individually, excuse-making places us at great risk. It can make us appear callous on the outside, but emotional and self-righteous on the inside. We'll pardon miscreant behavior in ourselves and others, while bizarrely judging at the same time.

We all need to be alert to this kind of justification, lest we lose our spiritual connection forever.

Humans have the potential for both intuition and instinct. The more dedicated to living out of intuition one becomes, the less *animal* we will be. Then, where we once justified our strange attachment to animal impulse, we now begin to live through spiritual insight. This is a completely different existence than most people are used to, but it is certainly preferable. It leads to a life that is free of struggle. Some will view this as a charmed lifestyle, bursting with miracles and true joy.

That's understandable. It is blessed with the stamina to overcome obstacles with grace. When threatened by illnesses, health spontaneously restores. Life-threatening diseases are reversed. We experience cures, as the body's immune system revives, recapturing its protective role. This isn't limited only to the body either. There's an overhaul of totality that includes a psychic healing too. We become mentally whole as well.

The narcissistic personality is incompatible with a mindfully conscious, God-connected mind. Accordingly, once awakened, relationships that have been broken by self-serving attitudes begin to mend. Selfishness drops away. A healthy altruism replaces egoistic thinking. We discover an inner enthusiasm for self-sacrifice that we never had before. All bitterness for others neutralizes. The clash of the self-obsessed Titans ceases. Immediately, vices lose their grip. Gross addictions fall away as obsessions mitigate, finally dissolving as if into thin air. If all of this sounds miraculous to you it should. Miracles await all those who stop trying to install their own happiness and turn life and will over to God's care.

You develop usefulness in ways you could never have before imagined. Life then becomes a progressive journey toward becoming a faultless, spiritual being where eventually there's freedom from character defects and ill will. But the excursion ends unfinished, and we remain broken, the moment we stop moving toward the Light. Don't think you can never become perfect in this lifetime, that it's okay to accept abandonment to animal indulgences. It is not okay. That would be surrendering to dark madness and a fatal suspension of natural momentum toward your Creator.

Excuse making is deadly balking. It represents inner dishonesty, altering direction and drive, sucking out all natural enthusiasm for life and progress. Once we stop growing spiritually, we immediately lose human purpose. Perfection in this lifetime is possible. To cease growing toward perfection means yielding to the negative force of an alternate universe. Evil wins. You lose.

Allow me to demonstrate for you where these two universes are. I call it *DOSE (Distance Object Space Exercise.)*

Please follow along and see if you can do *DOSE*. This is perfectly safe. I know exactly what I am doing.

First, look around where you are sitting right now. Notice the objects in the room. Perhaps various furniture or items lying on top of furniture. It doesn't matter what these are. Maybe a lamp, a pillow, a coffee maker, or a mirror.

Now, visually select four of these items.

Once you've made your selections I want you to look at one of the items, and then begin to gently shift your eyes from that item to another and then to the next, until your eyes have seen all four. You can repeat this several times if you like.

Do it now once more, and this time I want you to notice what has been happening. You can "hear" the mental sound of your own voice. It is as though you speak to yourself, inside your head. Notice how this internal language labels each item for you? Go ahead and allow that now with several of the items. All of them if you like. I'll wait while you complete that.

Finished? Good. As you shifted attention mentally and visually from one item to the next, your consciousness acknowledged the existence of each item. At the same time, intellect automatically intruded, tagging each item with the appropriate name.

So, a lamp registered in your head as "Lamp." A coffee pot registered as "Coffee pot," and so on. You took an intellectual inventory of each item, mentally converting each visual image into a word. Once an item received a name, intellect then told you what to *call* it, so you could remember it. It was as though you had anticipated a quiz at the end of this exercise, right? Okay, that was your intellectual mind at work. Quite normal.

Now, let's do the same thing again. But this time, I'll add a little extra twist, to finalize the point of this demonstration. (Don't worry. There is no quiz.) The next two paragraphs contain the full directions to complete this mini-demo, so do not actually begin until you've first read through to the end, okay?

This time, instead of moving your sight across all four objects, I'm going to have you mentally select just one of them. It doesn't matter which. Then, at the end of this paragraph, you will stop reading and simply look at this object, but, this time, I want you to notice the thought telling you what the object is.

For example, if it's light switch, be aware of the internal language of words popping up that tells you, "LIGHT SWITCH." As you direct attention toward that single object, instead of registering and moving onto another as you did before, simply hold attention to this one item. Again, just notice. Become conscious of this internal voice.

Observe how there is some distance between you and the object, even as your thoughts try to break through consciousness to speak to you. Space. Time. It is there and you are here, separated by an invisibleness you can sense with your mind, but cannot optically see with your physical eyes. Just notice this.

Become aware how it is you who is doing the noticing.

In other words, notice yourself and how you exist separately and apart from the object—that you are relative to it, and not it. There's space between you and the object as well as the voice that utters the name of the object to you.

Go ahead and do this now for a moment. You can experiment and reread this if necessary. I'll be waiting for you at the next paragraph.

Are you done with that now? Good. Isn't it odd? Go ahead and try it again if you wish. This book isn't going anywhere. It'll still seem peculiar the second time. I'll wait for you right here at this line of type.

The experiences between the two mini-stages in the exercise I just showed you are different from each other, aren't they?[147] There is a very profound reason for this. Let me explain what just happened.

In becoming aware of the distance between you and the object, the space becomes occupied with your consciousness. Consciousness instantly activates, rising to meet and fill the space. The connection between you and the thinking intellect is instantly severed and cannot push through consciousness to tell you things—about the object, about me, about you, about anything at all.

There are metaphysical reasons for this, which I explain elsewhere in this book and in the exercise recordings. For now, simply see how thinking occurs on a physical plane. This is the realm of intellect. Conscious awareness occurs on a metaphysical plane. Not the physical. This is the realm of the spirit. The fine line of balance between the two realms is where all of mankind's eternal life or death is determined. Ultimately only one side can win out.

The main point of *DOSE* is simply to demonstrate both the physical and non-physical realms of existence. You have just now received personal proof. It may be repeated anytime you care to.

Our human mission is to develop and grow within the spiritual realm. Our progress begins with the first twinkle of consciousness, a state of being that improves as we continue to experience the Presence, in the present, more of the time. In exercising awareness, we'll naturally begin to live more of the *now* each day. We lose the inclination toward negative thinking, doubt, and disappointment, but instead become inveterate, constructive thinkers.

The journey toward perfection is best measured with a chronometer rather than weighed with a scale. With this kind of spiritual growth, fear of the unknown transforms into enthusiasm for opportunities to come. You become a natural optimist.

The day you cease practicing living in the moment, you'll be immediately carried away in time, toward spiritual stagnation. Doubt will be your new companion and you'll become mired in misgivings and hesitancy over opportunities which would otherwise be plain. A doubtful Spirit will dominate, instilling fear and a torturous tendency to procrastinate.

Allow the mindful lens of consciousness to increasingly become a part of your daily life and your spiritual growth will be marked by a naturally uplifted attitude. You'll become a natural optimist, not a forced, positive thinking, artificially motivated robot. As you become hopefully confident and lose your distrust of the future, fears will fall away. Life becomes tempered with courage before the unknown.

This isn't reckless bravado. It is the competence to move elegantly into any unknown that lies ahead, free from the binds of unreasonable expectations. This is faith.

"Around here, however, we don't look backwards for very long. We keep moving forward, opening new doors, and doing new things, because we're curious and curiosity keeps leading us down new paths." ~ Walt Disney

Walt's practical perspective contains a valid lesson. His immortal words support the point that we must always be making progress. Stagnation is a sure way to negativity and fear.

Whereas in the past the only way you knew to stop beating yourself up for your defects was to compensate by patting yourself on the back, now you can see the insanity in either. As imperfect reality becomes clear, also realize the need to remain humble. Don't resent your own imperfect nature. Stop judging the faulty, defective you.[148]

See the certainty of living in a flawed world and though you may not be perfect either, in cultivating conscious contact with your Creator, at least you are improving. You're headed in the right direction, toward perfection.

By turning thinking and thus behavior over to intuitive guidance every day, you make a vital admission about your life. You acknowledge your imperfect nature and need for Supernatural help without which there can be no progress. Now relinquish spiritual indifference. Commit to the journey on the path toward perfection, moving forward in the direction of the One and perfect God.

You can become *saintly*. Once truly dedicating your life to the will of the Creator, natural morality expresses through your presence. Virtue becomes elemental in your approach to living. There is no need to put on a deliberate, saint-like performance. If you were already one you'd have no cause to read this book. You wouldn't need me to point you toward practicing God-consciousness because you'd already have it all the time.

The idea of being a saint can hold different meanings depending on who you ask. For some, there's the implication that you have already become perfect. Christians know they can't be Christ. But they can become Christ-like, meaning they can move in His direction, over time becoming progressively perfect, just as He is already perfect. Being Christ-like doesn't mean walking on water or turning water into wine. It does, however, mean *no longer hating*, always forgiving and not *playing God* through emotional judgment regardless of whatever cruelty, unfairness or harms are imposed. This amounts to true love and forgiveness for all while being concurrently filled with God's love *as we love others*.

There's no good to come out of pretending to be perfect. Continuously moving in the direction of perfection is about all we can do. Starting with the few and small things in life, love progresses from there. It's a process. If you were already a saint you'd never have to act like one because whatever was your behavior, that lifestyle would automatically demonstrate *holiness*. You won't become a saint by pronouncement, but you can be someone who's becoming one. Then one day maybe it'll be so. If you keep moving forward, exercising conscious prerogative, you'll have a wonderful life along the way.

Correctly done, curls and dips strengthen biceps and triceps, ensuring that when called upon we can easily lift heavy objects without straining. The body fortifies through physical exercise. It is exactly this way for the spirit too. Like going to a metaphysical gym to work out, a steady flexing from consciousness to thought-involvement and back will strengthen your ability to remain awake during the normal course of each day.

By practicing the cycle, entering and then abandoning thought-immersion repetitively, we gain spiritual strength. We build the spiritual muscle to meet life on God's terms. We move toward becoming *Christ-like*. Exercising consciousness is what effective meditation is. That's all it is. It allows the metaphysical arousal of dispassionate receptivity to the will of the Creator to awaken. Think of this non-contemplative meditation as a *stress rehearsal,* preparing you for the unavoidable stressful temptation each of us endures every day.

In flexing consciousness any time that you can, you'll learn to cope with the inequities of living by going through each day's encounters with the imperfection in others. As injustice and error are thrown your way, the actions of thoughtless people tempt you to become resentful.

Sometimes there's an urge to strike back. But if we're mindful and conscious, we can step back from these harmful stresses and not retaliate. We can watch emotions as they approach without them overwhelming us. Simply notice the Dark Nature puff up as It prepares to feed and cast judgment on others. Then, continue to watch as It deflates in defeat for having been denied It's nourishment. If you have ever wondered what true humility is, this is your demonstration.

Each time we experience this we grow closer toward God. It can be many times each day. When met with a mindful attitude, free of selfish motive, these brushes with unfairness strengthen the inner resolve for justice. Objectionable events place us in a position to be saved from anger while we grow through the experience. Adversity no longer beats us up. The slow, painful deterioration of mind and body toward death is forestalled. We age gracefully, retaining our vital facilities and remain productive until finally one day we simply expire with dignity.

Our passing won't be due to a dissipated lifestyle or emotionally induced disease. It will come naturally from ordinary old age. Time in this material realm will simply be up.

Emotionally overreacting to debris encountered in the stream of life decays and shortens lifespan. But, as you become aware consciousness frees you from the life draining grip of pessimistic thinking. The negative force contained in resentful thoughts will always tempt, but now they no longer overwhelm your mind and body. Your lifespan enriches and lengthens. You defy genetic predispositions, environmental contamination, and even the pathology of infectious disease.[149] Without the constant heaviness of worry and fear, you'll know good health and longevity.

Be cautious, however. Don't try to forge grace you don't truly hold. You cannot effectively counterfeit *conscious contact* with God. Be genuine. *Acting as if* is an ambitious attempt to create a self-fulfilling prophecy. It never works. Similarly, the essence of *fake it to make it* is a lie too. Ultimately it won't help you combat negative thinking. Being dishonest with yourself and other people never has the positive effect you hope it'll have. The lies you tell yourself and others aren't as harmless as you suppose. Morality and principled philosophies cannot be *faked* into existence safety.

Beware of your own white lies. All dishonesty is disruptive to relationships with others. Once they sense your phoniness, decent people with whom you might otherwise have become fast friends will automatically protect themselves, avoiding closeness.

Meanwhile, indecent, emotionally touched individuals who're at least as artificial as you will eagerly latch on to your companionship. They cannot help but exploit your lying consent to help fund their own deceitfulness. Either way, you foster unwholesome exchange-relationships that pollute your social environment. If you regularly find yourself surrounded by negative, needy people then this what you've done. You have created an adverse atmosphere yourself. Very unlovely.

I know you want to do *good*. You would very much like to pack positively into the environment, making useful contributions to the world and those around. But goodwill can't be forced. People sense bilge and they resent phony, self-righteous helpfulness. The tiniest, seemingly harmless dishonesties contribute mightily toward a tarnished reputation. Never having been taken to task for your duplicity, you may think you've gotten away with small indiscretions. You haven't.

Others might ignore or even encourage your pretense, the self-centeredness you bring to relationships serving their selfish need to judge you. They may fear losing your approval. You foster the company you keep. But they'll also not trust you. Why should they? You aren't trustworthy. They may not even be fully conscious of the wariness they have for you. Now, with a reason to resent your lack of virtue justified, the suspicious environment you've created becomes charged with an unpleasant energy.

The more time that you are awake and aware, the more people you'll affect in a constructive way. Some will sense a bond with you and wish to join you, and be a part of your life. Others, who are less sincere, will be inexplicably appalled by your integrity and drop off. They'll want nothing to do with you. This is wholesome divisiveness—a phenomenon causing the complexion of your immediate milieu to evolve over time. Just as negative energies infect those around you, the positive effect of consciousness is also contagious to your world. Goodness is as pandemic as evil.

The world remains imperfect—at least for now. Not everything is to your benefit or liking. Should you walk around with a grim outlook when life isn't going as you would prefer? Not at all. But there's no need to plaster on a phony grin either. Gratitude is natural optimism, a satisfied security that comes with the confidence in knowing that you're genuine, no matter what.

We may not always get what we want in any situation. Patiently trudging with dignity, albeit empty handed, builds character and the strength to endure. Natural appreciation and true gratitude develop for the *good things* honestly earned by virtue. No virtue, then no gratitude, and no growth.

By now I hope you've begun using the *Non-Contemplative Meditation*™ exercise. If you have, then you've experienced contact with God. If you haven't yet begun, then please do. If you do as I ask, meditating exactly as proposed, then within days you'll know joy, peace, and usefulness that goes beyond the single, spiritual awakening experience. It'll extend *awakening* into your daily life and routines, increasing in length as days go by. You'll need to stick with it, remaining committed to living a God-conscious life, making the daily commitment to your Creator through meditation.

Do this and a blessing will descend on you that extends into family, work and any environment in which you find yourself. You become free from the binds of a tyrannical dark nature. Then going forward, you're able to happily let Him supply all you need. You'll look back one day and marvel at the course your life has taken, realizing how all you've ever done was place faith in God through consciousness.

Once turning your life and will over to His care, He provides a much better life for you than any you could have given yourself. Experiencing security and peace each day, you develop a sense of redemption and increasing confidence. Your demeanor becomes the bright reflection of a new you.

Lack of consciousness results in an attachment to thought. It's a trap. It's a setup for failure. It can paralyze you with fear, preventing you from enjoying a proactive, productive life. *Conscious contact* frees you from negative thinking. You become an optimistic realist about life instead of a phony, strained positive-thinker. You come to know true *acceptance*.

Wake up and you will enjoy life in all its flawed inglorious-ness.[150]

There is a difference between being *inspired* into action and *motivated* into action. *Inspired action* expresses through wordless understanding, subsequent to Gods vision. It fills us, emanating silently from the heart. Then, in stillness, we cease acting through Self-will. The will of our Creator comes through.

Motivated action is behavior founded on wordy knowledge. It emanates noisily out of the thinking intellect. Sometimes it comes in your own voice. Other times it may sound like someone you've resented or worshiped in the past. It could be the spirit of a teacher, a happiness or prosperity pundit you've venerated in judgment. It is most probably a parent, a cruel teacher or a long gone bully. Either way, a bizarre inner mentor, supply's excuses, proffering profane judgment on others and on you, condemning or uplifting, telling you how wonderful or inferior you are.

The intellectual Phantom stands by to give advice and self-serving counsel at any moment—Self's vision of how life ought to be. It demands that you set aside intuited reasoning and rely on It for Self-centered reasoning. As long as you remain attached to this chattering consultant, you won't be able to help but act on Its will projected into you—now *Self-will*. To return all will and life over to God's care, give up Self-will.

Stop struggling to fix everything. Allow a leap of faith to keep open a path before you that cannot be seen until you arrive at it, in each moment. Do that and each next action will always be right and apparent. Life becomes graceful and propitious. People will ask, "How did you know?" The only answer can be, "I just did."

Realize the distinction between *motivation* and *inspiration* and you'll never resent indecision for as long as you live. Come to rely on intuited discipline as it arises through stillness. In living *now* your life will be effortlessly filled with positive, intuitive activity. Lots of it too.

Allow me to give a real-life example of how living in the *now*, in *conscious contact* with God works. It has to do with an encounter my wife Nancy had in trying to obtain a school bus pass for my daughter.

Keep in mind, being married to me for over 37 years, Nancy began meditating as I first showed her back in the mid-80s. Unfortunately, she gave it up shortly thereafter. (A willful business executive. You know the kind.) But for the last several years she has recommitted herself to consciousness. She's been coming around well too. There had been several health scares, both of which have long since resolved through this way of life.

That said, just a few years ago, on the opening week of school, the bus pass folk didn't have my daughter's bus pass ready. The agency in charge had fallen behind and the passes were delayed a week.

The women who run the local school transportation office in our area have somewhat of a reputation. When dealing with parents their attitudes are known to be a bit off-putting. I've only had to deal with them a few times over the years. But I clearly recall the sense of delight that seemed to overwhelm these women while they exploited their administrative power over others. There was an abusive quality to their attitude that tempted annoyance. If you've ever dealt with a bureaucrat, say at the DMV office, then I'm sure you're already familiar with this power-tripping phenomenon.

So, Nancy drove down to the office to see if she could expedite obtaining the bus pass. As expected, she's met with the bellicose attitude.

Let me add here that whenever you're awake, aware and conscious, you can see as you wouldn't otherwise. A certain prescience kicks in. You usually don't even realize it as it's happening.

She walked into the bus office and immediately sensed something was wrong. It was as though a dark veil had been draped over the room. Nevertheless, she approached fearlessly. A woman at the counter immediately tempted Nancy into a spat. But she didn't react. She remained conscious and steadfast in her awareness.

Not getting a rise out of my wife, the counter-woman then stepped it up a notch. She became louder, more argumentative. Hearing the potential for major hubbub about to ensue, another woman came rushing out from the back office to join it. Now a tense cloud of negative energy hovered over all three ladies. Still, Nancy remained awake, aware and conscious. She knew how, because she had been practicing, meditating, only hours before. Over a few months, she'd gotten the hang of it.

This had the effect of automatically drawing her into a neutral, calm position where she became naturally patient and tolerant. She remained calm, explaining the situation to the two ladies once more. Asking if we could somehow receive our daughter's bus pass prior to mailing them out. As she spoke, Nancy also watched as the temptation to latch onto the dark energy arose in the room. She wasn't overwhelmed by it. It passed. She was safe. Just as remarkable, the two ladies were saved too, rescued from the anger within them. Within seconds, the mounting emotional state was completely diffused. It just melted away. Nancy and the women were laughing together, as the first counter woman happily handed her my daughter's bus pass.

Nancy's presence in the room had a calming effect on these otherwise harried, emotionally driven and fight-ready ladies. She loved them, by *not hating* them. In turn, they were freed to love her in return. It all happened within moments. The women with the reputations for meanness were not really mean at all. Something mean inside them was instantly subdued and love could enter. The dark veil over the room lifted immediately. How did this happen? Nancy's no saint. She didn't have to be. All she had to be was *saintly* in this instance, and the potential for a negative outcome was neutralized and turned positive.

Jesus had this calming effect on certain irascible people too, even over a tempestuous sea. Nancy didn't still a stormy body of water. But in the moment where she was Christ-like, harmony ensued. There was order where previously there was discord. In the absence of hate energy, she didn't judge. The negative energy in the room neutralized. *Conscious contact with God carries powerful consequences through us into the surrounding world.* Each new *now moment* becomes a different *present* than would otherwise be.

Each day is just like this because once awakened we now begin to live a heavenly existence—on Earth, as it is in Heaven. Experiencing the tiniest taste of the fourth dimension of existence, we can never be the same. You'll either love it or hate it and for the rest of your life expend all your energy either embracing it as a way of life or else avoiding it like the plague. Whichever is to be will depend on your inner proclivity.

There is never a need to make excuses once we're confident and connected through consciousness.

If only Hitler hadn't gotten it right. *The evil bastard.*

Stop Making Excuses

*Have you told anyone a single lie today. . .even to yourself?
Deceive anyone, even yourself, often enough and you degrade as
a human being. Evil always steeps Its victims in Self-deceit.
Where there is resentment there are lies, unhappiness, and the
corruption of humanity. Rationalizing anger, justifying
bitterness begets more bitterness, each deception a further
descent into an inhuman existence.*

Point Eight

The Eighth Chapter

By which you see how losing your fear of today, tomorrow and yesterday comes quite simply once you take responsibility for your actions. Inner accountability frees you from faulty self-reliance and you begin to place faith where it truly belongs.

I like it hot. You like it cold. I'm loud. You're quiet. I eat meat. You prefer tofu. We all have our personal preferences. How uninteresting life would be if not for our dissimilarities. Despite the differences, we all want people to be pleased with us. No one enjoys being disliked or despised by others.[151] The more peaceably we get along, the more harmony there seems to be in the home, in the workplace, and within our social circles. Still, there are bound to be personality conflicts with abrasive differences of opinion.

In order to *play well with others,* there are times when we have to acquiesce to the wills of other people—at least to some extent, however small. It would otherwise be impossible to keep proceedings pleasant for long.[152] However, this becomes dangerous once it is to selfishly *appease* others. Then, it becomes compulsory. If you notice that you have a predisposition toward obsessive people pleasing, you should know what you're dealing with.

Upon reading this you may think, *Not me. I don't care what anyone thinks.* That's likely true at some level. But please also consider that approval seeking can also be much more subtle. You can become so embroiled with an obsession to find love and acceptance that it's difficult to see you've become a subservient patsy.

Allow me to show you how this tendency develops.

People pleasing is an emotional anesthetic. It's a trait that quickly becomes a habitual crutch. It inures us into a fawning existence, empowering others with the ability to control us. Underlying resentment creates an obsessive need to gain other's approval. Just as drugs and food numb the pain of guilt every resentful person feels, so does appeasement. Isn't it ironic how easy it is to unwittingly turn life and will over to the control of people you've hated?[153]

It's good to do nice things for others, to be helpful and useful, making positive contributions into the stream of life from which others can benefit. But it must be done expecting nothing in return, not even for the feeling of usefulness.[154] Feelings entail an unwholesome exchange of emotional energy. What may have begun as genuine altruism soon converts into an obsessive need to please.[155] We become servile approval junkies, turning to others for emotional inebriation, drunk on *good deeds* so as to rise above the pain our judgmental nature has brought upon us.

Obsessively giving or receiving approval is not only debilitating to you but to others too. It saps individuality, turning us into co-dependent performers who scrape for appreciation. Ironically, once this occurs you'll find yourself selfishly contaminating and destroying the relationships you so desperately try to preserve.

Everyone experiences the impulse to people-please to some degree. It can appear at any time and under the most unsuspected circumstance. Look how easily this can crop up. Several years ago, I was warming up at the local gym. Spinning away on the elliptical trainer, I noticed out of the corner of my eye, someone climbing aboard the adjacent machine. I briefly turned to see it was one of the gym's trainers, Elise, who I used occasionally. She had taken some personal workout time. We didn't speak. Headphones and gym etiquette prevented that. We just gave each other the obligatory gym-nod and grin then continued with whatever we were doing. I kept going. She began her exercising.

While we both flailed away at our cardio routines an odd thing happened. I found I was strangely compelled to compete with her. I've never been a competitive type, not even in my younger years. I didn't even play sports in High School. Yet here I was in silent competition with her.

Totally conscious of what I was doing, I sped up my stride to match hers. Soon I was going faster than her. I could feel a surge of motivation within, wanting to demonstrate to Elise how well I was doing with my cardio exercising. It was apparent to me that I wasn't trying to win a race with her. That was the furthest thing from my mind. I was in sucked into a private drama inside my head to curry approval with Elise. I got a small rush of satisfaction, just imagining that she would take notice of how well I was coming along. This absurdity only lasted for less than a minute before I became aware of it. Even so, the urge remained strong for at least five or ten more minutes before my awareness slowly neutralized it away.

I began to wonder, *Why the heck did I do this? Why did I experience this compulsion to pit myself against Elise?* The answer came immediately. I was compelled to seek Elise's approval. But another question remained. What caused that? I have no affiliation with her beyond a few hours of training now and then.

Later it struck me.

About eight months earlier I had called Elise to schedule a session with her. I left a message on her voicemail. She never returned my call. BINGO! It irritated me. Several days later I met up with her at the gym and we set the date.

I asked her about the message I left and discovered that she simply hadn't checked her voicemail. She never got my message. But that information came too late. I had already gotten annoyed with her, and instead of handling it in the proper way, I buried the frustration. Stuffed it.

Now I needed her approval to compensate for judging her. The original irritation was immediately converted to judgment, resulting in pain for playing God. She had no idea this was going on under the radar. We were on good terms. But you can easily see the dynamics of resentment and people pleasing here. Can you also see how low-key this phenomenon often is? It is easy it is to fall to judgment and resentment. It alters behavior and thinking. It's powerful.

This is just one example of many dynamics operating between the people we encounter every day. Everyone experiences phenomena like this. In this instance, I was conscious, became aware of the danger I was in and was therefore saved from it. This is why it is so vital that we live consciously. If not, we will fall into situations like this and never know. In personal or intimate relationships, people can develop parasitical associations, reciprocally pleasing and in turn receiving pleasure. Unless watched, these can become a sordid cycle of people dependency. You become obsessed with pleasing people for the satisfaction you get. You will be compelled into a servile scrapping lifestyle, continually looking for approval.

If you're an approval seeker, then compulsiveness will already be familiar to you. It is one of your character traits. But more than that, the behavior portends something much worse. It's an indicator of hidden annoyance, emotional irritation you may not even be aware you've suppressed. No matter whom or what you resent, you'll find you are oddly drawn toward assuaging the object of your irritation, just as I felt the gripping force wanting to please Elise. There's no need to struggle with it. Simply notice the odd urge. Observe the inclination to please or appease as it rises.

Unrecognized resentment alters thinking and behavior. It distorts our original confidence and independence. Once corrupted by bitter emotion, the approval seeking of those you hate becomes an irresistible compulsion. Sensing weakness, others are tempted to dominate, turning you into a silent victim. You'll find it difficult, perhaps impossible to speak up to others, less you run afoul of their approval. You will have become an appeasing approval addict.

This elicits more hostility inside. You freeze and go mute before a tyrant boss, an abusive spouse, a mean-spirited parent, teacher or bureaucrat. With no voice, you place other people in positions to take advantage of you. You won't have the courage to say, "No," even when appropriate. Your own children will be difficult to correct once you've allowed resentment to contaminate your relationship with them. They can abuse your affections. They can betray loyalties. They can't help it.

Just as for every seller there must also be a buyer, there's the *giving* of approval and *receiving* it. Be aware of either. Each becomes an addictive block to insight. Either of these can fill-in and substitute for other vices. What good is it to give up smoking and drinking, only to become a groveling people pleaser, spreading emotional misery to everyone within your reach?

Society gives approval to people who don't deserve it. Doctors, celebrity performers, and politicians are prime examples. Here, approval easily turns into worship. When someone earns your respect, watch for the tendency to make that person into your hero. Don't be the esteem grantor to any individual. If you see a politician make a speech or state a position you share with him in a media sound bite—even if it's obvious to you he is a good, patriotic person, just observe. If you become overly enamored with any person you are in great danger. Don't surreptitiously become their *fan*.

You can appreciate a good play or a movie. It's desirable to be entertained and perhaps participate in leisure and recreational activities. Team efforts and competitiveness contain valuable life lessons. They help develop character. Sometimes fiction writing or dramatic stage and screen performances can convey a powerful message to an audience. These do well as temporary indulgences, not unlike the natural enjoyment of sex or food.

Therefore, I am not proposing we should never enjoy a slice of pie with a cup of coffee. Or that a doctor, a lawyer or an educator shouldn't be appreciated for their acumen and skills. Neither should one be denied the fun of a good football skirmish, a night at the opera or a great performance in a play. But emotions evoked through excitement ought to be mild and fleeting, never exaggerated beyond their intended purpose. The joys of life can be heartwarming and delightful without the stress of emotionality.

Under emotional stress, the risk of hero worship and people dependency presents a danger. If something written here touches you deeply and you find it helpful, don't elevate me beyond what I am—merely someone who's happened to hit a sweet spot with some poignant words. Simply appreciate helpful people without placing anyone on a pedestal.

To *place on a pedestal* is just a metaphor alluding to the gushing of praise upon others. It usually means an exaggerated adulation, but it's also easy to subtly place someone on a pedestal without even realizing it. Secretly elevating another individual to a place of honor, or quiet hero-worship may seem harmless. It's not. It is extraordinarily dangerous to both sides.

When anyone receives our secret approval, we set up an invisible conveyance of power. Though from afar and without their knowledge, approval is still a judgment, metaphysically transferring authority they may not want, nor should they possess. Not only is it dangerous for you but it also places them in a risky position. Never decide who's good or who's worthy of your respect and love.[156]

When people do *good* it isn't because they are *good* people. It is because there's *good* working through them. What appears to be another's *goodness* is a virtuous nature emanating out of heaven within them. No one can become *good* on their own accord. It is only due to a good Spirit within that anyone projects virtue. Likewise, when people do evil, it isn't they who are wicked. It is a malevolent Spirit working through them. Either good or evil resides inside people. Only God is *good*.

Crediting others places them on a pedestal. Discrediting knocks them to the floor. Judging them in either manner is not a human prerogative. It's a super-human privilege reserved by God for Himself alone. Accepting approval from others encourages them to place you on a pedestal, playing God. Once people lavish blessing and reverence on you, they become your *God-maker*. Realize they do so only in exchange for your approval. In accepting their worship, you encourage grave defectiveness in them.

Though you may feel uplifted by their admiration, you exist only at their pleasure. They hold the seat of power over you. You sit upon a throne only for as long as they keep you there, where you serve their selfish need to play God. Ultimately, they'll come to resent and judge you, either for your need to grovel for their love or in disappointment for your failing to live up to their expectations. In elevating you they are, in effect, worshiping you rather than God. In accepting their adoration, you rob them of the opportunity to discover the true God.

Anyone who adores you degrades your humanity. Becoming puffed with pride you are mysteriously compelled to cater to them so as not to lose their love. The puppet master becomes the puppet. The slave master becomes the slave, and the slave is now a master of slaves. This is a demeaning way to go through life. Eventually, you'll come to resent the fool you've become and become sucked into the deep, dark tunnel of depression.

Everyone attempting to stand on a pedestal built for them by others sooner or later feels used deep within their psyche. Strangely addicted to approval, they can't help but *perform* in the attempt to regain the dignity they sense has been drained from them. Those you judge as *good* develop into your personal tyrants, at the same time becoming dependent on whatever approval you provide for them in kind.

Whether receiving approval or giving it, you'll never be content, healthy or secure sitting on either side of this table. You'll remain plagued by vices, bad habits, fear and emotionally induced physical or mental conditions. Get up and walk away from the game. It may be difficult to do. Approval is addictive and withdrawal is painful. It is also ubiquitous, so always be careful.

Clinicians have developed a method for identifying the person they feel is *likely to abuse* substances. Their concept of the *addictive personality* is essentially determined by scoring on a checklist of character traits. This method has such limited value it is practically useless. An "addictive personality" is better viewed as a vulnerable, psychotic state. It's a personality disorder where the individual's true identity has become overshadowed by a phantom personality within. This is not a metaphor. Something dark takes up residence inside every human being addicted to aberrant behavior or substances. It lies in wait, rising to any occasion It can to resent and judge others and become what It has wanted since the beginning. *To be God.*

A bitter attitude evolves and the narcissistic nature arises from within. Relationships begin to sour. Responsibilities become distorted. The real-life view is set aside for a fantasized existence where everyone and everything exist only in service to Self.

Now, an agonizing sense of natural guilt develops for having played God. Self feels the pain and cries out for relief. He is so identified with It and intellectually lost in his thought processes, the individual erroneously assumes the pain to be his own. Soreness of spirit festers, becoming a nagging wound and the burgeoning addict now becomes easily persuaded to indulge in any substance or behavior promising relief.

It could be a food or a drug but it might also include otherwise innocuous activities like reading books, cleaning or shopping. Anything that can relieve the pain will suffice. The most mundane human endeavors can be easily converted into obsessively self-centered activities he cannot stop. The phantom is now in control.

Vestiges of this phenomenon can occur on several levels. Some people develop fixations with entertainment, thrill seeking or even relationships. Education, study, work, pastimes often fill the bill. We've learned to add the *aholic* suffix to just about any human endeavor once those become abused and compulsory. Or there could simply be a mean pleasure taken through judging the errors and shortcomings of others. If you've ever chuckled at an inattentive man slipping on a banana peel or derived bizarre satisfaction out of a fellow employee passed up for a promotion, then you have experienced this phenomenon. See how perverse judgment can become in the spiritually ailing personality?

The baffling stubbornness of addiction isn't the physical craving for harmful substances and behavior. It isn't even the psychological aspects. What psychologists find truly daunting about addictive behavior is the piece they cannot quite place their fingers on. It's the supernatural element that predates all psychological study, going well beyond the limitation of intellectual disciplines. Here, in the attempt to be helpful, professionals are operating way out of their league.

To acknowledge the cause of the problem and the solution is to cut them out.

Once an angry individual's awareness has been anesthetized, he must refresh the consciousness-numbing effect repeatedly. Failing that, conscience forces the return to his natural state of wakefulness where he experiences horror and remorse for having judged and played God. It's either feel the pain of conscience invoked through anger, or not. A person with an addiction denies truth, refusing to accept the pain of being wrong. The only way he knows to escape the discomfort of visceral guilt is through a numbing indulgence. He finds it in pleasurable behavior and substances and once locked into the routine, continues to succumb to anger.

Negatively charged emotion is continually suppressed, as Ego strengthens, absorbing the harmful energy. Now he's trapped in a loop of emotionality, a virtual feeding frenzy for a Dark Self residing within. It's a vicious cycle that cannot be stopped by sheer will. This is the little-understood metaphysical origin of the "powerlessness" described in Twelve Step recovery culture.

Whenever you hate someone or something, you become addicted to the source of your irritation. Yet, a person who gives up their anger experiences the opposite. They lose all their obsessions, with food, sex, drugs, people, with anything.

Just waking up is enough and once anger falls away, with it goes all addiction to all things.

You could be told repeatedly that to become happy you must change your life, better your environment, get a new career, find new loves. You may even believe it to be true, and yet never find the courage or energy to do it. It seems like a sheer lack of motivation to change, but that isn't necessarily so. There may be ample incentive. It might just be the wrong kind.

Once motivated by emotion, you are no longer an independent operator. You devolve into a debased servant, easily enslaved to most despicable situations and people—a lifeless zombie, driven to immobility by unseen forces. Failure and sorrows fall upon your life like a shroud. Your loyalties become tainted with secret irritation, and you're spellbound to an unwholesome devotion by a force you do not understand. This is one reason why people become stuck in careers or in relationships with people they detest.

If *unconscious motivation* could be replaced with *conscious intuition* this would change overnight. Opening the connection between you and your Creator through consciousness ensures you'll never fear the unknown nor hesitate to live now. For you, there isn't a future. There is only *now*.

Procrastination is the manifestation of a self-fulfilling prophecy for future resentfulness. It triggers inaction, the locking up of progress, once we're overwhelmed by fear. To fully understand this, you first must recognize the simple dynamics of fear and resentment.

First, know how fear arises: Most of us are taught that fear originates within us. That is far from true. Fear is merely the name we use to identify one variety of resentment energy. It's the kind that projects from the future, as opposed to bitterness we experience during current events.

Appreciate this, then you can also see how it's possible to virtually freeze in your tracks, like a deer caught in the headlights of an approaching vehicle. Faced with the prospect of an uncertain future, just knowing that you may resent some imminent outcome can trigger wavering, now.

When presented with the likelihood of feeling bitter about an imagined doubtful outcome, we resent now that we might possibly resent later. Put even more simply, we resent the resentment. If you didn't resent, you could never be fearful. You would never hesitate to proceed toward whatever threatens to upset you.

Problems with procrastination are simple to conquer. The next time you notice hesitancy, a reluctance to check the mail or take a phone call that may convey unpleasant information, say, a large bill or past due notice—observe the spirit of doubt within that speaks of doom. Watch as It attempts to upset and pull you away from the present.

Develop immunity to resentment. Then fears melt away and procrastination is no longer an obstacle to progress.

***

Unless we're careful, ordinary loyalties to family, friends, employers, or anyone for that matter, can devolve into unwholesome allegiances. When devotion becomes obsessive or compulsory, it's a sure sign of deteriorating freedom, the giving away of life-force to someone else. Once initiated, this becomes an injurious exchange. It can convert the most common relationship into an addictive, living-nightmare. In time, the upsetting sense that you're improperly caught up with a personality turns you bitter. You will come to resent their authority, spoiling any chance of getting along well.

In the workplace: When secret hostilities develop, people will work hard and long for a boss they secretly hate. They'll become slaves to an unfulfilling job. Some employers will exploit this phenomenon.

In the home: A marriage partner will dedicate their life to regaining what they perceive as lost approval from a mate. Many marriages are shot through with this theme. Continuing for many years, one partner becomes master while the other a scraping, servile "pet."[157] When both sides are needy, relations become especially gruesome. What may seem to be devotion and selflessness is, in fact, an addiction.

By remaining watchful, you'll see your own motives. You will no longer form *unholy* alliances with people, occupations, or organizations that tend to develop when one side of a relationship has a selfish need.

In another example, adult children of spiritually corrupt parents can develop unhealthy loyalties to an aging parent whom they've never truly forgiven. Unable to love, they may attempt to make amends in compensation for the guilt of having repressed anger for many years. They may dedicate their entire lives to the care of a mother or father whose dissipations have rendered them mentally and physically restricted. The begrudging caregiver slowly dies on the inside while appearing to be saintly on the outside.

A battered spouse who resents a tormentor will find they are strangely drawn deeper into a dangerous relationship, unable to break free. Men will cling to a difficult, perhaps violent woman for the approval she affords him through sex. Women will *stand by their man* to secure long lost love of a weak or bullying father they secretly hate.

All marriages start out with certain elements of approval giving and receiving. A man brings into the relationship his need for mother's love, now transferred to a wife. She nurses his Ego, providing the approval he craves to feel *manly*. But, unless the man is growing away from this perverse reliance on female validation, the marriage will be doomed. It could end in bitter divorce, leaving children without the benefit of a natural family unit. Or it might continue in failure.

Even if such a relationship endures, the union will not foster the wholesome environment necessary to raise unaffected children. Then as adults, they will repeat their parent's error with their own mates. This is part and parcel to the disturbing legacy of generational *spiritual disease*. It's carried by weak men who've never forgiven mama,[158] bearing through life with a sick hunger for female approval. Most men are like this. What a disappointment. *Sorry ladies.*

And as for you men . . . *grow up, will you?*[159]

In immature, selfish man-woman relationships it is the weaker individual, typically the male, who may gush, "You complete me," to his partner. With this needy attitude, a sense of wholeness synthesizes out a parasitical, weak nature in him. Traumas from the past have created a hole he yearns to fill. He must find a victim out of whom he can draw approving *love*. His prey is a woman to make him feel *manly*. God help the woman who becomes emotionally involved with such a pathetic creature. God help the man whose nature has deteriorated into such a feeble state.

As the woman becomes host to the parasite, even a hug or a *hand-hold* becomes a hazardous contact. She can feel his *affections*—really a need, sucking the life out of her. In time, it becomes too unpleasant to bear. She'll resent it, remaking the relationship into a love-hate challenge. She will start to be repulsed by him and withdraw.

His need responds with clinginess in the attempt to recapture what he senses is being withdrawn. Fearing he is losing his source of approval, he may shower her with gifts and fatuous affection only repulsing her more—his weakness now even more apparent.

A woman who encounters enough weak men like this will come to despise all men. Traits which once held the relationship together will begin to slip away. He no longer seems attractive. She judges her potential mate's childish need for her approving *love*. A cloud of acrimony forms over them and the once exciting union turns rancid and self-centered.

Depending on her own self-centered needs, she will either marry him or dump him. If she dumps him, he is crushed, cut off from the *love drug* he craves—a woman's approval. If she marries him, may God help them both. . .and their children.

What could possibly come of sick bonds such as this, but resentment? Your lower Self has an incentive to addict you to unhappy relationships while It feasts on emotional food. Unwholesome romance only gives It license to judge and play God.

It's good to do good deeds. But doing good deeds as if you can become good from the deeds you do is a delusion. People pleasing can become an obsession, just like drugs. If you were good, then no matter what your deeds were, they would all be good. Men of good will are not capable of bad deeds. *Faking it until you make* it is insincere. It is an attempt to fool yourself into believing you've become good simply because you do deeds that look as if they are good.

Though done in secret, the most commendable conduct for the benefit of others can still be abused in the theater of your own mind. Self-installing gratuitous kindness by acting generous isn't true altruism. It's an intoxicating element of egoism. Once under its influence, you'll give money, assistance or aid to the wrong person under the wrong circumstances and ultimately harm them—while helping you form an image of yourself that only nurtures the dark side of Self within.

Of course the sick and disabled should have help from those who are yet healthy. Likewise, difficulties in marriages need to be mended whenever possible to avoid divorce. But relationships that foster mutual dependency are often ruinous for both sides. As a conscious being, the need for people pleasing dissolves. Relationships fashioned for the purposes of nurturing approval become irrelevant. You begin to clearly see what do to and when to do it as each occasion presents. Then unwholesome affairs cannot form.

If you have developed needy attachments where people have become the focus of your existence, now those will become less important. You're becoming free. Some of them may feel a painful withdrawal, as they wean off the addictive life-force you once supplied. There's nothing you can do about that. Family, friends and business relationships who are worthy of saving will reform, becoming wholesome. Now, you'll establish fellowship with them in healthy ways.

Some may still be needy but you can deal with them lovingly, at arm's length, neither exploiting their need or allowing them to exploit you. It isn't likely others will very much appreciate the change in attitude. They could become bitter, causing some relationships to collapse entirely. Be prepared to let parasites go. You're becoming truly altruistic. People who genuinely get along make for a pleasant atmosphere, coalescing productive coexistence, free of rancor and bitterness that always arise out of *people pleasing*.

As you practice living disconnected from the dark entity, your approach to everyone you meet becomes easygoing. You'll find you are free from the influence of their judgment, while at the same time, you cease judging them. A discerning, dispassionate attitude fosters an atmosphere of true love where no one is either worshiped or demeaned. Know that no one is *Reverend*. There is no one to venerate. No one is better than or less than you are in this world. Not one single human being.

No Longer the People Pleaser

Who are you trying to please? People pleasing is an emotional anesthetic, setting up an invisible conveyance of power by which others can control us. Giving or receiving approval degrades our humanity, trading healthy altruism for the obsessive need to judge. Be helpful, expecting nothing in return, not even gratitude.

Point Nine

The Ninth Chapter

By which the compelling case is made that you are never alone because God-consciousness can be accessed anytime and anywhere. Survival amid all obstacles sustains progress toward fulfillment as life becomes packed with purpose and meaning.

We are each born into the world with what we need to survive and live well. We are conscious creatures subject to our Creator. This is a psychic state in which we receive the ultimate love God has for us. We are, after all, His children.

For as long as we remain bonded to Him through consciousness we remain in-filled with intuition and the understanding to perceive with clarity and make correct choices in life. This is His will flowing to and through us via supernatural link.

It's only when we begin to resent and turn bitter that this connection becomes severed. We begin playing God, judging others, either condemning them or else placing them on pedestals.[160] We lose our proclivity to live consciously. What used to be our normal and natural state gets trammeled by the dulling influence of intolerant parents, teachers, and other trusted adults. These are people who should have loved us. They should have passed on their own capacity for forgiveness and patient endurance. But they had none to give. They had their own tormentors early in their development.

Without realizing what they were doing, they did to us what was done to them, instead of doing to us what they would have liked to be done to them. Thus, our consciousness dulled and instead of going through life as vibrant, awake individuals, it seemed that life was going through us. Disenfranchised from the source of intuitiveness, we lost the natural ability to make correct, spontaneous choices and not much that we ever did turned out right. Even when it did it was only by chance.

By reacquainting ourselves with what it is like to exist mindfully and consciously in God's Presence, we find the increasing ability to recoup what's been lost. We can practice deliberately, but without willfulness. This practice is *meditation*.

There's a great metaphysical mystery here. God grants a small bit of His own will to those who earnestly seek Him. It's a force drawing us in His direction as He also moves toward us. Once we have regained this knack for mindfulness we must take our show on the road, so to speak.

This is what I do in family life, business dealings, and all relationships. In working with others, I make no bones about mindful living and the effects of God-consciousness since I can demonstrate how others might conquer their issues through the example set by my own life. This is also one reason why I write. I cannot directly awaken anyone out of their dull state who's not ready for it. But I can help facilitate consciousness and plant seeds for the future in those at least willing to finally let go, even if they cannot presently.

The main point of my work, indeed of this book, isn't that people must learn how to meditate so they should buy my book and feel better. If that were the case, I'd simply create a pretty meditation APP from which to croon spiritual-sounding sweet nothings into people's ears, soothing their jagged nerves, addicting them to the pleasing sounds of music, bells, babbling brooks and titillating affirmations.

But that is not the case. Instead, I lead others to the door opening to understanding, and the simple idea that in becoming God-conscious we can bring a mindful awareness into our day, living to carry our Creator's vision forward into His world. I show exactly how it's done. If this premise is accepted, they are amazed and immediately begin to experience a quality of life they could never have provided for themselves—not in a million years.

I express these discoveries through writing, in working one-on-one with others[161] and also through lifestyle demonstration. I enjoy a mode of existence others may see as attractive since it is free from much of the heartache that their problems have caused. I enjoy peace, ease and a creatively productive lifestyle. In being transparent and honest in all my affairs, I know that I'm a good role model for my wife and children as well as an effective ambassador of mindful God-consciousness for all.

None of this is to boast. It's to reinforce the point, how once we make the transition from unconscious spiritual slumber to *mindfulness* we can bring conscious awareness into our daily activities. Only then do we maximize usefulness, conveying the highest value to our fellows at large. The world changes positively in the moment we allow the Spirit of goodwill to enter. We are spared negativity and life fills with purpose and meaning. We begin to bring our best into all our affairs as we never have before. This is the way it has been for me. And if you sincerely pursue this *conscious contact* it'll be exactly this way for you too. A new life for you and others will unfold before your eyes.

The famous *Book of Life* is a powerful metaphor written into a Scriptural song, for centuries referenced by holy men since it carries immense truth. We are either in it or not. We've become perfect or we haven't. At the moment when we physically die, we leave behind any mortal chance for atonement and further progress toward perfection. There is no reincarnation. We don't get a *do-over*. The object is to become God-conscious as much of the time as you can, but it'll take a lifetime to progress anywhere near perfection.

There's no mystical accounting department keeping track of the time you spend being *mindful*.[162] Subsequently, meditating for the purposes of accruing *good time* toward happiness or earning spiritual security doesn't work. All that matters is *now*. You cannot experience whatever loss or gain the future holds until the future arrives in the *present moment*. You need to experience each moment solely for its significance in the present. Any future value of consciousness is only theoretical. Consciousness is only in the present.

When we're conscious we trade passing time for timelessness. We begin living more in the mindful state each day, and the timed periods of our physical existence become less, while timeless, spiritual portions increase. The timelessness overlays time, as we come into the Presence of the Creator to experience a tiny sliver of the ageless realm, widely known as *the 4th dimension of existence.*

If you are aware and God-conscious, you experience it every day. It's like a little heaven on earth. Those Big Book co-authors weren't making it up.

He descends to meet you here, *now*. The more you live in this dimension, the more ordered and enriched your overall existence. You come under God's will and whatever other will had previously overseen your thoughts and behavior now weakens and becomes shattered.

Sometimes a person I'm working with will wonder, *Do I have to meditate to live well?* The answer is, "No you do not." But I also remind them that, "To live well you must first become God-conscious." If it takes meditation to do it, then for them it is necessary.[163]

While it's true each of us may have the capacity for God-conscious, it is also true that we have all veered off the original course that might have led us to it. Instead of living under God's will each of us has, to some extent, become attached to a

Self-will. This has ultimately caused us discord and even calamity for some.

All bright, awake people have had their fair share of dark moments. Those are the times that help shape who we are depending on how we meet them. There are degrees of brokenness. Some of us have been taken further off the path than others. But we aren't beyond rescue. If we return to an awakened existence, we'll once again experience intuitiveness. Immediately our errors remedy.

Meditation is simply setting aside time to practice the original conscious state we are meant to live. Once we do, order restores. We progress as spiritual beings, embracing a mindfully conscious existence day-to-day, as we go along. To fully benefit from this spiritual lifestyle, please practice the objective condition daily so the state of awareness will carry forward, moment by moment, and hour by hour. Without commitment, there isn't much value to practicing meditation.

But that isn't so difficult to find. In tapping into the Source of Light within, your resolve for Truth modifies. It becomes incumbent upon you as an awakened individual to extend grace to others, giving freely what has been given to you. This is a distinct variety of charity. It doesn't involve money or materialism of any kind but is the kind written about in Scripture. When you affect others through virtuous example, they automatically sense the Source of your inner peace and attitude. Many come to appreciate the positive energy of the Light within as it projects onto those around, bringing peace. This is truly *giving*.

As for those who are repulsed? Well, I think I've alluded to those in earlier chapters. Jesus once spoke of this polarizing phenomenon when he said, "Do not think that I have come to bring peace to the earth. I have not come to bring peace, but a sword." Now, just as then, there is Something in people that just doesn't want them to have what you have found once you awaken. You can only *give* to those who will *have*.

Living *now* isn't just for meditation time. It is for all the time. You won't be able to coast along on some wonderful meditation session you had earlier in the day or a week ago. Once you experience God-consciousness, becoming familiar with it through daily practice, you'll naturally hone an increasing ability to reconstitute awareness as you live through each day. Soon, you'll find you can become meditative or conscious seemingly at will. Not using your own will, of course, but by God's will—*on loan* from Him. In this regard, consciousness is perfectly portable. Access it wherever you go.

Positive energy exists in the *present moment* all around us in never ending supply. This handy feature of consciousness is what makes it so powerful. We can access the light of conscious awareness anytime and anywhere.[164] In this respect, psychic conditioning can be likened to a computer operating system. It contains a divine programming. Whenever during the day it crashes, becomes sluggish or infiltrated by malware, it can simply be rebooted. We immediately reconnect with our Source of discipline and intuition.

Once you've made a commitment to living in the Light of Truth as indicated by your willingness to practice—to meditate each day, you'll find your connection with God can be refreshed a thousand times a day if necessary. He never says, "No." A fresh start is always available.

By taking the meditative state with you into your day, you'll meet each new situation with composure you didn't previously possess. God-directed *uncommon sense* from within will displace self-directed common sense. Willful decision-making will become a thing of the past as the path before you becomes obvious, without the uncertainty of *decision* versus *indecision*.

Doubt may always be in competition with faith, but faith cannot fail as long as you remain awakened.

During each moment that we are awake and aware a new present unfolds and we're no longer making decisions. We move effortlessly through each moment, viewing events and prospects through the lens of consciousness. There's no need to get involved in decision making because each fresh possibility appears in crystal clarity. What to do next is always apparent and opportunities we might otherwise miss do not escape. We become activated from within. The actions we take are no longer fueled by willfulness but supernaturally driven by intuitive grace.

To the observer, you may appear to be an admirable *action figure*, demonstrating energetic accomplishments in all your affairs. To them, it seems like you've got the world by the tail. Yet your enthusiasm and uncanny vigor have nothing to do with your own will. You are compelled by a Power having no origin inside you. It's a Godly nature flowing in, through and then outward.

In abandoning decision making, I do not mean decisions like whether to turn right or left, selecting boxers over briefs or picking between chocolate and vanilla. I'm talking about key existential decisions. These are the critical life-choices having a built-in potential to alter the courses of yet to exist futures as they emerge to become the present reality, moment by moment.

There's no error in the God-conscious *now* because *now* you're no longer calling the shots. Each event is exactly as it should be, even when flawed by what initially appears to be mistakes.[165] Though tempted by doubt, once you've lived consciously for a while, looking back you'll see how life has been as though you were endowed with the *Midas Touch.*

All that you touch won't feel like it is literally turning to gold. In fact, your fortunes won't feel like anything special at all. Still, all of life's endeavors will be affected. For you, there can be no *praying* to affect outcomes. You'll see the folly in that. For the awakened person, there's no petitioning of spirits or summoning angels and dead relatives to alter the course of events for you.[166] These willful activities are all fantasy. You'll simply have a positive effect not only in your own life but also in the lives of others without effort. Some people won't like this effect. They may even become envious or oddly repulsed by it. Others will be comforted in your presence and appreciate your connection with their lives.

Will you experience this perfectly? No. It could take a lifetime to develop continuous grace. But even in the beginning, days previously burdened by fear and hesitancy become less. Noticeable peace and ease will begin to permeate the shroud of doubt. With each passing day, you will sense disciplined direction.

You'll experience a stabilization of emotions and a new, steady attitude will gradually translate into physical healthfulness. You'll know when medical doctors are right and when they are wrong, when to seek their services or products and when not. You may experience spontaneous cures for ailments and conditions that have not responded well to clinical treatments in the past. These will be miraculous events. For these to happen you must practice consciousness anytime you can. This means you first seek the Kingdom within you before all other things, even before cures. But they will happen if you're ready for them.

Your circle of friends will tend to be smaller than had you lived differently, but the quality of those relationships will be wonderfully wholesome. The positive energy among your close-knit associates will far outweigh anything that could come of a being a social butterfly. This isn't to say you'll isolate. God forbid. But those with whom you feel visceral rapport and brotherly love will be compact and potent. You'll never feel lonely.

***

What are you thinking at this very moment? How far down into the rabbit hole have you gone? If you are involved in your thoughts, consider then, please, how *rumination* becomes *ruination*.

A *ruminant* is a rank of animal that chews the cud, predigested food out of the stomach. The practice naturally serves these animals well. But for humans, ruminating food is revolting. In fact, there's a condition known as *Rumination Syndrome* where humans chronically vomit meals they've eaten and swallowed into the mouth. Don't even imagine what that would taste like. It's a disgusting thought, to say the least. But the animal loves it.

Getting tangled up in old thinking, or ruminating, is like a camel chewing cud, digesting already experienced food brought up out of its own belly. Before long, savoring the sour flavor and grainy texture of the past becomes attractive. Self acquires a perverse taste for regular feedings of bitter memories.

Isn't the inability to let go of a grudge a form of human *Rumination Syndrome?*

Until turning life and will over to God and experiencing freedom from the bondage of Self, no human being can resist the rumination habit. Once *chewing* on daydreams, no matter how bitter the flavor, you'll remain under a compulsion, continuing to pull up the past, deriving selfish value out of old visions stored in the memory banks of your brain. As scenes replay across the screen of your mind you pass judgment on other people as well as yourself—good, bad, approved and disapproved, worthy or unworthy.

Chewing on mental cud is a dangerous preoccupation because it places you into a vulnerable dream state. This spell must be broken. There's a difference between simple remembrance and reminiscence. One is a practical tool, the other a dire distraction from *the present.*

I have a good, real-life illustration of this for you. This morning my wife and I were about to leave the house to do some chores around town when I remembered my daughter was off from school. "Is she still in bed sleeping?" I asked. Nancy confirmed it. "All right. Guess we'll get her up after we get back," I said. She agreed. "I'll get my coat and let's go." I left the kitchen and headed toward the bedroom.

Walking down the hall, my thinking mind instinctively went to work. It calculated how long to allow my daughter to remain in bed, estimated the age that teenagers sleeping habits change, and for some reason, *I think I'll have peppers and eggs for lunch today . . . better make sure we have fresh peppers in the fridge.*[167] Once in the bedroom, I pulled my coat out of the closet and put it on. I discovered that my car keys were in the pocket and appreciated they were there because now I wouldn't have to search for them. Turning around and facing the direction of the bedroom door it occurred to me I should be sure that Nancy was mindful and aware during the ride so she could approach the rest of her day consciously. (I'd later take her through the exercise, something I do regularly for all my family members.)

Out of the bedroom and halfway back down the hallway, I wondered for a second *what I would write when we returned and how much time there would be before lunch to get some good material down for this chapter,* but immediately discarded these questions. Finally, near the end of the hall and just before re-entering the kitchen, an image popped into my mind's eye. It was the dark wet spot in the driveway under the Trailblazer. I was reminded to check the power steering fluid before pulling out of the driveway.

I was back in the kitchen. Roundtrip? All of 90 seconds. But more happened in that brief time than one might suppose because in those moments, my brain did a lot of work. All on its own. Except for the *peppers and eggs* and the temptation to plan my writing, both of which were immediately disregarded, there were no words. I did not engage in any conversation inside my head. No mumbling to myself. I did not latch onto a single one of them, converting ideas into language. There were just gentle reminders and notions organically passing through the lens of consciousness, each now done and dusted.

Stepping into the kitchen I was free of thought, instantly available for Nancy and ready to go. There was just one problem. She was still standing right where I had left her just moments ago. She peered out from her skull at me and said, "Should I go wake her up?"

Wait! *(SFX: Car tires screeching to a stop.)*

During that whole time, as my brain automatically processed and organized what I needed to do as the immediate future arrived, Nancy deliberated. Now here she was, still on the original subject. Though in my realm the matter of our daughters sleeping had been asked and answered, she continued to mull it over, rolling the subject around in her head like one might roll a hard candy inside of one's mouth. Nancy was stuck there ruminating. For her, life did not advance and she remained mired in our recent past, unaware of the new *present* which by now should have become the reality for both of us.

All we had to do was synchronize our conclusions, but for Nancy, no conclusions had been drawn. She had nothing to offer the situation except to confuse a mutual conclusion we'd already come to minutes before. She was stuck in time, preoccupied with a *then past* instead of living with me in the *now present*. In that moment, we were incompatible as man and wife, living on separate planes of existence. As life continued to unfold before me and I moved through time effortlessly, Nancy had seized. She became frozen and jammed up against time, struggling in the stream of life to *get it right.*[168]

Santayana's laconic phrase, "Those who cannot remember the past are condemned to repeat it," is a good adage for fortune cookies and pragmatic argument. But it's a very bad philosophy for daily living. Learning from mistakes is of course desirable, but that is very different from wallowing in the past. You can step back from intellect. In pausing, and allowing the Spirit-Self to rise over the lower Self, you'll instantly find that you are no longer mentally engaged with the stream of thought.

Images and internal dialogue from the future and past fall to the side and something truly astounding happens. Instead of living in the fantasy of another time, you begin to exist in the *present moment*, now. It's as if you've left some parallel universe behind and arrived in a new place. You have. It's the universe of the living God. His Kingdom has *now* come. His will can finally be done, on earth as His vision projects from His heaven, through you. Consciousness places you in the Presence of God where you are His protected agent. There can be no failure here because you aren't in charge. Only He is.

Now, with each passing moment, you begin to gracefully coexist above the thinking process, becoming impervious to whatever alien energies might otherwise convey through the continuous loops of thoughts streaming past, into your psyche. Plots, plans, *what-if* analyses begin to descend below your rising consciousness. As the spectator to your own thinking, you become an aware observer. This is akin to viewing a movie, watching a projection of your thinking as thoughts move across an internal screen. You see the pleasant thoughts as well as the objectionable ones. But now you can watch without prejudice, remaining composed and unruffled no matter which.

Don't be fooled by deliberate, pleasant thoughts. Becoming lost in enjoyable thinking is like sucking on candies. Sweetly positive sounding ideas swirled around in the imagination seem like a sugary treat, making you forget how bland the natural saliva in your mouth is. Meanwhile, your teeth begin to slowly rot.

Positive thinking is artificial sweetener to the starkness of a soured reality. It only helps to willfully fabricate delusional sense and phony lifestyle. It's *playing God* in the ambitious attempt to improve on what would otherwise naturally play out in a world we do not control. Like negative thinking, positive thinking quickly turns into a self-centered preoccupation with fantasy. It carries us away from the Presence, preventing us from being *here and now*.

Kindly thoughts are just as distracting from the *present moment* as rancorous ones. Rumination, whether intentionally optimistic or unconstructive, is still ducking out of the sunlight and into the shadows of knowledge where Self rules. *Positive thinking* can be more treacherous than *stinking thinking*. It delivers a false sense of security. Please don't fall for the *positive thinking*, vs. *stinking thinking* trap. The willful participation in either will cause you to miss the *present now*.

But don't worry. Once you give the God-conscious lifestyle a fair shot you'll be astounded at just how useful you become without trying, simply by remaining awake and aware. You'll find that you carry forward a world vision that's far superior to any vision you might have invented on your own. Your environment evolves without wresting all you can to maximize the world's usefulness to you. People around adapt to your new-found inspiration. They don't that know they are. It's spontaneous. Living moment to moment, above thoughts is the game changer. Welcome to the land of the living.

***

You are but one spiritual individual among many. There is a real universe. This life is not a drill and yes, there really is human existence with which you had no hand in making. The world isn't a dream or a collective fantasy in the imaginations of men, and despite the Self-seeking mutterings of a Dark Nature to the contrary, no, you aren't the Creator. Not even close.

If I could convince you to accept a philosophy where all the things in life bringing you suffering or dissatisfaction are mere illusions, just part of some bogus reality manufactured inside your head, I could get you to experience a burst of relief for your troubles. Once feeling better, it would also become a simple matter to persuade you to believe that you are *Creator*. Then, through the illusion of an imagined mental capacity to alter outcomes, I could easily help you fabricate an artificially blissful existence—right inside your mind. Your self-esteem would become so exhilarated, it'd have to be kept up. You would never want to lose me as your friend and mentor.

As you became increasingly reliant on me to help continue feeding proof of your divine nature, you would place me on a pedestal and I'd become your source of inspiration because your existence as *God creator* would depend on my constant reinforcement. Not only would you be mysteriously drawn to my philosophy but also personally to me and soon anyone who can supply you with an elevated sense of worth.[169]

World cultures, including our own Western society, are brimming with "We are all God," and, "There's no such thing as Evil," or, "All is an illusion," cults. Members cling to the words of life coaches, trained mentors and self-styled mystical leaders for constant validation. Seething with suppressed guilt, they want to know for sure that they aren't bad. They want to live as if there's no price to pay for egoistic indulgence, that they might safely continue to judge others and *play God*. Is it no wonder there are so many self-help gurus and spiritual charlatans successfully pandering to the dark nature that is within all of us? It's name is Pride.

There is right-wrong, good-evil, and true-false. Illusion exists in the minds of those who remain in denial of the ever-pursuing conscience hounding them to give up Pride—to return to reality and become *present* in God's realm of *now*. Non-duality and cultic mysticism are hideous hoaxes and yet remain enormously popular. To become God in your own head is to separate from the true God. I implore you to ignore these theoretical by-ways. Eschew people who peddle seductive philosophies designed to set you up to become God. If you've considered these in the past, then you must abandon this self-centered streak now.

There is a reality. Life is not all an illusion. Accessing your birthright ability to make discerning distinctions is imperative to exist peaceably and grow in the real world. Never minimize the work of your Creator, pretending that what He has created is a mirage, the universe some perverse fun-park to serve self-seeking humans. Something sinister wants us to be dismissive of what He has made. It murmurs into the thoughts of the distracted mind, suggesting, "All is an illusion. Think and create your own happiness. You are God too."

If ever tempted to view the world as Star Trek Holodeck-like fantasy, imagining that life is some simulated man-made reality subject to human will and wit, just remember that even in Hollywood, just beyond the sci-fi there is also a real world. It has shape, substance and there are consequences for the actions we take in it.

Someone has constructed this world. And it wasn't you.

There's no denying there is a definite physiology to our existence. Our human neurology and physiological functions are largely comprised within the biochemistry of our brains. It's a little-understood organ engaging mysterious processes, but we know it's capable of affecting wonderful things. At some level, the human brain can even coalesce matter into form.

As remarkable as this is, it doesn't mean that we stand at the gearshifts of the universal apparatus. We were meant to explore and discover some of the pedals and levers governing the universe but then humbly surrender the choice to take them over for ourselves. Always remember to ask, "Who created the matter that forms the biochemistry?" To purloin the controls away from a Creator is to play Creator, and there is a painfully high price to pay for spiritual larceny.

With each new discovery, imagining he's coming closer to proving the supremacy of mankind, the scientist only digs an intellectual hole. Ironically, the deeper he goes the closer he comes to dispelling his intellectual fantasy. As our understanding of the universe becomes more refined and closer to detail, the finer facts of our material existence unfold. Still, we just keep encountering more to learn. That's because creation is infinite and will always elude our finite abilities. We must conclude that all begins and ends in One Source. The human brain, no matter how well educated or assisted by invention, is still just like a big, scientific dog chasing its own wagging tail. *Arf!*

***

Nearly everyone I show how to meditate eventually gets around to asking, "When is the best time to meditate?" My answer is always the same, "You need to meditate all the time."

Consciousness is for *always*. What they really mean to ask is, "What is the best time of day to practice *the meditation?*" The best time to *practice*, to engage in the non-contemplative, God-consciousness exercise, is anytime you don't need it. Just as the best time to work out your body's muscles is when you aren't using them for other things. That way later, as you do need them, they're in shape. Trust me, *later* always comes. Eventually, once the future of our imagination arrives and becomes the present-time reality, we are prepared for whatever happens. We are totally confident in each new *now*.

Weight training at the gym strengthens the body, preparing us for lifting groceries, holding a baby or defending against an aggressor. Similarly, meditation strengthens in spirit for the inescapable emotional encounters we all experience moving through each day. It is a metaphysical exercise preparing us for easy action. Just like physical exercise, slacking off in the metaphysical regimen will result in regression.

After reading this book, some of you are going to begin meditating, experience God-conscious living, only to get lazy about it later. The clamors of life will pull you back into the noisy stream. The wounded Ego will cringe in fear over the prospect of Light returning to shine on It. It will begin judging and seek anger to nourish a damaged pride in opposition to your return to consciousness. It may resist this meditation, putting up quite a fight.

As fear and anxiety remount, It may attempt to steer you toward pointless intellectual pursuits. It might lay other spiritual methods at your feet to entice you with inspiring ideas, religions, or cults that promote escapist meditations. Medications, drugs, alcohol, anything to sedate you back into unconsciousness or preoccupy the mind may seem attractive.[170]

The Light is too much for It and It may blame meditation or me for the pain It feels.

This is not your pain, but It's pain. While relapse of any kind is not preferred, if your motives have been sincere, there's nothing to fear while experiencing a setback. Think of it as a test through which you can become firmer in faith.

Simply remember your inheritance of consciousness, restart and you'll begin to move back in the direction of your Creator. If you're reading this right now and find you are this position, you can have another new beginning right this moment. *The Kingdom of Now, which is God and of God,* is always at hand. It can be accessed anytime you go within to discover it.

Feel the sadness. Then allow joyful reality to restore sanity. Just re-commit. Make it your steadfast practice once again and you'll be all right. Don't let a half day go by without practicing meditation. When you've been freshly conscious, having recently practiced, you won't fall so deeply when the inevitable difficulties crop up. Although you may become unconsciously lost in thought and distracted from the present, you'll notice it. The simple discovery of your failing is enough to immediately snap you out and away from danger.

Don't make meditation a habit. It isn't one. It's the anti-habit, eliminating all other habits, making obsessive routine a thing of the past. Becoming an obsessive meditator indicates improper motive and will result in other obsessions never being dealt with. You can abuse meditation turning it into just one more thing you do to hold onto your willfulness. You'll never break from obsessive bad habits if you make meditation just another one of them.

A young woman in Mexico who was new to meditation and consciousness, once told me, "My brain keeps going to dark, painful places and memories."

"Yes, Julietta. That's supposed to happen!" I reminded her. Her reaction to consciousness is a common one when we're yet new to the experience. As tempting as it is to fight the inner chatter, go into each day as the observer to your thinking. Never imagine yourself as a combatant warrior fighting against thoughts, no matter how negative or vile they may be.

Struggling with thoughts turns life into a continuous inner battle, breeding only more thinking and insecurity. The cycle of resentful resistance against your own negative emotions must be broken. As long as you believe you can rid yourself of the mental chattering in your head, you'll never get free from their stressfulness. Instead, remain above thoughts as much of the time as you can during the day. You'll stay free and neutral, unaffected by them.

Just observe thoughts as they as they approach, without fighting them, no matter how depraved or how beautiful. Take no sides. Allow God to protect against stress. Do not war against it. This is not to say you aren't courageous or strong in the face of difficulties. It means you aren't combative, willfully engaged in mental mêlées waged against windmills or monsters out of the past, present or future.

After a while, you won't be haunted by a regrettable past nor provoked into fear by the prospect of the uncertain future. As you experience *now* in real-time, you develop the strength to endure in God's real world. Life becomes peaceful once we develop resilience to hate.

We are all born into a world where *hate* is rampant. It is an unavoidable evil power emanating out of an energetic field, as real and ubiquitous as any other universal force. Hate is a negatively charged emotional force. It evokes out of our willful resistance against truth and nourishes the voracious alien Ego identity within.

The mechanics of this terrible force at first seem formidable. Without Supernatural help, for us humans, it is. But protection is possible. We can "Let go" quite simply, once we understand what it is we are giving up.

We use the expression "Letting Go" because it's quick and accurate enough conversationally. But the truth is we cannot willfully rid ourselves of emotion. That is not within our power.

Yes, negative emotions do get inside us. And in time, it may seem that they've become a heavy load. However, the mass of resentment within doesn't accumulate. The intensification in bitterness we feel is from an expanding "Self" that grows as it becomes nourished by negative hate-food. The fatter It gets, the more "Selfish" we become. Every self-centered person houses an anger-feted Ego-entity. *And probably doesn't know it.*

Memories do not store resentment energy per se. They can, however, trigger the coalescence of anger out of *thin air*—out of the universe. Heaps of negative emotional energy are fed to the Ego-entity, using thoughts to spin resentment into helpings of bitterness.

Resentment isn't something we collect and keep in a sack like stones. Undoubtedly, you've heard of this concept. The idea is that if you could just rid yourself of the emotional "rocks" stored in your sack, your burden would lighten and life would become easier to bear. It's a cute thought, but just a metaphor, probably conceived by someone who didn't understand the metaphysics of love and hate.[171]

"Letting go" isn't a bad term, but it is more accurately described as *allowing* the temptation toward willfulness to fall away by simply observing thoughts, thereby disengaging from the intellectual stream, cutting off the food supply—and not struggling to be rid of them. (Or encourage them if they happen to be *happy* thoughts.)

The act of "letting go" is really *letting go* of the Ego-will that would otherwise struggle and indulge in It's own power. Ego becomes weakened and feeble, perfectly managed once It is observed, without our fighting against It.

So, observe. Watch, without becoming sucked into the vortex of thought and fantasies in your head. This simple principle will allow you to become free from anger. Although it may at times seem so flimsy an idea, that it shouldn't work, it does work. Magnificently.

The only prerequisite here is faith. Placing total reliance on God instead of Self gives us instant accesses to the most powerful Force in the universe. It is a Force that always defeats negative emotions, driving out fear and anger. Then these despicable culprits no longer dominate our thinking.

The world is full of folks who have seen this truth, yet pick up swords rather than allow God's defensive shield to become the only protection they would ever need. Had Jullieta's thoughts been bright and optimistic, she never would have complained. Instead of agonizing over the negativity of her *stinking thinking*, she'd have been mesmerized by the *happy chattering* of thought flowing through her mind. When this happens, we abuse our thoughts the same way we might abuse a drug.

Happy or painful, thoughts are distractions. They pull us away from living *now* in *real-time*. Jullieta's memories from her past were revealing. She'd have to see the truth of whatever that was. But she also had to see how nagging negativity embedded in her thinking serves to prevent meeting life as it occurs, setting her up for future pains for having not met events gracefully.

Once angry, you lose control of your life, becoming subject to even more injustice. The basis for the negative effects of all stress lies in your negative emotional responses to cruelty or unfairness. Disturbing events, big or small, may be self-inflicted or they could be caused by other self-seeking people. Whichever, each moment of temptation to become upset that's not met with properly spins into negative emotional energy, eventually harming us physically and mentally.

Only by remaining awakened and, therefore, neutral to each new stressful moment, can you survive the brutality in the stream of life. Not only will you endure but you'll grow from it, coming closer to perfection with each new victory over the pressure of evil. A lifetime of spiritual progress comes long before sainthood.

Just on the other side of survival, there's joy, success and the peace of mind for which every human being searches. The alternative is to surrender to cruelty, becoming subject to misery and human failure for being overwhelmed by lethal emotions.

Awaken, please, and become a survivor. You won't find another way.

The Kingdom Travels with You

Are you ever truly alone? The portability feature of conscious-ness is your lifeline to peace, ease of living and serenity. Practicing develops the ability to become mindfully conscious anytime, eventually living in the moment continuously. This is where your Creator lives. Welcome to the Kingdom of Now.

Out Into the World
The Tenth Chapter

By which you've begun to awaken, watching the world and living consciously . . . in real time and in all your affairs.

If you're old enough you may remember a hit TV police drama from the early 80's called *Hill Street Blues.* At the end of each morning roll call, Sergeant Phil Esterhaus would send his platoon out to their patrol shift with the cautionary reminder, "Hey! Let's be careful out there."

Despite the warning, no matter how "careful" the show's colorful characters were they still met with all sorts of danger and intrigue. There'd be no point to a TV police drama without it.[172] Anything less just wouldn't resemble real life. Just as with the TV cops in the line of duty, it is also an occupational hazard for all human beings to meet the daily stress of emotional attacks.

Perils faced in the real world hone the intrinsic virtues of the good guys, or else nurture the inequities in the bad guys. Resentment and fear must be faced and survived without overwhelming. Like the TV show, there'd be no point to our existence without conflict. With it, we thrive as spiritually improving human beings.

Through the stress of daily life, we meet with a continuous stream of opportunities to reunite and perfect a relationship with our Father within. Consciousness makes this possible. With no temptation to play God to overcome, we'd have no path to redemption. Simply being awake and aware of the incessant diversions that would otherwise block the path, we conquer every hurdle, becoming better *cops* through *on the job training*.

We strengthen by the rigors of living.

Hopefully, by now I've convinced you to give the main proposal of this book an earnest try. If so, then you are already finding you are better prepared. You've begun the *Non-Contemplative Meditation* exercise at least twice a day, once in the morning and right before bedtime. You've been experiencing the twinkles of light within your head and you're extending that brightness into your body in the special way indicated. Subsequently, you've begun to wake up, and all that I predict in this book has begun to manifest into your life experiences.[173] You are going to have a wonderful life, a much different one from the life you were going to have prior to this time.

Many of you have already given up bad habits like smoking, drinking, and recreational drugs as the direct result of this new awareness. Your family and friends have noticed the transformation in your demeanor. The rest of you, at least those who have begun to meditate in earnest using the exercise, are well on your way toward freedom from these symptoms. A renovation of being is underway. Be patient.

As mentioned in the preceding chapter, consciousness is not only for meditation time. While charity does indeed begin at home, once initiated we must also carry a loving nature out into the world. Going forth consciously is how.

You are sure to encounter diversions from consciousness. Some of the most common temptations will be the most mundane. To remain safe from these all you need is to "Be careful out there," watching, but not struggling. Ongoing vigilance is now your new way of life. You have the tool to maintain it. Observe the temptation to engage in behaviors drawing you back into a state of unconsciousness.

Once you begin to live in the awakened state not only do you perceive your surroundings with increasing clarity, you'll also distinguish some of the finer aspects of the role you play while dealing with other people. Illuminated by the Light of consciousness, some relationships could be exposed as shams, not the wholesome connections with others you once thought they were. Your part may not be all too flattering either.

Calmly step back without judging yourself. Everyone has at one time or another made mistakes, errors in judgment and wrong decisions based on emotionally dulled intuition. We've all been mopes. But bitterness for errors made in an egregious past guarantees you'll repeat them. By not resenting old blunders, new prospects unfold in plain view—opportunities that would otherwise be missed.

Anger, unrecognized resentment, clouds awareness. But once free of emotional bitterness, *the next right thing* becomes obvious and clear. Sanity returns. Now instead of repeating mistakes, we truly learn from them. It is one thing to recall and lament the past, it is another thing altogether to take the lesson well enough to experience change. Such transformation will sometimes seem a revolutionary upheaval. Other times they will be more subtle. But a positive modification of attitude will happen simply and without effort, once you've begun to practice existing in *the present.* Just watch your emotional reactions to the pressures of the world—big or small.

When I say *watch* I do not mean to see, and then willfully attempt to stop yourself. I want you to simply observe as each inevitable temptation arises. See your proclivity toward these things. Realize its origin while remaining objective to the inner hunger for emotional drama and danger. What follows are a few of the most common ones that need to be especially watched.

Watch for the temptation to fix other people. Rather than making sure others *get it right*, set a personal example of virtue. The way to change the world for the better is by becoming an agent for progressive improvement. Never relish fault in others. Secret judgments are smug diversions. They dull awareness away from facing self-imposed chaos. You never find a solution for any of it. Why should you? You aren't really looking for any.

There are constant skirmishes within the stream of thought. These are subtle dramas, operettas and passion plays where not only are you a cast member, stagehand, and stage director, you're also the sole person in the audience. Then to make the production even more bizarre, you become the theater critic, reviewing the production for your single reader—again, it's you! This is busy time serving a nefarious purpose. It all happens inside your head. No wonder you're exhausted by the end of each day.

Do you find yourself daydreaming much? It's easy to forget about how people have upset you once you've vanished inside a fantasy. As long as you remain preoccupied inside your own mind, judging others, supposing how they ought to run their lives, even when it's to find their own happiness, you'll accomplish little. Anger, impatience and a lack of tolerance for people are opportune[174] and spring up at any instant when you are caught in a dream. Pondering offers no real protection except to generate a comforting defense against the unpleasant truths about yourself you dare not see.

A fixation with thought is a sedative distraction. As you stuff away the memories of past irritating events into the subconscious, the intellect forgets. Painful shame borne out of improperly meeting emotional stress seems to diminish. Meanwhile vestiges of guilt for having judged your tormentors remain. Anxious and guilty, you may no longer recall the events causing you to feel so edgy and restless. In time, mental blank spots develop, inviting obsessive behavior.[175] Over long periods of time, voids of recall can become numerous. This is responsible for developing memory lapses, bizarre conduct and eventually more serious cognitive disorder.[176]

Stress can drive certain anxious types into *do-good* careers like law enforcement, the military or medicine. Police and firefighters often come from long lines of dysfunctional, alcoholic families where emotions regularly run high. Nurses and those in the caretaker industries often select their line of work out of an anger-sourced need to restore feelings of well-being through the only means they know. *By making sure others are well.*

Military recruiters will focus on teenage men and women from broken, anger filled environments. The sense of fighting for right compensates for the ill will projected into a child from birth. In each of these examples, there's a great need for correction of what is wrong within them. But they can't bear to look. And so, they divert attention toward correcting what they've judged as being wrong with the world instead. The pain of judgment draws out a self-centered need to fix other people.

While issuing sanctimonious correction, you ignore your own shortcomings. It's dishonest but relief is a powerful motivator. It allows a dark nature to feed on unchecked resentment. Angry police officers, soldiers, healthcare staffers are a blight on society. They are unable to perform their duties with either grace or patience. Their careers and personal lives will demonstrate a slow degeneration away from self-sacrifice and honor, moving toward self-service and corruption.

You'll personally encounter such people. In a quest to rid the world of injustice and pain, they can't help but wield unjust authority over others. At work. At home. In the field. With the family. They've grown awkward, even vicious. Forgive them. What was done to you was also done to them. They had no defense, as you once had none.

If you're one of those, then see what secret anger has done to you, and give it up. You have become what you've hated and are out of control. Police, Firefighter, Soldier, Doctor, Caregiver, Social worker—the course of your life and the lives of those you have set out to help can change right now if you'll become conscious and let the Light inside. Allow it to drive out what has taken up residence inside you. Become the dignified ambassador for good will and order you once were, by doing nothing more than stand back and cease struggling. We need your talents, skills, and love for truth. It's there. Step aside and let it through.

Loving members in any of these noble professions uplift and improve the quality of life for all. Those are the truly altruistic heroes of humanity who run into collapsing buildings, who every day perform honorable deeds under the radar— admirable conduct serving God and man for which they'll never seek or allow reward of any kind. These are the few teachers, civil servants, and clergy who are a different breed from their peers who will never be recognized, but who quietly carry the world with love.

When it comes to spiritual matters don't try to remember spiritual themes or savor mystical directives you hear or read. Watch the temptation to study and learn spirituality. Personal transformation and growth do not come by thoughts projected into the mind through words. You cannot be trained into enlightenment.

Clearly, obtaining a degree or license in the furtherance of a personal trade or career requires study and the use of mental skills, such as memorization. However, study, for the purposes of learning spiritual principles we hope will lead us to God, get in the way of conscious contact with Him. A preoccupation with the thought process takes us out of consciousness. Thinking about God helps supply a pious impression of ourselves, but ironically, also pushes us further away from Him.

The combination of virtue with educational credentials contributes positively to the whole personality. Intellectual pursuits made from a conscious state of mind tend to enrich, of course. But you can't be taught wisdom. You can't self-help your way into consciousness or goodness either.

Spiritual progress and enlightenment will come but not through your efforts to self-install them. These attributes are for the patient few who wait, sans ambition. They're made possible only through the discovery of stillness within.

Whiling away hours, pondering God's existence and spiritual principles is the ultimate spiritual death trap because it seems so... *spiritual.* It is spiritual. "Look at you! Studying and learning about God. You are becoming so enlightened," some dark spirit mutters. Really? Is this true? You must wonder.[177]

There is a healthy way to spiritual discovery. It isn't through learning, studying or absorbing the spoken words of gurus, lecturers or even writers like me. The mindful, conscious contact exercise in this book will open your psyche to receive a spiritual education that isn't otherwise possible by any means.[178]

In Latin, *educare* means to draw up and to lead out, as an unfolding of latent knowledge. When something is *educed*, underlying understanding is revealed from within. Ignore *out-sight* and allow *in-sight* to fill you, revealing what you are to know. With inspired insight and a spirit-filled heart, your very presence will spread true enlightenment to others, improving your environment in ways you can never imagine. The world becomes a better place by merit of your existence in it.

Watch for food. The difference between an individual who abuses a sugary donut or a shot of whiskey and someone who snorts cocaine up the nose or sucks nicotine out of a cigar is . . . *none*. Not when any of these acts are solely intended to dull the pain of a guilt-plagued conscience. Each of these arouses pleasure center activity in the human brain.

Varying surface manifestations are obvious. Somehow a Krispy Kreme habit doesn't seem so bad when compared with snorting lines of cocaine. Many people are uncomfortable with their nicotine addiction, but oddly less so when the drug is delivered through an impressive thirty-dollar cigar. The indignity of chemical addiction is overwhelmed by an illusion of self-worth. The need for narcotic effect is just as *in-force.*

Certain worldly activities have a vital place in our lives. Eating food, drinking wine, having sex within reason, each for their intended purposes is wholesome. There are many circumstances where even certain prescription medications can be useful. But the proof of abuse is apparent once any of these become addictive, unable to be regulated by normal human power.

Whether they care to admit it or not, cigar and cigarette smokers, nicotine vapers, food or heroin addicts and alcohol abusers, all ride in separate cars on the same train. It's a high-speed express, careening down a tragic track bound for derailment and death.

Just how a person anesthetizes the pain caused by repressed anger or rage, makes little difference. Regardless of substance, each will provide a sure shut down of consciousness. It's moving away from mindful contact with God and always leads to a tragic finale. The emotional need for nicotine is an indicator of ongoing dishonesty and spiritual illness.[179]

For the sake of maintaining appearances, an individual might stick to the most socially acceptable abuses. A person in a religious society for instance, who risks shunning by peers for so much as a nicotine habit may substitute food. He'll become obese.

A person who wants to maintain favorable standing in a Twelve Step fellowship must remain abstinent of alcohol and narcotics, but might instead take up cigars or e-cigarettes. If they personally despise smoking, there are many alternates to nicotine too. They might become promiscuous or begin gambling for example.[180]

The calm, collected smoker is a consummate liar. He has deceived himself and subsequently the world under the sedative chemical effect the drug of his choice supplies. He can seem at peace. It appears to himself and others that he's escaped forever-nagging anxiety. But its cause remains. Underneath a composed exterior, the raging Phantom lurks. The body and mind are slowly destroyed by the suppressed emotional energy that continues to feed a ravenous Self.

Cancer, heart disease, strokes and aneurysms in a nicotine addict aren't directly caused by the drug itself. These physical sicknesses are spurred by the emotional nature of the spiritually sick individual, harboring traits that nicotine has allowed to cultivate. All anger brings death. All smokers who use nicotine to escape from consciousness are angry, dying drug addicts.

Watch for sex for the same reason as food. It isn't a stretch to see how sex and food are closely related. Both rank highest on the list of essentials for human existence. Without either, humanity would not proliferate. Sexual reproduction multiplies the numbers of the race and food provides the energy to have the sex. It's quite basic. God, in his wisdom, has hooked these two vital activities into the reward circuits of the brain to ensure our survival.

We eat and it feels good. We have sex and it feels good. But like food, the potential for abuse of sex is enormous. Foods, like sugar or alcohol—and sex, like intercourse or masturbation, are at the base of all of mankind's most troubling issues. Converted beyond their original functions, piggish *screwing and eating* obscure the vital discomfort we are designed to experience once we've been resentful. It's no wonder so many of us fall for their allure, becoming obsessive and addicted to unwholesome relationships with food and sex. They help us forget what judgmental, God-playing fools we've become.

Watch people dependency. No one has the answer to give. The local preacher doesn't. Neither does the self-help guru. I don't either. Answers are always found within. Exclusively. Intuition is one hundred percent trustworthy. There isn't a single edict in this book that is the answer to any of your problems. What you'll find instead are guidelines pointing toward the perfect answer. When feeling unhappy or unfulfilled there may be a temptation to seek out easy schemes purporting to install happiness—courses in spiritual therapy, diets to follow, programs to live by, pharmaceutical regimens, life coaching, even religious movements through which to walk lockstep with other lost followers. These are foolish abandonments of intuitive connectivity and the reinforcement of a doubtful spirit.

Once these ambitious efforts to make ourselves happy prove unsuccessful, we become desperate. Surmising it must be our lack of information or the right method that has failed, we'll scour the horizon in search of the greener grass. "If only I could find the trick, hear the magic words, hook up with the right teacher, or adopt the right plan," we think. Therefore, rapid weight loss diets, programs for happiness and other quick fixes become so popular. Such undertakings appeal to an impatient nature. Yet nothing satisfies. Be wary of any tendency to place too much reliance on the advice of others.

Yes, consider good practical guidance. But don't turn your life and will over to any human being in exchange for information. Reserve surrender for your Father. Hear what people have to say, but be sure to remain conscious and clear-headed before receiving opinions, especially from those who've been placed in positions of authority. This is critical, especially when they've elected themselves to those seats.

Everyone shares the same dilemmas as you, whether they display them or not. You'll never know with one hundred percent certainty what is going on deep in the back-story of another person's life or within their heart. Most people are too busy caring for their own welfare to be of much meaningful help. Even the most well-meaning Samaritan who seems to only exist to serve may really be more dedicated to servicing his own self-esteem by his deeds.

Of course, a good doctor may have some useful technical knowledge. A special cleric may be filled with insightful understanding. A spiritually awake friend may have experience living God-consciously to graciously share. It's right for people to give and receive loving aid from each other, even to buy and sell supportive services if necessary. It's desirable to use the good advice people offer but it should be without fostering personal attachment to them.

Keep in mind, however, that putting anyone on a pedestal encourages ties of dependency. Elevating others creates an exchange of energy signaling the temptation of your personal hero to assume unhealthy control. This tendency could allow human-will to displace God's will in your life, making you subject to the wills of other people. By maintaining mindful access to conscious awareness you'll keep active the internal ability to properly discriminate—neither judging others as praiseworthy or contemptible. Awareness opens the eyes. It prevents the development of co-dependency.

Be careful not to capitulate to scheming groups of people who brainwash and take advantage of those who've misplaced their gift of discernment. Cults and imperious fellowships are full of followers and students who've been conditioned into blind obedience to undeserving authorities. They've thrown in the towel, so to speak, abandoning their original intuitiveness. The ability to think critically for themselves has been lost.[181]

They must turn to New Age shamans, occultists, and other mystical guides and gurus advocating pseudo-spiritual philosophies designed to seduce those harboring a wicked enemy within. This is an Entity that longs to be God. Anything that confirms this idea will be irresistible. Through God-consciousness, safeguard your divine endowment and spiritual autonomy. Then you'll remain free.

The ever-present threat of bondage to your own Self is bad enough. Don't further complicate life by unwittingly subjecting yourself to the bondage of a Self-tyrant that resides in other people. Move towards receiving all discipline, direction, and inspiration from Him only. Don't look for great truth or wisdom from others.

When someone says something substantial or meaningful, don't boast just for hearing it. Don't think, "I have to remember that," as if you might repeat it to others, uplifting yourself in their eyes for your ability to recognize impressive wisdom. That isn't enlightenment. It is an egocentric practice. Instead, watch in quiet. See the significance, but discover by inner revelation. Truth awakens from the inside. Watch the temptation to analyze. Just observe, free from emotional patronizing.

Most enlightenment comes through inner revelation during events in everyday life, not through purposeful speeches, lectures or sermons. Absorbing the content of this book won't lead to enlightenment either. A truly enlightened person realizes he is unable to give you enlightenment any more than he can give it to himself. It can't be taught or learned. Each person establishes an enlightened, personal connection with God by invitation only. He draws you toward Him. Anyone claiming to have some exclusive relationship with God that you can't have except through their aid is lying to you. Forgive them. Something residing inside them seeks devotion and is willing to deceive you to obtain it. It wants to make you dependent on them for your happiness.

The potential to realize truth isn't exclusive. There aren't any special, divine appointees. We're all intended to receive the same God-consciousness into our lives. A few of us seem to advance first, ahead of other people. Others more slowly. Many, hardly at all. Each of us will have our own experience. But whether it's accepted or not, a capacity for mindful conscious contact with God is the spiritual inheritance of every human being. Enlightenment is always within reach. We are all meant to become mystics.

Sometimes the Self will put on an intellectual front with which to masquerade as a sage or assiduous student of wisdom. This is spiritual flim-flam. Once broken free from the intellectual reliance on written and spoken words, rote knowledge no longer stands in the way of understanding. We gain access to true enlightenment. We can't fall to self-deception or drivel from people who have themselves been deceived.

Due to past recklessness, it's possible to become suspicious of our own instincts. You may think, "I can't trust myself." Your reservation isn't unfounded. All error is instigated by an inferior Self, not the real you. When pulled into the stream of thought, instead of contemplating past errors, step back to observe morose thinking. Allow consciousness to rise above the never-ending maelstrom inside the chattering brain. From this perspective of spirit, you'll observe the false Self—a dark phantom, sitting proudly on It's throne of intellectual reason.

Be on the lookout for an *inner voice* that attempts to draw you into a dialogue with It. It speaks in your own voice. It could also come in the voice mimicking a parent, or someone you've resented, feared or perhaps appeased in the past.

Every time you engage in a dialogue with the voice in your head, you reinforce the bondage of Self—for it is the false Self who speaks. It's not you. It is not God. It isn't an angel[182] or a dead relative who wants to guide you through life from the heavens. It's an unholy entity residing within, masquerading as you and as others. You can learn to separate from this nature of darkness or else be forever controlled by forces you may never otherwise notice.

"How do you know? How do you know?" It trains you to ask. Here's how:

True guidance comes from God. It is a wordless communion between Him and His children. It is by far a more sophisticated communication than language emanating out of the dark pit. The will of our Creator comes effortlessly, in each moment. It is a silent transmission of understanding by intuitive inspiration, never through motivation, thinking or muttering inside the head. You cannot *dialogue* with God, only with some vile Thing that thinks It is God, that hungers to replace Him in your life. It'll *talk* to you in a heartbeat once you've been conditioned to trust It's drivel. Avoid cults, and spirituality and occult movements that encourage chattering with and the placing faith in this unholy Thing.

Whenever a voice or even multiple voices rise inside thoughts, simply step back to observe. Do not believe it. Do not disbelieve it. Just see it. It goes away cursing your awareness and devotion to the Creator. It won't like your watchfulness. It hates that! It hates all of this information with an unholy passion. Tough Turkey!

Just keep growing by remaining awake as much as you are able in each moment of each day.

A continuing improvement of consciousness is essential for a productive life. If not, then in time you'll reach the day when you won't be able to distinguish where the real you begins and where the Ego-creature inside ends. The noise in your mind will increase. It could become louder than the people speaking in the room. You'll experience an identity crisis within, not knowing who you are, creating all sorts of confusion in your life.

A clear majority of everyone you meet is already in this predicament. Don't fear this. You are being shown a vital fact about the world and yourself.

A lifetime living a Jekyll and Hyde existence will have made you apprehensive and subject to chance. The insecurity you feel is the outcrop of bad decision making for having placed your bets on a lower Self. There is a true Self you should trust. It's a Spirit expressing as the conscious being you've always been.

I know you have objectionable thoughts. These can be a source of consternation. Just watch them. Do nothing about them. It's a mistake to try and install any new thinking over old negative thinking. Positive thinking is a plaything for a miserable person struggling to turn happy thoughts and contented fantasy into reality.

Once a thought-obsessed person becomes besieged by his own negative thinking, he is thrown into a panic. In desperation, he may try to retrain his thought-addicted brain in an anxious attempt to get free. The hope is that he can feel better by forcing a positive attitude, willfully refilling his troubled mind with constructive thoughts.

He just might succeed at it too, temporarily. But he's like a fearful boy who keeps his spirits up by whistling past the graveyard, forgetting the dangers he's imagined lurk in the shadows. His mind will remain easily overwhelmed. He'll meander among the pleasant, artificial thoughts rattling around inside his head. Instead of cutting through life gracefully, with confidence, life will go through him, like water goes through a leaky boat.

Positive Thinking is just as dangerous as *Stinking Thinking*. It's a sweet-scented distraction used to cover up the stench that would otherwise be exposed by conscious awareness. Internal *happy talk* is the false-positive version of judgment. Self pitches thoughts to trick us into remaining vulnerable to cruelty and injustice in the field of negativity. Resorting to *Positive Thinking* is a fool's tool to manage stress and alter outcomes. It always fails. Always.

While manufacturing indulgent fantasies that *all is well*, that you are *good*, that you have become empowered with the will to ward off adversity simply by thinking it so, you become mesmerized. You lull yourself into a fictional world where *consciousness* is lost and unseen forces are free to have their way with your mind.

You won't know while it's happening, but the narcotic effect of affirmations and positive thinking are no different in the brain than psychoactive drugs. These chemicals perform the same physiologic function, inducing an identical mind-altering chemistry as the most potent antidepressant prescription. Is it any wonder then that people become addicted to their own thoughts?[183]

Engage in *positive thinking* and you'll feel better temporarily while becoming worse over time. You could become so hypnotically influenced, it may seem you are becoming empowered to do the impossible, like God. But you're drugged.

You are high on self-worth, operating under the influence of powerful chemicals infused by a supernatural force. It is now at the helm of your mind and your life.

Positive thinking, platitudes, or concepts like, "Fake it till you make it," do not lead to genuine contentment. Positive thinking gurus, self-improvement schemes and thought modification training are all gimmicks designed to install pleasing, *new-thought* style programming, replacing objectionable, old-thought conditioning. There is fleeting relief at best, and these are popular for this reason. But they fail to address the underlying cause of all problems, and you regress. You become worse off while enjoying artificially induced blissfulness that exists only in your mind.

It is like the insane *Birdman* who leaps off a skyscraper roof, blissfully flapping his arms as though he might fly. He's plunging to a tragic death below.

The grand idea that man can turn his thoughts into reality, affecting outcomes through sheer willpower, is an offer that a highly developed Ego-Self simply cannot refuse. It's an irresistible glory of imagined greatness, nearly impossible for the egoist to defend against. A lower Self gains the upper hand in controlling his mind and he is suckered. The con is complete. He's trapped inside a self-induced dream state and save for reintroduction to consciousness, he'll never wake up to live sanely or soundly again.

Do you remember when you were a little kid and you were warned never to put on a classmate's eyeglasses? That's because each pair is designed only for the person for whom the prescription is written.

Placing someone else's corrective lenses on your eyes might strain and damage them. An incorrect prescription will force an out-of-focus image to the retina. It gives an indistinct picture that may resemble reality, but much like a fun-house mirror at the amusement park, it is surreal and inaccurate. You begin to move in a distorted world that may have been fine for one person—but for another brings confusion about what is true and what is false.

This is true on the emotional and spiritual planes too. People will attempt to fashion new lenses for you. They want you to see as they do. They will suggest that you focus on their vision for your life. But allowing other people to apply their prescription for good sight becomes a handover of dependency. It is the rejection of *insight* in favor of *out-sight*. It places the wills of people before your Father's will within.

Your vision may indeed have become impaired. You may need correction. However, see how wearing other's glasses, even if freely offered, adopts their vision for you, not God's vision for you. Like the fun-house reflection, that image too is distorted.

Through the inner connection with Him, God can actually heal broken eyes, restoring your own natural sight. God's vision for you is "For your eyes only," Only He knows what that is. It's a vision you share with Him once revealed through conscious contact. Accept no one's vision for you, but His. What others visualize for themselves or for you is no substitute for God's vision.

Nothing can replace seeing truth for yourself. Each of us is on our own personal journey. The discovery of enlightened reasoning comes independently through our personal conscious contact with God. Each day that we live consciously we become filled with insight from our Creator. Mindfulness of this kind places you in a position to accept His power, automatically bringing His vision into the world—without anyone telling you how.

Others may share their discoveries, but when it comes to matters of the spirit, God forbid that you call anyone *teacher* or *guru*. Only God is qualified to supply insight. The capacity to experience His perfect vision for us comes directly from Him. Once we allow the lens of conscious awareness to reveal His will, we sidestep the flawed and biased spiritual teachings of other men.

This isn't to say we should flat out ignore everyone. There's no need for smugness. Sometimes we may feel that someone inspires. They do or say something to stimulate us through a heavenly volition that doesn't force or threaten us to move by their will. If it does, that's motivation, not inspiration.

Anyone who excites you into taking action or to think a certain way is exerting unhealthy energy. Imitate no one. Not their success. Not their lifestyle. Not their "look". Not their speech. Not their beliefs or disbeliefs. Not their "habits for success."

Be careful of motivational speakers, preachers or rousing lecturers who incite emotionality. Although mimicking good intention and purpose they will often put forth a good face to gain confidence. Speaker-talk is often a variety of mass hypnotism where the will of the mesmerizing orator projects into a listening audience. Here, the ultimate aim is to convert you into an extension of the motivator. You lose your own ground of being. As the orator speaks you become him, at the expense of your own identity. Fascination overrides God-given sensibility with which we're all born.

Don't be motivated by others. Become inspired instead. Inspiration allows a natural proficiency to unfold from within. We'll know and do what we never knew we could do or know before. It can be tempting to allow others to take control of your emotions, to stir and excite you into ambitious action. Matters of business, religion, health, and spirituality seem especially prone to this. Anything or anyone pushing the God-connection aside in order to motivate gets in the way of God's direction—even if they speak of God, goodwill or helpfulness.

It's only a ruse since you cannot be useful in this world while remaining subjected to the wills of other human beings.

When I worked on Wall Street, one way we Securities Dealers would get investors to buy stock in high-risk companies was to excite our stockbroker sales teams into a feverish pitch. We would create an atmosphere denigrating low-producers while exalting the extravagant lifestyles of high earners. Tempted by their own ambitious need for a high sales commission, brokers would transfer their excitement into clients.

Once activated, self-centered energy would project from broker to client. It was like a virus. The air of excited human emotion would supersede all rational thinking. It was so contagious it could be transmitted at will, over the phone. We raised many millions of dollars this way, moving huge volumes of shares in companies in which few investors would have otherwise been interested.

Through over-the-top sales meetings, rousing religious revivals, stadium events filled with stagnated souls hoping to hear words that might ignite an emotional fire and motivate them into action, it's easy to create a frothy atmosphere for artificial stimulation.

People can become too easily excited and seduced by the right combinations of words. A cunningly delivered talk can become an opiate, stimulating feelings of well-being without actually altering circumstances. Once intoxicated with adrenaline, a vulnerable individual cannot help but become overwhelmed with artificial feelings. A sense of invincibility is conveyed the moment he reaches the right emotional threshold. In an emotionally charged setting, Ego enlivens and surges with Pride. But this is a cruel setup.

The chase of empowerment is nothing more than a superhuman fantasy. It's an egoistic indulgence in self-approval. As all fantasy, motivational speech numbs the unfulfilled individual's consciousness away from a nagging malaise carried during the course of daily life. Emotional inebriation comes as a welcome relief. Getting drunk on motivational speakers is a very dangerous, addictive avocation.

Whenever we become fixated to an external motivator, our humanity is debased. This is an enslaving phenomenon easily turning the unconscious individual into a somnambulant zombie. Once a person is no longer at liberty to exist as his true self he'll become a reflection of the will of a mentor. He is compelled to return to that personality source for emotional recharging or else quickly lose motivation. There can arise a fanatical allegiance, developing an instant preoccupation with a hero.

Whomever or whatever reinforces ambitious drive becomes God. Whether through a sales manager, a preacher, a spiritual guru or self-help pundit, once disconnected from Higher Reasoning and reconnected with the will of a charismatic leader, the capacity for humility diminishes. Self-centeredness begins to metastasize, soon directing the life of the devotee. He digs himself deeper into the comforts of worldly attachments, becoming dependent on whatever comforts his mentors suggest.

Thinking he's found a better life for himself through the guidance of a hero, ambition still betrays him. Now, life turns for the worse, not the better. Unmanageability rises and he is compelled to return to the tent for his fix of hopeful ecstasy. Just like alcohol or drugs, this induces a mock sense of well-being. Ultimately, it's life threatening, because it supplants God in the life of the ambitious.[184]

It's good to lead an energetic, active life. But, please realize there are two kinds of human action.

There's one type that is egocentrically motivated. When fueled by an ambitious nature and self-centered nervous energy, we propel against time and the natural world. The stress ages us quickly as we hurtle toward death.

The other kind is a direct product of humility. It's fueled by a positive force of energy flowing out of the universal spring of heavenly grace. Founded in a timeless realm, this type offers a protective resistance to evil stress. We remain youthful in thought and countenance.

Whichever of these two types you employ will spell the difference between having an anxious, bedeviled lifestyle wrought with struggle, or else a peacefully serene life that's free of worry and fear.

Most people are self-activated, not God-activated. The Lower Self goads them into action through the promise of greatness, happiness or some other reward. Be careful not to emulate their kind of achievement. Don't be impressed by their acquisitions. There's nothing admirable in Godless ambition.

Looking to find God in others before discovering Him within ourselves is a grave error in prioritization. It leads to reliance on people for guidance and direction—management over our lives they aren't qualified to provide. The activation of mind and body must come from within, not from *with-out*.

Once we're humble, we become true to a superior guidance rising through the heart. This is God's vision for us, in us. Conversely, when we are self-guided we become subjected to an inferior voice leading into an ambitious temptation to play God. The idea of giving up self-reliance can be unsettling.

Nearly all of us have been preconditioned by the world to place faith in ourselves and in people over inner guidance. Unless broken free of this conditioned response, you'll never be saved from the inclination toward anger and God cannot enter to properly disciple your life. Becoming free requires conscious contact with God. Nothing else. Not bliss. Not enlightenment.

Not relaxation. Not health or peace of mind. God-consciousness should be the only aim of meditation because solely through accepting His will and power to employ His vision do we receive all we need. We become disciplined by God within. This is humility.

Therefore, simply step back and observe any discomfort. Realize it isn't you who takes offense, who fears being found out. The lower Self bristles with indignation whenever It is reminded of its inferiority. The Ego intellect hiding within doesn't think of Itself as an inferior entity. It believes It is the superior supplier of higher thinking. It worships its own reasoning and intellectual ability. It takes pleasure in the God-like judgment of others. It places them on pedestals, creating little gods to serve the need to verify its own false supremacy as god-maker. Far from Supreme, this inferior Self detests exposure.

Whenever light is shed on It, It feels embarrassment, angrily shrinking inside your psyche like the shameful coward It is. It may speak to you through intellect to convince you It's shame is your shame. It lies by word and thought. But when you are awake, you move beyond the confines of the limited brain.

As vital as the intellect is and how magnificent a creation the human brain, the limitations of the thinking mind must be acknowledged. Without the benefit of conscious awareness, the brain is nothing more than a highly evolved, vital animal organ. However, with the introduction of consciousness, this mass of intricate neural networks transforms into the crown jewel of humanity. It becomes a spiritual gateway through which enters either heaven or hell on earth.

Our only choice is which type of consciousness we will agree to. Will it be Self-consciousness or will it be God-consciousness? Whichever we chose determines how we exist—the quality of our lives, our death, and our afterlife.

There's a functionality of the human mind that is beyond animal thinking. It serves a purpose that goes to a metaphysical connection between Heaven and earth—between man and God Himself.

Watch for thoughts. Even thinking can become an addiction once it is abused. We all have a brain capable of processing information and ideas. It's magnificent. But realize that thoughts and ideas that seem to emanate out of this incredible organ are not ours. In mindfully rising above mesmerized thinking, you won't find it too difficult to relate to them properly, unselfishly.

No doubt you're familiar with the term, Critical Thinking. It's a well-studied thought process, often perceived as an intellectual discipline. It helps us respond practically, without outward prejudice, to virtually any situation we're presented within the stream of life. Out of Critical Thought stems rational behavior. We develop an ability to solve problems. While practicing self-correction, we learn to minimize error as we go along. The less error we have in our lives the more we feel life is going well for us. As you can see, this is vital to our personal security and general well-being.

Critical Thinking is an admirable quality. It will take us far in life. But it doesn't take us far enough. Be assured that there is another discipline to augment Critical Thinking. It's an autonomous Authority, not of the brain but of something far superior to the thinking mechanics of reasoned thought. You may know it as Intuition. I call it *Critical Inspiration* and it emanates out of the human heart of anyone who's allowed it to fill within.

The word critical derives from the Greek κριτικός (kritikos) and translates into *discerning judgment*. A shrewd judge will adjudicate right from wrong without emotional prejudice.

To inspire literally means to breathe life from within. When we're inspired, we have been *in-filled* with a will that stimulates our inner being. It moves us into action, independent of thought or anything outside our psyche that may otherwise sway our thinking. Once independent of external motivators, we think and act from an energetic Source moving from the inside out into the external world.

How do these two types of thinking compare? Critical Thinking is a process. It relies on obtaining external data, then processing that information into reason. Critical Inspiration, on the other hand, goes beyond the external, accessing inner understanding. This is a spiritual element which when added to Critical Thought, powers finer reasoning and observation, free of prejudice and error. This reflects true open-mindedness. The more we allow inspiration to direct us rather than thinking, the fewer mistakes we make.

If you would combine Critical Inspiration with Critical Thinking, *in-spired* reasoning would automatically take precedence in your life. You'd become guided by unsinkable, dispassionate creativity. With your intellect now directed by inspiration, you would think and behave with practicality and uncommon sense. Once Critical Thinking is tempered by Critical Inspiration, the combined mental and spiritual energies become a powerhouse of mastery over all things.

The proper use of will becomes automatic as inspiration directs the thinking mind. Then we'll access the complete human faculties we have been given. Thoughts are like tools, and inspiration is the congenital, wordless instruction directing us, showing how to properly use them. Draw upon thoughts without becoming entangled in them and you will have learned the appropriate use of the thinking mind.

Critical Inspiration is a means by which one can come to conclusions based on intuition. It's a way of knowing whether anything is true or false, moral or immoral, without being told. It's a divinely brilliant practice leading to abilities that can't be learned or taught. They become an automatic knack once established. Yes, intuitiveness rules, delivering a Power behind the ages-old spiritual axiom to *Let Go, Let God.* This capacity to access intuition is what differentiates us from other living things. We aren't mere beasts who just happen to have lucked out by developing a better reasoning brain. We are spiritually founded beings, purposely created in the image of God.

As an Inspired Critic, you experience the God-guided, God-disciplined state of mind where we reason at the highest human level. It's unselfish, nonjudgmental and morally God-centered. People who combine the power of the thinking mind with a regulating spirit within, enjoy balanced lifestyles. They are empathic, keenly aware of the inherently flawed nature of unchecked human thinking. They can recognize imperfection as it arises in them, and they develop a nonjudgmental sense for when others err too. This endows great advantage in all their affairs.

Perhaps now is your time to find what they've discovered. Before that happens, you'll need to access consciousness. Become mindfully aware in such a way that your lower Ego Self shrinks and God can fill you with His spirit and vision. Unless you've already achieved perfection, then this consciousness can only be experienced through *Non-Contemplative Meditation*™.

If you will follow the directions, then long after you've put this book down and for the rest of your life, you'll participate in a lifelong educational journey that will continue for as long as you remain awake and aware.

You will have discovered the answer to all the troubles of mankind since the beginning of time. You won't need any additional praying, religions, gurus, spiritual guides, or mystical undertakings beyond this. The daily activities of your life will become your progressive journey and the training needed to live long and well will come from within.

You won't need to go on retreats or travel and sit at the feet of any guru to discover truth, because everything you need will be revealed directly, in God's own time and in His own manner. Sure, there are people to meet and discussions to have about your discoveries. Some fellowship is healthy and desirable, as long as it doesn't dominate otherwise purposeful living.

Your enlightenment won't depend on other people or any activity other than this one thing, *to be still so that you will become humbled.* The dark nature within you will become right-sized and you'll go about your days being the real you, taking direction only from what is delivered by wordless, inspired reasoning.

Keep a Watchful Eye

Are you ready to take the leap of faith that every human being must make? The world is filled with self-appointed masters of both reality and illusion. You've been one yourself, bewildered in the morass of intellect, your unconsciousness the only reason you've ever suffered.

Wake up now. Leave behind the dark illusion of imagination and begin living in the real world. You'll become instantly free from the bondage of Self. It cannot survive in the Light of Reality. Just let the Light inside.

I Have a Big Problem

The Eleventh Chapter

By which I further make the case that how you meditate matters. It matters so much that I wrote this separate chapter just to address the subject. There are many methods available, but there is only one way to safe and effective consciousness. This is the one.

By the title of this chapter, you might at first think that I'm about to confess some dire personal transgression. I do have my human deficiencies.[185] That, I can assure you. But right now, this is not the case. I am, however, confessing to a serious communications problem. It is the biggest single difficulty I face every day.

During the course of my work and in my writing, I explain the single cause and the only solution common to all of mankind's problems. Every single reader, whether they're conscious of this or not, and whether they like it or not, can identify on some level. I know that I do a good job at getting the point across. I explain the disturbing nature of evil and the means we humans have at our disposal to conquer it—by discovering God, of course.

Then I show how to discover where He is and how to reach Him. There's hardly another living person in the world who can convey this subject matter as well. But we are dealing with the Supernatural and there is something about the nature of the Self and of the Spirit that places them hopelessly at odds with each other. They clash, and in the collision, there can arise a certain *psychic-cognitive bias*. It gets in the way.

The Self is stubborn. It's also intelligent and cunning. It doesn't want to be found out. The moment It senses that a person is waking up It immediately goes to work, building a wall of doubt and denial to block out understanding. Try as they might, nothing much ever changes.

If you've read much of this book or have been meditating regularly, then you already know that the culprit lies in *trying*. Though I remind people of this fact a thousand times, stubbornness remains a problem for some. Intellectually they see the value in giving up ambitious trying, but there seems to be a line they simply cannot cross.

I say, "Give up anger," "Stop hating," "Stop being willful," "Forgive," and they just cannot do it. For them, it seems forbidden.

Subsequently, they remain stuck, unable to honestly approach this meditation, touch consciousness or earnestly seek God without ambition rising to spoil it. It successfully interferes with meditation, constantly getting them to do it incorrectly. It keeps them willful.

Willing away willfulness becomes a never-ending cycle and they become trapped inside their own heads, struggling to get out—or else surrendering to the voice of depravity within.

In these cases, there's usually a degenerate spirit, abetting the lower Self that needs to be brought out before such a person can get free. This is not the scary experience it may seem to the casual reader. It can be dramatic or easy—but it has to happen.

Is there hope for any of these people? Of course, there is. The key is to keep up with the meditation exercise as prescribed. Once you begin, do not stop. I cannot overstate the importance of this.

You may have heard there's no wrong way to meditate and that it doesn't matter much how you do it, only that you do it.

This isn't at all true. It matters very much how you meditate. Unless both motive and technique are correct, you could end up losing your identity and your sanity, making yourself worse off than you were before, although it may not seem so at first.

The very special technique in this book is a metaphysical exercise. Just as with physical exercise, if you do not follow the directions precisely, not only will you not see the desired results, but you will also injure yourself very badly. Used as prescribed, *Non-Contemplative Meditation* works wonderfully. Change it because you think you know better and you will not be happy with the results. There could, in fact, be grave consequences. This technique is not your yoga instructor's meditation or some New Age gimmick. Tampering ruins it and not only will it not work, but you will hurt yourself. This isn't a toy.

Many people have become so conditioned and attached to their lower Self that they're unable to follow the simple instructions I give.[186] They take liberties with the non-contemplative technique I use in my books and recordings. They might combine foreign contemplative elements they've learned elsewhere. They'll fiddle with the times or the frequency.

One of the biggest obstacles to progress is a lack of commitment.

A good number of people are going to try my non-contemplative meditation. They'll take to it immediately and begin experiencing wonderful benefits. Their health will improve. Relationships with people will normalize. They'll begin to know peace in their lives. Families will take notice and share in the benefits too. They will begin to prosper. They'll visit my website, read my books, and articles. They'll enjoy listening to my recordings. But then, though feeling better than they have in years, they will begin to cut down on practicing God-consciousness. Meditation will fall by the wayside. First to just once a day, then once or twice a week, and finally only when feeling anxious or upset.

They'll revert back to their prior state of spiritual stagnation with a headful of talking points gleaned out of my materials. They'll speak of resentment being the cause of problems, getting free from anger, meditation, and consciousness. And though perhaps talking a good game, they will still backslide, falling prey to anger once again, becoming selfish, self-centered and full of fear. Knowledge will have begun to substitute for understanding. Eventually, Something inside will tell them, "See? That didn't work!" But it is they who gave up and abandoned God.

It seems that some people are just unable to be consistent. So, let's address that now.

Non-Contemplative Meditation isn't some pop fad or gimmick. It's not something you just do once in a while when you feel a little off-center, like popping a Motrin, muttering some *happy* affirmation or getting a back massage. This may be the case with other forms of escapist meditations found in dharmic, pop cultures or New Age cult practices, but not in the method I demonstrate and offer in my books.

Non-Contemplative Meditation is not ordinary meditation. It is a powerful metaphysical tool that leads you directly to God. All your troubles are removed, your problems answered, you begin to lead a wonderfully productive and peaceful existence. Then you live forever.

It's no small thing.

For it to work, it's first necessary to commit to the conscious realm, never letting up. It is something to do for the rest of your life. The directions I give are short but very explicit. Practice using the recording (i) once in the morning, (ii) right before going to sleep at bedtime, (iii) sometime during the day and finally, (iv) let consciousness occur increasingly during all your waking moments. The first three of these allows for the fourth. It is as simple as that.

Meditating just once a day won't do it. Ten times a day, three days a week won't work either. Skipping mornings, avoiding evenings and you will not receive the full benefit, and there could be a negative benefit.[187]

Only exactly as I direct works. I can write another whole book on the metaphysics of why this is so, and perhaps I will, but please know that these directions are based in success and errors made myself decades ago, as well as experience working with thousands of other people. I am showing you what works, and all that works.

Short-lived commitment and rebellion at following the simple directions aren't the only pitfalls. Sometimes earnestly seeking "meditators" will initially commit, but then misuse the recordings, ending up enthralled by the sound of my voice. This effect is averted for the most part. I use a very special anti-hypnotic[188] technique, known only to me that is extremely effective.

However, there are still some who willfully attempt to break through this protective hedge. They may meditate for hours at a time deliberately trying to mesmerize themselves into blissful oblivion. Again, this is contrary to the directions and very dangerous to do.

Now about the recording. Let me state it as plainly and directly as I can: *You must use the recording.* It is very special, having fundamental qualities that cannot be easily duplicated. It's typical to need it to meditate using this recording for quite some time. For some, this will mean many months and even years. For a rare few, it will be only days and weeks. (Upon hearing this the Ego entity sometimes chimes in to suggest, "You are one of the rare few." If it speaks, it lies.)[189]

Be wary of that voice that tells you "You've got it now," attempting to persuade you to drop the recording. It knows that It will soon reinstate It's willfulness inside you once you do.[190] I know exactly what I am doing on that recording. It has been produced in a very specific way that cannot be replicated and cannot be meddled with and still work. There are metaphysical reasons for why this is necessary in the beginning. It is just a matter of how long that beginning is. I have met only a handful of people in my entire life who can "Go commando," all the time, and perhaps a few more who can go off the recording on occasion.

My son, for example, usually uses the recording once a day and meditates without it the other times. My wife Nancy uses it morning and at night, but not during the day. Others keep easy access on their smartphones for use anytime.

Some meditate for a few months or years and drop the recording only to quickly slide emotionally sideways and suffer greatly. *They weren't ready.* Others are ready and they do fine.

Typically, a person will have to use the recording for at least a year, gradually losing the need for it while continuing to practice the meditation. After years of daily practice and experiencing a mindfully conscious lifestyle in all their affairs, conscious contact with God will have improved to where they are constantly awake, aware and impervious to resentment. They will be free of anger. Then they will not be able to meditate much anymore because there is a constant state of conscious awareness. Eventually, they may not meditate at all. This will take decades. The journey toward this state and finally perfection is designed for a lifetime.[191]

Another issue lies with the power of consciousness to generate self-transparency. Before you can live to full potential, you must become receptive to truth. You have to see through the lies to the *first truth* so that *first lie* to which you've already fallen can be obliterated. Most people are not truly self-aware. They *think* they are. But the *Self* of which they have become aware isn't really them. This is the truth about yourself that I write about throughout all the previous chapters. To become truly "self-aware" you will have to see the truth about Self.[192] But even more importantly, not resent what you see, no matter how disappointing.

Every human being who remains attached to their dark nature evolves a lifestyle around avoiding truth and seeing lies as truth. To see the truth is painful, especially the truth about yourself. Subsequently, the message in this book competes with an untruthful nature in people to which they have become addicted. They just want to feel good. They want to think highly of themselves, often higher than they really are or deserve.

People want to feel good even if they live badly. This is a principle behind internet marketing schemes, religious evangelism, phony spirituality, many government leaders, and even employers. Restless, irritated folks who're discontent with their current way of life can be seduced by supplying them with mental tricks to help them feel better than they deserve. *Get Rich. Get Saved. Get Happy. Get Fit. Get Powerful.* Surely, you've heard many variations of such themes.

But I do not trick or charm people to make them feel good. To them, I become *persona non-grata*. My proposal is that if they could just endure the pain of the truth about themselves, then just beyond that is enormous peace and joy that isn't conditional on me or anyone else making them feel secure.

I once heard someone say, "You will never convince anyone whose mind is already made up." Oh boy, is that ever true! People who cannot get beyond their need for fast relief will seek out pleasure, eschewing anything that fails to immediately assuage the guilty conscience. They'll resist truth, becoming offended and upset by many of the things I say. This is a variety of resentment that is impossible to avoid. I don't even try.

Another issue is what I call *mish-mashing*. Certain individuals will take the non-contemplative technique and mingle it with other methods, not only combining the directions but also go so far as to insert dharmic philosophies and practices. All of these tend to insert religious ritual and pantheistic philosophy. This is an extraordinarily bad idea. Philosophies deriving out of contemplative meditation practices will inevitably become counterproductive.

In *Non-Contemplative Meditation*,™ there is no philosophy because there is no intellectual knowledge or thought in consciousness. There is only wordless truth called *understanding*. Inserting any philosophy at all automatically pits truth against man-made design. It converts the non-contemplative exercise into a thoughtful endeavor, ruining it.

All thoughtful reflection, even on spiritual themes, is distracting inside the psyche and irregularities can soon follow. Then when suffering increases or bad things happen, the meditator will blame the technique for his failure, when he has not earnestly used it at all. So, don't *mish-mash*. It's a very bad idea.

If you thought meditation meant mantras, hypno-music, droning sitars or mental visualization led by a syrup-voiced spiritual guide, then hopefully I've already successfully disabused you of this idea. If not, then I've failed. Please reconsider practicing *Non-Contemplative Meditation* at this time of your life as the resulting psychic conflict will place you in great danger.

Surely, you are already aware of the enormous health advantages attained through any kind of meditation. Experts cite measurable improvement to immune system response, lowered blood pressure and slower heart rates.

When purposed as a relaxation tool, certain forms of meditation begin to yield some beneficial effects. But anything that helps you relax will do that too. If your motives for meditating are selfish you can easily find a technique to support a self-seeking attitude. This is a grave mistake.

Some of you have physical ailments or mental incapacities and are hoping to be helped by meditation. All right, fair enough. If you follow the directions and begin living consciously you will have those benefits. But if the heart rate is to stabilize, if blood pressure is to reduce, if cognitive abilities are to improve, then those improvements and the healing benefits which follow cannot come from outside influences. To have any lasting value, development has only to unfold from within. It is spiritual progress and occurs only through spontaneous, mystical healing. It never happens by physiological manipulation.

Predictably, meditation found on the internet, in popular self-help books, in APP Stores, and through spiritual cults teachings are typically guided recordings—using music, mesmerizing sound effects and soothing vocal modulation to trigger a mild psychotic state. It's a seduction.

Professional hypnotists call this *induction,* where the meditation facilitator or spiritual guide is free to aurally introduce suggestions into a subject's mind. This can be anything from simple positive affirmations like, "You handle the situations in your life effectively," or, "You feel peaceful and happy and well rested," to pointless suggestions such as, "From now on whenever you hear a car horn honk you will feel an overwhelming urge to bark like a dog."

If this reminds you of a stage hypnotist, you are correct. Most meditation is nothing more than self-hypnosis. All this does is temporarily alleviate some of the most objectionable symptoms of deteriorating virtue.

In allowing a compelling personality to access your mind in this manner you are being conditioned. As your consciousness is dulled, you lose awareness. It appears that you feel better. But the underlying reason for whatever trouble drove you to seek relief from the hypnotist will continue to ravage your being from the inside out.[193]

I'm not saying these don't work. Many of them do work, but it's the way they work that is gravely problematic. The apparent benefits don't last long and in the longer-term have a deleterious effect on the body and mind. You will notice those who engage in these practices becoming physically and emotionally degenerated as time goes on. It's important not to become upset when seeing their error and the consequences.[194]

Be especially wary of any meditation using mantras. Mantras are meaningless, conscience-canceling thought-sounds. They are especially hypnotic. The way they work is simple.

Since it has been thinking that has caused suffering in the past, the dispensation of negative thoughts through mantras generates a contrasting sense of euphoria. An ecstatic sense of well-being seems to emanate out of sheer nothingness. In manufacturing this void of thought, there's a perceived lessening of physical and mental stress.

When continuously repeated in your head, the empty word evokes a mental vacuum. Through mantras, you ambitiously blot out the conscious awareness of the flaws in your nature. Just like drugs. Just like alcohol.

It's imperative that the mantra holds no meaning or else the cover-up doesn't work. The insignificance of the sound produces a contrasting hollowness against the stream of thought traffic. A person laden with repressed emotional energy, such as anger, discovers this blank, altered state, with no meaning attached, and experiences an immediate, short-termed feeling of relief. In what seems to be nothingness, he thinks he's found heaven. Each time he returns to sit in his special pose, repetitively muttering the special words or mantra in his head, the subject experiences a sense of freedom, as he detaches from the corrective conscience that rightfully caused his original unease.

Restlessness suspends. His irritability levels off. He begins to feel better. It's a welcomed break from the pain of his guilty conscience. He feels as though he's letting go of his troubles. He really is *letting go*. What he's letting go of is his conscience, and a lower Self basks in the false sense of manufactured well-being.

Once placed into this altered state the natural connection with God is defeated. In its place forms a direct link with the lower Self. He's disconnected from his inner regulator. It feels like heaven. To the Ego, hell is. Now connected with this lower entity, It deceives him. It tells him he is united with God—part God, part man. In accepting this pleasurable fantasy of Oneness, he is conditioned to believe his newfound faith in his Self. The false knowledge of his own divinity feels like enlightenment. He's now in a fantasy, psychic anesthesia numbing the pain of conscience. He no longer feels the embarrassing sting of God's corrective love. It's no wonder that mantras and similar devices have become so popular.[195]

But this is a counterfeit serenity and a false sense of empowerment arising out of Self-consciousness. In time, he'll become idyllically devoted to a Self that will train him in how to willfully block objectionable thoughts. He will learn to swap worry with new happy thoughts supplying hope. Eventually, his thinking will become so self-manipulated and contrived that unless deprogrammed, his spiritual self may never see the light of God's day. He has gone to the dark side, intoxicated with an imagined oneness with the universe.

Do not become upset watching those who engage in contemplative meditations as they slowly go mad, become ill and die of emotionally induced sicknesses. Those who survive longest are adored masters, parasites really, who've learned how to exchange collective life-force with many others. When the sources of this diminish, or their need grows too large, they too will succumb. Please be wary.[196]

Non-Contemplative Meditation ™ is simpler but metaphysically far more advanced than the types of meditation typically found in the pop-spirituality culture. The meditation approach I propose is not intended to produce blissful Self-consciousness. That's what any escapist behavior or a substance like alcohol, gambling, sex or porn does. Engage in meditation solely to find happiness and you may as well just light up a cigarette or do something to gain someone's approval. What this meditation will do instead, is permit an autonomous state of presence we call *God-consciousness*. Once broken out of your dream-state, the one you don't know you are in, you spontaneously begin to discover and face personal truths that had previously escaped you.[197]

The immediate physiological benefits to the organs like heart, lungs and the brain that often accompany rudimentary relaxation techniques will, of course, come. But, when compared with the enduring benefits, these are only a trite beginning. God-consciousness alters more than the physique and thinking. It also modifies human character. It instills spontaneous virtue. It allows God's heavenly will to access earth through the life of a conscious human being. Not only will you feel better but you'll be becoming a better person, and your wellness will express through your body as well as your mind. You'll amaze as well as *be* amazed. Living a God-conscious life is this way.

So, let's go over some of this.

First, there is the issue of sound. Piano man Billy Joel once said, "I think music in itself is healing. It's an explosive expression of humanity. It's something we're all touched by. No matter what culture we're from, everyone loves music."

Music and ambient sounds tend to have a soothing, seductive effect on the mind and body. They can alter mood and thinking. Music, for example, is well known for the narcotic tendency to distract, motivate or induce relaxation.

There are recordings of babbling brooks and crashing surfs to lull you into a sense of serenity and wellness. However, these remain only superficial mood enhancers. The effects of the most moving orchestral classic, raunchiest rock and roll or peaceful sounds of nature are at best short-lived for their lack of depth.

Music has its place of course. It's a universal tool for human interaction and communication. But like mantras and sound effects, music should never be used as a sedative while meditating. Rhythm and melody get in the way of true peace and serenity whenever they're used in this manner. Will you feel blissful? Absolutely. But artificially altering the mind or physiology in any way also short circuits the healing effect of God-consciousness.

For these reasons, you'll notice that the meditation exercise contains no music or sound effects. There are no chants, or bells and no syrup-voiced, hypnotic chatter to seduce you into a spell. There also aren't any clocks, counters or metronomes, not even the mesmerizing rhythm produced by your own body like the heart beating or lungs breathing. The reason for this is vitally important.

With *Non-Contemplative Meditation,* there's just pure conscious contact with your Creator—a metaphysical condition that will change your life forever, beginning now.

Mantras running through the mind, droning sounds like music, ringing, incantations—are all just hypnotics, supplying substitute blissfulness for true conscious mindfulness. These popular hypno-gadgets arouse a judgmental, power hungry Ego into believing all It has ever wanted to know since the beginning of time—that It is God Almighty.

Devices help invoke a self-indulgent fantasy of Supremacy, existing only in the thoughts. Never use imagination, images or sounds in meditation. For meditation to be effective, consciousness must rise above contemplation, never joined with it.

Non-Contemplative Meditation frees the true you from the bondage of a false Self by separating you from imagination. Let the fact that other people meditate in hypnotic fashion have no bearing on the sheer simplicity of your own conscious contact with God. It is enough to know in your heart what is true.

Another problem is when people try to reinvent the technique or refashion it. They'll use the left hand instead of the right, notice their eyelids but not the fingers, energize their fingers but disregard the eyelid direction. This is the ego trying to sabotage the meditation by taking the reins, and ruining what would otherwise be a very simple and effective tool.

These are opposite to the advice I give and despite warnings that these modifications can be very harmful, they do it anyway. I've noticed that about half of everyone who begins practicing my Non-Contemplative technique benefit immediately. I believe that'd be 90 percent or better if more people possessed a true capacity for honesty and the willingness to commit. It is, after all, a commitment to their Creator.

Hopefully, I've persuaded you that meditation for selfish motives and through improper techniques is hazardous. Please consider my many years of experience and success in this matter. If you look around online and in bookstores, you'll find innumerable proposals for what is touted as meditation. These are nearly always affiliated with underlying religions or specific spiritual movements and organizations attempting to recruit and indoctrinate new members.

The consciousness exercise I pass on isn't like any of those. More to the point, Non-*Contemplative Meditation* is precisely the opposite. The object of becoming still is to allow understanding to fill you. This meditation is the simple exercise of stillness. It brings you to consciousness, the very doorway to heaven within, where the Kingdom becomes at once accessible. It is a lifelong commitment to conscious contact with your Creator. Once established, you experience a mystical association within, a metaphysical existence in the 4th dimension.

First, you are rescued from the dull, altered state into which you've unknowingly allowed the world to seduce you. Then as you perceive reality you are freed, discovering forgiveness within for your trespassers. You experience true communion with your Creator and you live forever.

Feeling Good Isn't Becoming Good

There are many ways to feel good while becoming worse. Just like alcohol, drugs, food, and sex, there are meditation practices designed to temporarily blot out internal pain and conflict, masquerading as progress while undermining true wellness.

How This Came About

The Twelfth Chapter

By which I summarize my personal story and clarify a few of the credentials that allow me to say and to write as I do.

Folks who contact me looking for help will sometimes refer to the exercise I use as, "Your meditation," or, "Danny's meditation." It's understandable that they would put it that way. After all, *Non-Contemplative Meditation?* is something they've never heard of before. It is an innovative term. It piques much interest and even speculation.

Even I have been known to refer to it as, "My meditation," to distinguish it from other types. I am, of course, the originator of the name *Non-Contemplative Meditation*. But that is all that I own. I cannot take credit for the clockworks of the technique nor for its creation. No one can. It isn't an invention. This has been around for a very long time, before any of us were ever born, and it exists through our discovery, not by human creation. Becoming still, and awakening to realize that Something in you wants to play God, then separating from It to allow the One and only true God flow within, is not a recent development.

I regularly speak with people who, once being shown, recall experiencing this method spontaneously when they were very young. As it turns out, practicing God-consciousness is a natural phenomenon—a proclivity already deep within us all, whether we realize it or not. We come into the world with the inborn potential to move toward Him. This very special exercise is simply a convenient device leading to the threshold of God-consciousness, the yearning for which is already embedded into our being.

So you see, practicing God-consciousness this way is nothing new, just something forgotten. All I've done is give it a descriptive name and reintroduced the approach to these people. Through practice, they rediscover their true personality. God-given intuitiveness returns to them. It works. Really well too. The term *Non-Contemplative Meditation* is my only conception, mere words to describe the single divine deed we humans can safely make.

I was blessed with recognizing it as *a thing* early on in life and I've been able to latch onto it. I don't know why that is so, I only know it is. Although I've have abused it and suffered, I have also discovered how to do it right. I mean *perfectly*.[198] I share my discoveries with as many people as I can through this vocation, writing—hoping others coming across my work will benefit from it.

This technique isn't at all complicated. In fact, it is the sheer simplicity that is key to the powerful effectiveness of *Non-Contemplative Meditation*. There is nothing else like it in the world and nothing else works. Believe me.

If you've been meditating as shown, then you already know that there are three simple components to the exercise. The first two are obligatory. It doesn't work without them. The third is optional but highly advised. There's the *eye-head* part and then there is the *hands* part.

To be interesting and informative, I'd like to share with you just how I began practicing this technique and set out showing it to others. I first stumbled on the *eye-head* part when I was a little boy.[199] It was truly a Godsend at the time. I know in my heart that from that moment on I was protected from harm, allowing for a great degree of spiritual autonomy and emotional freedom early in life.[200] What follows is exactly what happened.

For as long as I can remember, as a young boy, I had been toying with the *lights inside the head* phenomenon. (If you do not yet know what that is, please go to my website and give it a try. That's the only way to truly appreciate this description.) I'd go to bed each night, close my eyes and it would happen spontaneously. I did this on a regular basis and can recall as far back as perhaps when I was three or four years old, doing it every night. It became a private wonder I never told anyone about. I didn't really know what it was for, or even that there could be any future usefulness in it until I was around six-years-old.[201]

Then the purpose became quite clear.

Allow me to set this up for you, just briefly if I may: We were a broken family. I was the oldest of three with two younger sisters. We were each from a different father. One poor guy, let's call him *Man-Dad One*, who my mother actually married, assumed all three of us were his. (So did I.) He divorced my mother but came for visitations every few months.

A second *Man-Dad*, biologically my own, is to this day still at large and remains unidentified. *Man-Dad Three*, who sired my youngest half-sister, managed to maintain a part-time relationship with us. He already had a legitimate wife and two kids on the other side of the borough, so he couldn't very well just move in. But he'd come and go when *needed*. Being the real father of my youngest sister, he was inexorably linked to us Schwarzhoff's.

It was through this third *Man-Dad* that I first learned how useful my little *starry-headed*, inner light practice was.

One would not immediately *call Man-Dad Three* a creepy person. But he was weak for having fallen to my mother's charms as a married man.[202] With a lifestyle so patently in violation of his strict Catholic background, the double life was too much for him. He became a violent drunk who regularly hit all of us. The fatherless household became infected by both physical and verbal abuse. He'd pummel our mother pretty well. The screams in the middle of the night. The bawling. The black eyes. Black and blue marks. The sounds of punches and smacks, mommy begging for the hitting to stop. The vile smell of the most pungent vomit imaginable wafting through the apartment. My sisters and I would hide our heads under the covers to escape the stench. I once got up in the middle of the night and slipped on a trail of blood on the foyer hall linoleum. My pajama leg streaked with the blood of... I wasn't sure whose it was. We all feared *Man-Dad Three* terribly, and subsequently, our feelings evolved a classic love-hate association with him.

One day it was my turn for a beating.

I didn't like the school lunches served at Holy Family School and could hardly bring myself to eat them. My mother told me if I didn't eat the lunch I'd be physically punished—by *Man-Dad Three*. Of course, not being my biological father he had no authority and had already earned my contempt for his drinking.

One lunch served was some horrible baloney and butter sandwiches with canned prunes. I wanted so much to obey my mother. I didn't want to go against her. I wanted to be a good boy. I certainly didn't want to be punished. I tried to eat it. But gagged and couldn't swallow. It was awful. I just couldn't eat that lunch. I managed to squelch my *sin* for much of the day. Every time I remembered what I'd done, *or not done*, I'd simply distract myself with something else. On the walk home however, I knew reckoning was getting closer. I trembled. The fear became all consuming. It was all I could think about on the way home.

My mother met me at the usual spot to take me across the boulevard and home. She grabbed my hand and we crossed. I was a dead man walking. As expected, the moment we got inside the apartment she asked the question, "Did you eat the lunch today?" It did not occur to me to lie. I started to cry. I knew the words that were about to come out of my mouth would bring me a beating. I don't know exactly the mechanism that caused it, but for some reason I yelled out, the truth at the top of my lungs, "NO MOMMY I DIDN'T!" My eyes were so swollen I couldn't see out of them. She told me to go to my bed and stay there. I did. For hours. Until *Man-Dad Three* arrived.

He used a thick leather belt. As he was hitting me fear and anger rose. I closed my eyes and immediately experienced the eye-head phenomenon that I was already used to having at night.

This time however, instead of the normal curiosity I usually felt, something different began to happen. The lights inside my head coalesced and formed a bright center, like an opening in a cave, the walls of which were my head. I could see ahead, outside the cave a complete brightness and sensed a protective Presence just outside the cave entrance. Here is when it happened, the phenomenon that changed my life forever. Immediately the hatred for my mother's boyfriend melted away.

The fear of him just totally vanished. I felt profoundly protected. That I do my best to describe in this book but which is impossible to adequately convey by words. You have to experience it yourself. Today, this is elemental to how I live each day and what I write about. It is called *forgiveness*.

Oh, don't get me wrong. My butt was sore. Angels didn't descend with flaming swords to defend me. *Or did they?* My mother later became angry at *Man-Dad Three* for leaving such bright red welts. "Oh, he didn't really hurt you. Just your feelings are hurt, that's all," she consoled herself. I went to bed that night with my bottom stinging. But I also fell to sleep without an ounce of animosity toward this man and found I could be kind to him ever since.[203] He never got to me again. In fact, that was the last time he ever hit me until my teenage years. Unfortunately, my mother and younger sisters did not share the same discovery as I and consequently did not survive it. No one survives anger. We all need protection.

I continued this practice for many years thereafter, subsequently also becoming aware of an inner attitude that was strikingly different from that of my peers. To me, my views seemed normal. But it would be surprising, often shocking to learn of other opinions and attitudes about life, the world, and human relationships. They were so apart from my own, seemingly without virtue or guidance of conscience. There's much more I can say about this and the experiences have varied over the years, but this is just one book.

Then there is the looking at eyelids and the extension from *head to fingers* elements of the Non-Contemplative exercise. These are very good physical devices, both of which I picked up from a similarly blessed man who had helped me when I was in my early twenties.[204] These added components are so good in fact, that I combined them into one technique. I took my original *eye-head* element from childhood and put it together with the *finger and hand extension* into an original meditation exercise that I developed specifically for alcoholics.[205]

I recorded and began distributing the technique to alcoholics and addicts who were drawn to me, my lifestyle and meditation. It changed their lives. Today I include these with the approach presented in this book not only to alcoholics and drug addicts, but to all.[206]

Finally, there is *the hands in-front* suggestion of the exercise, which surely you can recognize as the classic *praying* position.

If you've seen artist's depictions of saints in prayer throughout the centuries, then you already know where that method comes from.

Out of this mixture of elements into one technique, emerges a meditation experience replicating how Jesus taught his disciples to become still and realize that they are not God— that only He is.[207] It suggests we do not try to eliminate mental noise in our heads, but that we fall back, becoming objective to our thoughts, neither struggling to be rid of them or embracing them. It is not aggressive, nor is it a passive activity. It is conscious neutrality that is free of thinking, despite the relentless stream of thought.

Any willful redirection in mental focus, concentrating on ideas and thoughts, positive or negative, is an extremely dangerous practice. Although it can stir fleeting degrees of euphoria, it also takes the individual out of the present reality and into imaginary streams of past or future events which are artificial.

Learning to mentally generate positive thoughtfulness, supposes the power of the mind can manifest desirable outcomes. This is egoistic conditioning that trains into an *unsane* attitude, irrational behavior, and finally, complete mental and physical breakdown. As knowledge, prestige, and possessions accumulate under such schemes, there is also a simultaneous deterioration in spirit, mind, and body. I've been a witness to this principle many times over the years, in my own family, my life and in working with others.

I've since discovered true personal well-being and health by letting go of artificially generated optimism and instead allowing a gentle disheartenment of ambitious spirit so that true confidence unfolds from within. This attitude has caused the suspension of interest in selfish things and generates a keen awareness of the needs of my fellows.

Even under the most stressful circumstances, willfulness yields and I'm able to step back to become a neutral observer, calmly watching the chatter generated in the mind without prejudice—neither believing or disbelieving any of it. This has proven to be an advantageous perspective, where there is a reduction of Self, simply by becoming uninvolved with It's vain prattle.

With Self diminished, life-victories evolved naturally, comfortably, and indefinitely, without struggle, wear or worry. With the stillness came peace and ease, a fearless state of being. I'm free.

I realize how lofty this may seem to some, but I assure you it was quite effortless and automatic the very moment I became mindful of the Dark Self existing inside every person and defaulted back to the original state of God-consciousness I recall as a child. You might say that I had an exorcism. I *definitely* say that. Now free, I exist in a conscious state that is not self-consciousness but what I know to be God-consciousness.

Whatever your opinion on my technique may be, whatever you think of me or how I came upon this way of life, please know that as the result of nearly four decades of practice, I am awakened. I write and speak from the perspective of a mindfully conscious human being. I share real-life experiences borne out of living in this realm, not merely estimations about how I think things should be.

This *Non-Contemplative Meditation*, exactly as I propose, is directly responsible for the way my family lives too. It saved my life many years ago. It's currently saving my wife's life. My entire family uses it daily. It remains key in developing my children's lives, having an enormous impact on their social and academic progress.

It's also currently changing the lives of many people with whom I've worked with over the years helping them overcome their troubles.[208] The well-being of entire families has come as the direct result of conscious awareness through *Non-Contemplative Meditation*. Among those helped, there are people in media and business, major household name personalities of whom I have firsthand knowledge, are using this technique very successfully. You would be astonished to learn who they are.

Change, Transformation, Whatever You Call It

Although perfectly content to leave me out of the discussion, I'm not at all awkward talking about myself whenever appropriate. The backstory of an author's own personal transformation is pretty much mandatory in a book of this kind. I've determined this a suitable place to tell you just how I came upon all of this. The first section of this book proclaims that my presentation is not like anything you've ever seen or experienced before. Having read this far, then by now you've undoubtedly seen why.

Just a Brief Backgrounder
About Daniel J Schwarzhoff

By which you learn some of the basics about Dan's background and life.

Daniel J. Schwarzhoff is a writer and author. His work centers on personal development through demystifying spiritual awakening, mindful living, becoming freed from anger and the elimination of stress induced obsessions—mainly fixations with food, sex, drugs, and unwholesome relationships.

Schwarzhoff's books and recordings help others all over the world discover personal autonomy, liberating them from the bondage of self and people.

His vocation is nonclinical and not linked with any religion or pop-culture spirituality. At the core of Dan's work lies the intrinsic conversion of being that each person needs to have in this lifetime.

He introduces others to a way of overcoming problems through the renewal of God-connectivity, developing a defense against harmful, emotional energies. His primary tool is what he calls *Non-Contemplative Meditation*™, a technique that stimulates *consciousness* and maintains *grace under fire* in a stress-filled world.

Leading through experience, Dan shows others how to wake-up from within. They effortlessly lose bad habits, recover from addictions, as well as physical and mental sicknesses through the unique, non-contemplative exercise he first discovered as a child. The practice results in a transformation, moving the individual out of a mesmerized state they don't even realize they're in, and into a state of psychic arousal.

Dan is not a doctor or cleric. He doesn't diagnose illnesses or prescribe medication. He doesn't preach a religion and is not a member of any organization. He considers his own autonomy to be a distinct advantage in helping others. He shows people how their problems can be overcome, diseases and conditions cured, without the use of psychology, medicine, hypnosis or conventional religious means. He traces the etiology of most physical and mental illness back to metaphysical malady. Metaphysical solutions to metaphysical problems are Dan's realm.

He's a strong advocate for seeking professional medical guidance and occasionally even certain medications that can assist in controlling symptomatic outbreaks, while concurrently addressing the spiritual origin of every mental and physical disorder there is.

Dan's proposals present a profoundly simple standard by which he has personally conquered clinically diagnosed major depression, anxiety and ADD, smoking, alcoholism, onset diabetes, obesity, high cholesterol, sugar addiction, drug abuse, colitis and other dysfunctions.

Drawing from over 30 years of experience with mindful consciousness, and overcoming obstacles intrinsic to the human experience, Dan's insightful, simple method has helped countless others discover how to allow true peace and fulfillment to unfold from within. It enhances the quality of their lives and the lives of those around them.

He's the author of the cutting-edge book *Real Meditation for Real Alcoholics: and those who love* them, and now *Go In.*

In 1999 he moved from Queens, New York City to Cape Cod Massachusetts, where he currently lives with his wife Nancy and their two children, Danny Jr., and Kristen. In July 2017, the Schwarzhoffs celebrated their 38th wedding anniversary. The Schwarzhoff family is a complete family unit, enjoying emotional, mental, and physical health and a harmonious lifestyle that is free from injurious stress.

And by the way . . .

Why is the term *Non-Contemplative Meditation*™ trademarked?

When we think of trademarks, what first comes to mind are those little legal symbols used to protect brand names, products or services against infringement by competitors. You'll see one such symbol attached to Non-Contemplative Meditation™.

As a writer, my intellectual properties naturally belong to me. I own them. That is a fact of copyright law. In the specific case of the term *Non-Contemplative Meditation (*NCM™*)*, there is also a much more important need for the trademark symbol.

If you Google the term *Non-Contemplative Meditation* the only result you'll get is from my writing and websites. The term doesn't exist, outside of me and my work. If this ever changes, if anyone ever tries to duplicate what I have already done, the original source must always remain identifiable. This is not solely a matter of commerce. For many, it would be a matter of success and failure, joy and misery, even life and death. *Non-Contemplative Meditation* is not a leisure activity, fad or plaything.

Right now, there are hundreds, perhaps thousands of various meditations available. There are websites, books. and APPs all disseminating some form of meditation practice. If all meditation techniques were the same, producing the same desirable results, there would be no reason to trademark or otherwise distinguish those from my NCM technique. But all practices are not the same and do not produce the same results, especially long term.

Along with my extraordinary understanding of meditation techniques, I also have a deep grasp of how the various methods work and what they do inside the human psyche. The effects of the NCM technique are drastically different.

I am deeply concerned about this.

There are legions of enterprises teaching meditation, promising to deliver the key to success, happiness, empowerment and good health. Most of these advance *contemplative* techniques. There are others that arouse introspection, prayer and promote varieties of cultured mindfulness that encourage the evacuation and replacement of thoughts with philosophical and theosophical ideas. The *Non-Contemplative Meditation* technique I practice and pass on is very different and special. There is no theology. No religious indoctrination. This becomes instantly apparent to the practitioner once he begins.

Rather than being hypnotic, as all contemplative techniques are, *Non-Contemplative Meditation* is anti-hypnotic. The words I use in the recorded guides are knowingly crafted and presented in a certain order, invoking specific psychic and spiritual response, bringing the practitioner to a very special state of consciousness that cannot be duplicated by any other means. There's something metaphysical happening that is just not possible with any other meditation method.

In short, NCM is the opposite of all other forms of meditation. It is precise but also risky unless delivered in an exacting manner, as I do in the Non-Contemplative exercise. To the casual observer, this may not be clear since it is going on within the psyche.

All meditations outwardly appear to have roughly the same procedure. But to the practitioner of *Non-Contemplative Meditation*, there is a world of difference requiring distinctive branding. It is vital that not just anyone use the term, possibly causing spiritual, psychic or emotional harm.

Because of this, there is a need to distinguish this meditation from all others. If *Non-Contemplative Meditation* were to become confused with any of the contemplative varieties of meditation, at the very least, there would be no effect and at worst, the psychic harms to individuals attempting to practice it could be substantial. Here a trademark serves to protect consumers, allowing them to identify *the real thing*, the specific technique that I practice and write about in all my books, as opposed to a facsimile.

With a trademark, others can be sure they are using the genuine article because no one can be trained to teach this technique or legally use the name NCM or *Non-Contemplative Meditation*, and anyone who does so is passing on a counterfeit.

Finally, there is also practical necessity for the name *Non-Contemplative Meditation* to bear a trademark. I believe that we are well into a new era in cultural development. The need for solutions to spiritual and social conflict among mankind is rising. As pharmaceutical and psychotherapeutic solutions are increasingly revealed to be ineffective, and as our society begins to harbor more anger and negative emotional responses to declining conditions, I predict that dharmic philosophies that advance meditation are going to figure heavily. Even more than they are already.

There's Transcendental Meditation. There are also varieties aligned with Zen and Vipassana. Others link with pantheistic societies. Many relaxation exercises relate to yoga and new age cult movements. These meditation procedures purport to produce a wide range of effects on the mind, body, and behavior. It has become a big business and getting bigger all the time. *Non-Contemplative Meditation* is unique in this regard.

Practitioners of my technique experience all the scientifically measurable physical responses that we see from other forms, but there is one more thing: *God-consciousness.* There is nothing else like *Non-Contemplative Meditation* on the face of the earth. Period.

Consciousness and conscious contact with God are not the creation of my mind. It's a preexistent condition that is as old as time. There surely are others in the world who also practice mindful consciousness through meditation this way. They are welcome to call what they do by any other name they wish. I hope they spread true mindfulness and God-consciousness too. They just can't use, "Non-Contemplative Meditation," since it applies solely to this original technique and is unique to my work. The trademark is a way of maintaining effectiveness and the purity of this very special method, helping ensure that future generations also continue to benefit from my life's work.

Restore Spiritual Connectivity, then the Body and Mind Heal

There's a passage in the book Alcoholics Anonymous where its co-authors make what to some may seem a rather weighty proclamation. They claim, "When the spiritual malady is overcome, we straighten out mentally and physically." This has always been axiomatic in the spiritual realm of human existence. The term "Spiritual malady" is not to say that the spirit becomes sick. Rather, it goes to the original spiritual relationship with God that's become corrupted, needing repair and healing. Consciousness re-establishes lost connectivity and a full picture of wholesome, human-spiritual purpose promptly restores. As we recover, the symptoms of a shattered relationship with our Father evaporate. We become whole once again.

Would You Like Some More?

Okay, so you're either peeking ahead or you've already finished reading this book. We don't have to stop here. I'll have more books, of course. There's also plenty of free stuff on my website. I'll be adding new articles, pamphlets, and videos all the time. Please go there regularly.

I'm a very active blogger, one of the originals going back nearly 20 years, with thousands of articles published. I plan to continue that tradition. I take questions. I give advice and answers. I also will be podcasting regularly in 2017.

So, there's no need to lose contact with each other. Just one warning. I highly discourage any kind of clinginess. Yes, contact with like-minded people is wonderful and it warms my heart to disseminate what have to those who need it. There's great benefit from fellowship with others in this regard. But there's no church, group, or organization to join.

I am not going to be your life-coach or anyone's spiritual guide. Mentorship and consulting is useful in business and occasionally in relationships too, but for matters of the spirit, it turns very unhealthy, very quickly. On the contrary, I help people get free from spiritual cults and people dependencies.

I do have an email list if you want to receive a periodic blog article. (In case you forget to visit my site. Staying touch at a long arm's length, if only for a while, can be very beneficial. But that's about it.

I hope to hear from you or maybe even meet up one day. You never know.

Dan

Here are all the links you need to stay in touch.

Mailing List: www.schwarzhoffmedia.com/email-signup/

Email: dan@schwarzhoffmedia.com

Website: www.schwarzhoffmedia.com

Facebook: www.facebook.com/danschwarzhoff/

YouTube: www.youtube.com/DanielJSchwarzhoff/

Twitter: @danschwarzhoff

Medium: @danschwarzhoff

Instagram: @danschwarzhoff

Periscope: @danschwarzhoff

Errata Grata

[1] Oh, how I do not want to use that word in this book. I am no preacher. Just as no one preaches to me, I am not interested in becoming anyone's rabbi or mentor. But this fits the, "practice what you preach," adage, so please cut me some slack here.

[2] Tragically, those outside our immediate family have rejected the conscious way of life I propose, the consequences have not been good.

[3] I can better address separate issues for those with especially stubborn concerns in other areas on my website. For now, this will do just fine. All problems have the same origin and are resolved through the same solution anyway. Just Google me and find it, or go to www.schwarzhoffmedia.com

[4] Yeah, I know. It's in the "Self-help" book section. I can't help that. It must receive some sort of classification. It's a publishing and bookselling standard. I don't mind at all. Just go with it, even though it's inaccurate.

[5] I sometimes hear from individuals who have at first held a deep resentment for me, my work and message, but after months and years of reading my materials finally have become receptive. They begin to meditate. They awaken, and through consciousness, their lives change drastically.

[6] This is the reason I don't read spiritual books. I can't even get past many of the titles if you want to know the truth.

[7] If you want to respect me and my work, fine. But never become a fan of me or anyone. (Ok, one exception: You can "Like" me on Facebook.) You'll see the importance of this later in this book.

[8] It's easy to find. There aren't any "click funnel" pages. You can also search YouTube with my name or "Non-Contemplative Meditation."

But the free streaming on my website is simple to navigate and can be bookmarked on your smartphone, iPad or laptop.

[9] There are no Eastern cultural influences, polytheism, non-duality philosophies or New Age beliefs promoted here.

[10] AKA the *Boob Tube.*

[11] Because of how I used these characters as a little boy, to this day I still carry a paternal imprint going to the real men who played the parts, William Shatner, Sean Connery and George Reeves. It's a vague fondness to their images, not connecting with these men, but with the memories of the characters they portrayed. It's a kind of reverence, an imprint that all human offspring experience in response to a fatherly image. I don't even know any of them, nor have I ever met them, and yet this sentimentality really exists. The closest I've ever come was a few weeks ago, as I was finishing up the final draft of this book, I heard a Tweet on my Smartphone. It was Shatner. He had tweeted, "Good Morning!" I looked at the clock. It was 10:15 PM. *What?* I tweeted back, "Where the hell are you?" A few moments later he responded, "Well, I'm certainly NOT there!" I cackled a bit. Nancy asked me what was so funny and of course I told her. Then it struck me. "Oh, my God Nance! I am standing here in our living room on Cape Cod, with a hand-held communication device, talking to Captain Kirk!" *Silence. Just let that sink in for you too. Look what have we done with our world? See, it isn't all bad after all, is it? All right now, please just go back reading my book.*

[12] Does a thirty-room home in Chappaqua with a heliport and a personal major domo qualify as the *American Dream?*

[13] At first, the depression seemed situational. But years later, after having suspended my non-contemplative meditation practice, I was diagnosed with clinical depression. In giving up consciousness, Self nourished Itself, first on the condemnation of others and eventually of me! A dark veil appeared over my psyche. I resorted to taking SSRI antidepressant medications (principally Lexapro, Wellbutrin and Effexor) that made me feel a lot better. I began attending 12 Step

meetings and took the advice of members to obtain these, legally of course through a doctor. *NOTE: When someone suggests that you to go a doctor for depression or anxiety, they are advocating antidepressant drugs to you. They might as well be authorized to write the script themselves because doctors routinely prescribe these medications on request. If you go to one feeling blue, you're getting the antidepressants. Believe me. And you will be on them for life.*

[14] Several years before the DeLorean DMC-12 hit production, I heard Larry King interviewing Patrick J. Wright, author of *On a Clear Day You Can See General Motors: John Z. DeLorean's Look Inside the Automotive Giant*. As an impressionable 21-year-old, hearing of John Z's life and career, the prospect of achieving success like his just blew me away. I wanted what DeLorean had. I guess we all know how *that* turned out.

[15] I had an attorney named Benjamin who also did work for John. He and his wife received *His & Her* Mercedes Coupes as Christmas gifts from John. One day we were at the *Palm Too* restaurant in New York having lunch and the waiter brought a phone to our table. This was before cell phones. It was DeLorean calling. He wanted Benjamin to pick up his *DeLorean* from the garage and drive it out to his New Jersey "ranch" for a weekend cookout so he could take a chopper home. I was agog. My mind left the planet, soaring into the not too distant future where I was John Z's new best business buddy. ("John Z" is what we who are close to John called him.) I totally forgot about the Filet Mignon, butterfly cut, on my plate.

[16] At least in my eyes, I was. The fancy Wall Street titles, *Investment Banker, VP of Mergers and Acquisitions, Stockbroker,* the custom-made suits, limousines to and from work, all suited someone of my highfalutin station. Nancy and I dined in the world's finest restaurants, had the best seats at any of the Broadway shows, owned a top floor, luxury apartment in the best zip code in New York City, and drove new luxury cars. It impressed the hell out of me. But it was a lifestyle we didn't deserve. It wasn't truly earned.

[17] No, I'm not a billionaire. Not even close. But don't' worry. If I ever become one, I'll write a book about it. Let's just say I have no money worries.

[18] There is a saying "You can prospect for gold or you can sell pickaxes to miners." This goes to the entrepreneurs of the mid-1800s California Gold Rush where those most successful weren't the gold diggers themselves, but merchants having the foresight to sell mining supplies to would-be successful miners. Most prospectors didn't find very much, but setting up shop to sell them the equipment to try their hand at it, became the true mother lode. Think of Levi Strauss, who, during the rush, built an empire starting a wholesale dry good business distributing clothes (Yes, jeans) and other necessities from the east coast to the west.

[19] It's only natural to wonder if I'm rich. Obviously, I cannot allow access to my banking records. Let's just say that I am financially stable. This is a little ambiguous perhaps, but I can say that when it comes to finances, I am better off than you are. My family and I want for nothing and we're the healthiest, most successful, happiest family you will ever meet. And it's getting even better every day. When it comes to money, this is the kind of security that is the most desirable, and that is true whether the values of your accounts and assets are more or less than mine.

[20] Money, labor, and wealth are profoundly fundamental to our spirituality, our human connection with God and His universe. How we relate to work and money impacts on our emotional and physical well-being as well as relationships with others, just as intensely as do food and sex. Even right now, if you're honest, you can probably notice at least a tinge of emotion arising inside just from reading about it. *And we're barely touching the subject. See? That's anxiety.* Toil, recompense, financial matters of all kinds, upset everyone-rich, poor and in-between, even those who swear it isn't so. And it's not by reason of socialization or culture. The natural concern for money is a spiritually inbred facet of our humanity. Just as each of us is born

personally invested in procreation and survival, so are we viscerally attached to money. Not currency. Not cash. Not Bitcoins. But money-yes, tender, as well as the wealth we accumulate and exchange for the things that bring us pleasure, security, and approval. There are supernatural reasons for this. It is right. As in all things, handle money well and be well. Handle it improperly and you'll not survive either affluence or poverty, whichever your station in life may be. People who say, "Money isn't everything," are consoling themselves for the umbrage they feel by not having any. Those unabashedly admitting, "It's all about the money," are defending an obsession with pleasure seeking. The truly contented person understands the enormous spiritual sway of wealth, financial security, investment, and work. They respect it. They are neither dismissive or obsessed with finance. A healthy regard for prosperity is automatic once we understand and live this way. Then we can begin living free, released from the anxiety that anyone still bound to Self experiences. It requires a deflation of Ego many of us have yet to know.

[21] Without the added propaganda, religious indoctrination or programming.

[22] Notwithstanding average life expectancy statistics, we each have roughly 100 to 120 years to get it done. Depending on your current level of health and emotional lifestyle, that can be considerably less, or more. In the U.S., our overall life expectancy is currently 79 years of age. In the U.K., it is 81. Considering our potential to reach perfection, both averages are *too soon*. Our time here on earth does run out.

[23] Something inside you may cower at some of the ideas presented here. It could try to distract, preventing you from understanding what's written. Sometimes you might have to reread small passages to break through It's fear. If you cannot and if the understanding still evades you, then just move on. Don't struggle with the words. Resist the temptation to study or drill information into memory. What you

need to understand will come later, once you've been meditating for a while.

[24] Overeating, overdrinking, alcoholism, drug addiction, sexual compulsions, relationships, to name a few.

[25] By "certain foods" I specifically refer to carbohydrates such as sugars and alcohols.

[26] This is the originating concept expressed by "Thy will be done," in what is known as *The Lord's Prayer*, contradicting *my will be done*. *Enlightenment* is a complete parallel to the words in that prayer.

[27] And yet upon learning this and even agreeing with it wholeheartedly, not one in ten thousand will pursue and live it. Hopefully, you're one of the few who does.

[28] These paradigms are just images manufactured in our heads. They become the mental metrics we use to gauge what we determine to be "success." They're entirely subjective, customizable and frequently not necessarily supported by reality. A successful person in Turkey is not the same as a successful person in America. A successful German is not the same as a successful Slovenian.

[29] There are characterless psychopaths who rise to prominence using knowledge, power or wealth obtained egoistically. I'm not talking about those types. They are failures regardless of what wealth they accumulate or their level of recognition and fame.

[30] Instead of simply being who they are at any given moment, people often create for themselves a fantasy world of what they want to be. This is why *Fake it to make it* is a complete sham. It's a lack of total honesty, that although it may feel good for a while, ultimately destroys the individual's character and chances for true happiness or success. The 24-year-old State University grad with a YouTube account pretending to be a Life Coach, because he became "certified" for a thousand bucks through a webinar, or because his parents have always *oohed and ahhed* at their grades, future prospects or good looks, is living in delirium. The self-help writer, portending to tell

others how to become successful in life without having met with much of it themselves is probably on the way toward a padded room. The spirituality guru who still gets angry, who's prone to resentment, fear and emotionally based disease, is not credible. Without living what they preach or preaching delusional theories they haven't themselves internalized for good, no one can never know real joy. If any of these would simply become aware and conscious enough to see and then learn to separate from their lower self, a whole new world order would kick into place for them. Instead of taking others on a fantasy tour into oblivion, they would first become well themselves. Then, they'd have something truly worthwhile to pass on.

31 The next time someone comes to your office and declares how they plan to, "Stay hungry and stay foolish," realize that you are not dealing with a whole person. And if that's you, then you've come to the right book. Trust me. Please don't be too offended.

32 Before writing this book, I didn't know all that much about Steve Jobs. I knew who he was, of course. I knew that he founded Apple, was fired from Apple, and later came back to propel the company to the top of the world. I just didn't know anything about Job's life, personality or affairs. I was never an AAPL promoter when I worked on Wall Street—was just never impressed with the company enough during the 90s to follow it. But now, looking for a name-brand example with whom many were already familiar, I went onto YouTube and watched several hours of interviews with Jobs. I read maybe twenty or thirty articles, each infused with views about him and his life, both pro and con. I also read and heard several opinions about the medical issues he suffered with, and of course the tragic ending. *(Those opinions were about as erroneous and inaccurate as could be expected. Terribly wrong estimations.)* With just a few hours vested in the research, I am by no means a Steve Jobs biographer. But from what I've discovered I say, "Boy, what an example," of how to do it, as well as how *not* to do it. If I'd have gotten ahold of Steve Jobs at almost any time prior to his death, even a few months, he'd be alive

today, still at the helm of Apple Inc. I am convinced of that. He came so close to truth early in his lifetime and it is crystal clear to me just where he went right. It is also clear where he went appallingly wrong. The error cost him his life. But I am certain that if shown, Jobs would have grabbed onto what I am offering you in this book and he'd have totally taken off with it. He was a very good candidate because he had already discovered the first half. Just one vital element was kept from him *(Facebook's Mark Zuckerberg is making a similar mistake by the way.)* I liked Steve Jobs and his story so much, that in the middle of writing the last chapter of this book, I went onto Apple's website and bought a brand-new MacBook Pro and an iPad. Not in tribute, but because of what I learned. It has become apparent to me that Apple products are the best there are. (At least for now, until Jobs' influence has been mostly absorbed and diluted—then Apple will no longer lead. It has begun already.) And this from a lifelong Microsoft devotee.

33 Of course, then you'll also have to deal with being placed on a pedestal by people. It could be millions of fans or just your own children, depending on your lifestyle and position. This important subject is adequately addressed in "Point Six."

34 As opposed to "all hell" which unless truly is Hades, then is rightly outlawed by Elmore Leonard. www.nytimes.com/2001/07/16/arts/writers-writing-easy-adverbs-exclamation-points-especially-hooptedoodle.html

35 I'm using the term "seeker" generically. I mean someone who viscerally longs to know the meaning of life, the origin of their existence, who they are and what their place is in the mix and actively engages a lifestyle toward that end. It's not a religious reference at all.

36 Many readers will feel a flinch within on first hearing this idea. That is the lower Self balking under the agony of just having been identified. It doesn't want you to have this information. It doesn't

want me to write about it. If you will simply notice It's reaction, in time It will lose the grip and power to influence.

37 The simple fact is that everything you've ever been told about the Ego, everything you have read or heard from psychologists, spiritual pundits, religious clerics, and university professors has been wrong. These aren't ignorant people. They are highly intelligent, well-meaning people, but their information and training have been corrupted, based upon a planned ignorance that not even they have been aware of. From this day on your perspective on life, and of every human being, is going to change with this one bit of information. Your life will never be the same.

38 In understanding just what Ego is, it is useful to know that Jesus Christ was born an Ego-less human. He was an individual existing solely as His true self, who could not be influenced by a lower, Dark Self because there was none in Him. His psyche was filled by Light, with no darkness at all, where only goodness from the Father could flow and project through Him. By this reason, Jesus is an extraordinary, supernatural being and could not be corrupted. He already knew that it wasn't He impelling paranormal events and expressing wisdom, but the Father, God, through Him. When we become conscious we are still, and in that separation from thought, we too can do wondrous things because we cease judging, acting as God. Goodness is not ours, except that it flows through us by our Father in heaven, when we are in that state of mind—the same state of conscious awareness that Jesus enjoyed for all of His time on earth. This is why although His body was destroyed, Jesus could never succumb to permanent death. You'll see TV preachers or church ministers jumping the gun, trying to perform miracles they are not metaphysically authorized to do, as Jesus was. They'll lay hands on the sick, portend to prophesize the future, try to alter outcomes and reality (especially financial realities) through prayer. These so-called "wonders" are modeled after biblical interpretations of Jesus's works. But they are not effects of true goodness projecting through God-centered individuals. Only one who's severed the connection with

Self in favor of conscious contact with God will facilitate supernatural phenomena we have come to regard as miraculous. Public, commercialized "miracle workers" are mimics, just practiced performers who know how to stage facsimiles of miraculous events. Within the realm of true miracles, they are rank amateurs. Miracles are possible. But, they only happen under the auspice of God-conscious individuals. You won't see them performed on religious networks or in churches. Those are all phony, every last one of them.

[39] Consciousness is like an amazing lens, making every thought and situation passing under it become crystal clear. Lack of consciousness is like a dulled lens providing diminished sight. The distinction between clear and dull can spell the difference between sane and unsane living.

[40] Sadly, they are often medicated into a numbed psychic trance, chemically stymied from consciousness. They're prevented from feeling bad enough to ever awaken to reality.

[41] People find it so difficult to get free of the obsessions that manifest in bad habits and vices because they cannot see the cause. But, once realizing how obsessions originate, they finally become distressed enough to crave freedom and receive the inspiration to allow it, even to look at themselves.

[42] Open minded means being receptive to new ideas. It doesn't mean automatically accepting what anyone says as truth, no matter what. That's gullibility. I am not trying to get you to believe or disbelieve anything in this book. I only hope that you receive it. That will be enough. You must see for yourself.

[43] "You can be anything you want to be." "Just believe and it will be so." "You can make it happen." Positive thinking theories, etc.

[44] This is where all atheists eventually find themselves. While proclaiming to themselves and others that, "There is no God," they do not realize that they've simply converted worship away from some

concept of Him, back onto themselves. As it turns out, they do believe in a god after all, except that their god is them.

45 There is a profound difference between motivation and inspiration. Motivators stress and press you into action, whereas inspiration is the gentle, loving nudge of spirit activating body and mind without self-will.

46 "Confidence," - "con fi deo," is literally "with God" and a reflection of the Creator's will as it flows through, automatically projecting into our world without effort. It comes by being still and allowing Him in. This phenomenon instills courage and only occurs when we are conscious.

47 Okay, Bullshitters. All right?

48 All hatred is bad. But if one hates what is good, terrible physical circumstances will quickly manifest. The smooth functioning of the brain and body become inhibited. Fatal diseases can suddenly erupt. This isn't some cosmic retribution or "karma." It's simply the naturally occurring metaphysical backwash out of the spiritual realm affecting the physical side of existence.

49 It isn't fame or the glamour of the entertainment business that destroys people. It's easy to blame the wealth or to say, "Too much too soon". Yes, these can be contributing factors along the way. However, the approval seeker's underlying brokenness precedes all obsessiveness. It develops into a penchant for excess. The metaphysics inherent to the first bow and applause supplies the "gateway" drug, providing an entertainer's true high. Addiction to it can be immediate for certain vulnerable types. Nearly all tragic show business suicides and overdose deaths occur among individuals who grew up without the protective influence of a virtuous father. A lack of security sometimes results in horrific brutalities, other times less so. The greater the cruelties, the greater the chance of extreme approval seeking and a compulsory attraction to recognition and ovation.

⁵⁰ Stage and screen acting, singing, dancing or playing music, all professional performance falls under this idea. Considering my own stage experience and having worked with entertainers, specifically stage and screen talent (well-known and not-so-well-known actors, singers and musicians), I can confidently say that occupational entertainment can indeed be done safely and for good, noble purpose, as long as it's practiced with the correct attitude. A wholesome relationship with an audience and a consciousness of message are essential. Both audience and performer together enter a metaphysical realm that either or both may not survive unless this understanding is clear.

⁵¹ What goes on in the minds and secret lives of individuals occupied by such overdeveloped Self entities are shocking. Believe me, you don't want to know.

⁵² Psychoactive drugs, often prescribed by physicians for these conditions, effectively mitigate the symptoms. But they do not treat the cause because that's way beyond their reach. Professionals have no idea what causes these conditions or how to cure them. They only have pharmaceuticals to alter the personality of the individual, mimicking calmness while the real problem continues unabated. The individual becomes artificial and repressed. The cause of these goes to metaphysical disturbance, remedied only through metaphysical means, not physical or psychological.

⁵³ I am not talking about the kind of visions we often attribute to the innovative producers of the world. The so-called dreams of such an individual are not the delusions of a person who's lost in fantasy so much as they are the constructive reckonings of a creative soul-intuited visions they can later decode into communicable language. This kind of "dreamer" is not really dreaming at all. He isn't sinking in his imagination. He's translating a vision that has unfolded within, while he was conscious, and fashioning an actionable plan he will execute. And then he does. That's the difference between the basement inventor who holds 1,000 patents on good ideas that will

never see the light of day and a person like Steve Jobs. Ninety percent of the great ideas, the Ubers, the microchip technologies, the Amazon.coms and the Smartphone APP sensations, sell products that have all been conceived a thousand times over by a thousand-different people. But it is the rare individual who possesses the conscious gumption to take action that does something about them. They become gifted with the confidence to bring their vision to our reality. It isn't their mind that does it. It's not their will. It is a mystical Will that enters anyone who discovers and lives through conscious awareness. We cannot create reality with our minds. Only God can do that. We can execute the Will of our Creator by becoming awake and aware, ready to work.

[54] Just some of the disorders that others I've worked with in this area have conquered, include, Cancer, Heart Disease, High Blood Pressure, Sleep Apnea, Depression, Anxiety, Chronic Pain, Neuralgia, Obesity, Smoking, Drug Addiction, Drinking, ADD and ADHD, Bipolar disorder, Paranoia, Dementia, and Schizophrenia.

[55] Stress-induced outcomes can be positive too, if they're met with properly. Without resentment. I'm only speaking here of the negative consequences following improperly met pressure so I can stay on-point with this chapter.

[56] This is how Isis, Al Qaeda, the corrupt politician, even a cruel lover will subdue and control their unwary prey. They can want to get caught in their misdeeds because once you become upset by the deceitfulness, you automatically fall weak to them. They've got you.

[57] Very simply? It's either God's or the Devil's.

[58] You may have read this idea in a bible or heard religious people speaking of it. You'll find this in the "Gospel According to Luke." Luke was a Greek physician, an Evangelist and close friend of the Christian disciple, Paul. AKA. "Saul." Someone asked Jesus when God's Kingdom would come. He basically told them to stop waiting for it to come out of the future and to stop relying on others telling them when it would be, because God's Kingdom was already there, now, within

themselves. He was referring to consciousness, the very subject of this whole book. I did consider calling this book, "Go to Heaven Now" but I thought it was too provocative a title for the time.

[59] Most meditation techniques are really hypnotic recruitment tools used by Eastern religions and non-duality cults to indoctrinate westerners, if not directly into their organizations, then at least to adopt their philosophies.

[60] These can range from mild endorphin and pleasure circuitry stimulation by heavy breathing or aroma "therapy" to physical gyration and "humping" masturbation to reach orgasm. There is no depth some will not sink to anesthetize the pain of a guilty conscience. And yes, as absurd as it seems, these will be character-ized as "meditation" techniques. I am not kidding

[61] If you classify yourself as one who meditates, you self-elevate, stepping up on a pedestal, judging yourself and others, feeling superior to those who do not meditate. Have no opinion of yourself. Stop keeping score. Just know that you should meditate without it becoming part of your imagined identity. Exist side by side with other conscious human beings without manufacturing a meditation culture with them or for yourself. The church is not literal. It is metaphysical and beyond intellectualizing. Just knowing you are awake and aware, in the world yet not of it is fine, if you do not fall to judging others. Because once that happens, you enter the realm of self-righteousness, becoming a useless, religious bore.

[62] God's true church is metaphysical, not physical, and though comprised of individuals, we are allied ethereally, not by formality.

[63] The suggestion to find God is sometimes met with, "I don't have to find God. He isn't lost." This semantic rejoinder is simply a way to dismiss or defend unrecognized agnosticism. It's kind of arrogant. But it is cute. So, whenever possible I prefer to use the word discover in this context, instead of find. But I do use them both interchangea-bly.

64 Some people read my books, blogs, and Social Media content and come to love what I say. They appreciate the strong insistence upon meditation and decide to give Non-Contemplative Meditation a try. But then, a voice from the dark side rises in their heads to inject doubt. Sometimes it is through others. They go and find some alternative technique, totally different than what I propose. Instead of exclusively using my Non-Contemplative Meditation they experiment with some POP-Psychology exercise or Eastern movement technique. Some take a cafeteria approach, mixing and combining techniques with mine. Then as they become worse off, some suppose that meditating at all isn't worth their time. Please don't do this. When I use the term meditation I am not talking about anything other than the very special kind that I propose. No other "meditation" works. I mean none. Only Non-Contemplative Meditation exercises conscious contact with God. You will be very glad if you do not tamper with, modify or scoff at this technique.

65 Even minute, psycho-stimulating effects contradict the metaphysical benefits that this meditation has in the body.

66 Deep breathing induces fast, exhilarating euphoria. When we were little kids we'd repeat fast, rapid breaths until we felt lightheaded and drunk. It was a cheap high. In less than 30 seconds, we totally forgot whatever problems we might have had in our lives-stressed home life, homework, social pressures. Suddenly we were in heaven, albeit briefly. Even a runner's high, the exhilaration of all those feel-good chemicals in the brain, norepinephrine dopamine, serotonin, and of course the body's own home-brewed opiates, endorphins (opioid peptides) producing a morphine-like mood enhancement to numb the conscience and relieve pain. Any reader who'd like to go into business with me, please take note: We could make a fortune opening a Breath Bar, where patrons come to sit at tables and simply breathe deeply-let's see, purified ambient air-and perhaps some special aromatherapy rooms for a steep surcharge. Add a touch of light trance music, some subdued lighting and of course, heavy breathing. Viola! Bliss. Katching! Given the disposition required to become a

member of a typical cult, we could develop the idea immediately. We could establish a cult called, The Breathers: High as kites, cosmically connecting with the universe through the artificial miracle of mild hyperventilation-coming to a foreclosed church property near you. I jest of course. My Non-Contemplate Meditation™ would run any Breath Bar out of town before anyone ever saw a profit.

[67] I won't go so far as to say that if you own a yoga mat that, "You're hooked." But I might at least consider it. You ought to too.

[68] Yoga is responsible for introducing a big conflict here.

[69] Existing and living meditatively is simply being awake and aware. I do not mean with your eyes closed and your hands, fingers, and torso vibrating.

[70] Others may notice this uncanny ability. To them, it seems you've developed some sort of ESP. It's natural and not so extraordinary once you awaken. I am not saying you will read minds outright or see directly into the future like The Oracle in The Matrix movies. But your senses will be heightened to an extremely advantageous level. You'll gain prudence and a proclivity for foresight and vision unfathomable to most people.

[71] This term is out of the book, "Alcoholics Anonymous" from what some in that fellowship call the Third Step Prayer. "God, I offer myself to Thee—to build with me and to do with me as Thou wilt. Relieve me of the bondage of self, that I may better do Thy will. Take away my difficulties, that victory over them may bear witness to those I would help of Thy Power, Thy Love, and Thy Way of life. May I do Thy will always!"

[72] The Matrix is a 1999 American science fiction action film from Warner Bros. Pictures, written and directed by Lana and Andrew Wachowski. Their film depicts a simulated world where nothing you see and experience is real, and the truth is kept hidden behind a life-like facade controlled by a tyrannical authority.

73 Don't you see that God has already forgiven you? He knows it wasn't you. He's known all along, before you were even born. Before any of us were.

74 I probably could have spelled that "boar" and metaphorically not lost an iota of accuracy. Don't you think?

75 This is the much talked about paying it forward principle that many have heard of but very few comprehend. We can't necessarily know of all the effects our actions have on others. Like George Bailey in the 1946 film, It's a Wonderful Life, if we are of goodwill we project will into the world in a positive way. If we are of ill will then we are like the Mr. Potter character, recreating the world into a sick, depraved environment, causing misery and harm to all.

76 This Non-Contemplative technique cannot be tweaked, improved upon or added to and if the attempt is ever made, not only will the ultimate result not be effective, but it will likely bring opposite consequences. This, in its current form, is all there ever will be and all that will ever work. It is not a toy. It is not an experiment. Please be warned.

77 If you are currently ill and haven't already begun the Non-Contemplative Meditation, then please start. If you already have, then as you read this book there could come a sense you are very soon to experience a miraculous healing. For at least half of you that will be 100% correct. For another quarter, it will take a bit longer and the rest of you will abandon this, move onto something else and not really benefit at all.

78 Yes, it took her that long to come around. We've been married since 1979 and believe me, it hasn't been easy. One day I'll write more extensively about just how I drove those spirits out of her (and others), and exactly what their natures are.

79 Not merely a suddenly violent or noisy upheaval. I mean literal Hell, that dark otherworldly abode of Evil and all the condemned

spirits that ever were. It's where Elmore Leonard does not live. At least as far as I know.

80 It isn't really love, of course. They're calling it love and believe it to be love, but it's the sick support for what is wrong in them that they seek from you, and that you may have provided too. Up till now.

81 I'm in my late 50's as I write this book. By the time you read it I will likely be at least 60. At this stage in life, I can count on one hand, my true friends. And believe me, it's not even nearly a full hand. I've hundreds of pals whom I love. I have thousands of wonderful acquaintances worldwide. But, I have less than a handful of close friends. Even so, we are free of each other and can truly enjoy what we each offer without obligation. I do not cling to people. If you and I were to develop a personal alliance, I assure you it would be very healthy and we'd be useful to each other, but we'd never attach as parasites. This is very wholesome—not in the last bit lonely and the relationships I have with so many people are beneficial on both sides.

82 If you've become separated from your children or parents because of your poor decisions and egregious deeds in the past, now there's a real chance for true reconciliation. Not a willfully forced reunion, but through a genuine amendment of dissipated lifestyles, there comes light at the end of the dark grudge tunnel. I've seen years of rancor vanish overnight. It may not happen, but at least if it were ever going to be possible, now it truly is. Miracles happen in this area. You cannot make them happen. They just do. Miracles happen regularly once we stop expecting them.

83 This does not describe a perfect family. I don't know perfectly what perfect really is, but I can tell you that though these ideals are in the right direction, they aren't even close.

84 If you're married, this is the worst time for sex. If single, don't masturbate now. Even if aroused, don't engage with sex, either real or imagined, upon awakening, or use excitement to invigorate the body. The effect is exhilarating, but the psyche will become dulled. Despite what you may have believed in the past, becoming physically

pumped by thoughts coursing through the brain, sexual or otherwise, is not a good way to begin the day or any endeavor. Just being consciously aware provides the right kind of vigor one needs and is far superior to being physically stimulated into action. It's the difference between being the cannon or the ball. You don't want to be the cannonball.

85 Others are people who need our approval to have much sense of worth, but who tend to suck love out of us to get it. These are psychic vampires with an insatiable thirst for our catering support. While they may pretend to love us, it isn't true love at all. It is the emotional funding of the wrongness that torments them inside. While they derive life out of us, becoming intoxicated with our loving support, we surrender our energy, becoming less as they become more. Our submissiveness forms sick, parasitic relationships with people and is the single root cause of all emotion-based illnesses like heart disease, neurological disorders and most types of cancer. If you could never hate, you could never die. But as you love, you set the pace for wellness of body and mind, living forever. If you've ever wondered what human co-dependency is, you just found as perfect a description as you'll ever come across, right here in this footnote. It's simple, isn't it?

86 If you've ever prided yourself on how compassionate you are for others, this may be difficult for you to accept. Compassion is seen in society as a positive human attribute and you've likely believed it. It is not. In fact, most compassion is a filthy emotional exchange. The sharing of psychic energies with others is not healthy for you or them. There are wholesome ways to be truly helpful. The psychic coitus of compassion isn't one.

87 I've just described what it is like to be nonjudgmental. You may want to go back and read that again, then begin the meditation exercise proposed, so you can begin living this way.

88 Of course, it was true. He did tell the good brother exactly that. Aurelian was no liar. The underlying question was, "Weren't you

really late because you snuck outside the building to have a Marlboro?"

[89] Animals receive their discipline solely from their relationships with their environment. We are to grow away from this animal-earth relationship for stimuli and move more toward God.

[90] This is the very instant where people do the things they don't want to do. It is the moment where obsessions trigger. IE. A drink is ordered. A call to a drug dealer is made. A person leaps off a subway platform into an oncoming train. A provocative tweet is sent. A biting remark goes out to a child. A sexual indiscretion is committed. A rock gets smashed into the head of an innocent passerby.

[91] Don't let these questions fool you. I am a staunch, practiced capitalist. A believer in American Exceptionalism, rugged individualism, and conservative economic values.

[92] "The cycle" is the cycle of addiction.

[93] There will also be co-workers, employees and business partners who'll become very uncomfortable in the work environment that evolves in your presence. They will not like working in an honest, open culture. These people will leave. Some in a fury. That is good. On the surface, it may seem you're finding it hard to fill positions or to fit in among others but this will be a blessing long term.

[94] Just what you are being saved from will be apparent once you practice. I am being intentionally evasive here so as not to create expectation.

[95] In the Twelve Step approach to recovery, the unrecovered alcoholic wishing to recover completes a written inventory of the people, institutions, and principles for whom he's ever harbored any sore emotion whatsoever. Invariably, at the top of the list is biological mom and dad. Both. Dead or alive. Divorced or together. Estranged or close by. Identity being apparent, or a mystery. This is an admission which, if honestly made, goes a long way toward a fundamental breakthrough of forgiveness within. It stimulates a spiritual

awakening experience discharging the individual from his fixation with EtOH.

⁹⁶ Don't confuse emotional ties and affection with love. They are not one in the same.

⁹⁷ I once worked with a fellow stockbroker who was sure he came from a wonderful, loving family. There was no divorce. His parents rarely fought. His dad owned a profitable business and they lived in a nice home. They had the means to put him through one of the top private universities in the state. Yet he became a food and drug addict, as well as an alcoholic. He insisted it was never his upbringing that was to blame for his problems, and he had the pedigree to prove it. Interestingly, he also confided that his father regular ripped off his customers in business and that his mother once bragged of getting free cans of tuna at the supermarket when the cashier failed to ring up all the items before bagging. Do you see what happened to this poor man? Who knows what other disappointments he endured growing up in his loving family. In truth, his parents were anything but loving.

⁹⁸ Bill Wilson had a dramatic spiritual awakening experience while at the hospital. Subsequently, the obsession to drink alcohol had been temporarily removed.

⁹⁹ They truly believe the information they receive from their netherworld connection is legit. The truth is demonic spirits lie, and so they believe the lies of nefarious entities. Now they project those lies onto naïve, searching folks.

¹⁰⁰ You may recognize this as coming out of the "Lord's Prayer." We need strength each day to set aside thoughts and allow consciousness to be our everyday standard. "Daily bread" is a metaphor for accepting some of God's power to assist. We haven't any muscle of our own. But we get some of His to use. On loan, so to speak.

¹⁰¹ These can include Alzheimer's disease, arthritis, atherosclerosis, asthma, cancer, liver disease, COPD, type 2 diabetes, heart disease,

metabolic syndrome, high blood pressure, high blood sugar, imbalanced cholesterol and triglyceride levels, osteoporosis, stroke, PTSD, depression, and obesity.

[102] Once realizing your powerlessness, you could finally resort to the old last standby. People call it, "the power of prayer." Yes, prayer is powerful and miracles happen through it. But not the way any of us have ever been told. The problem is that hardly anyone knows how to pray. The way you've been taught, how you've supposed, has not been correct. Incantations, recitals, beseeching, or praising dialogues with God, out loud or in the imagination, are not prayer. Yes, the religions, the movements, their clerics and leaders have mostly gotten it wrong—to the delight of Darkness. Of course, there's beautiful sentiment that can express through songs, poetry and other writing. But that is all they are. Writing. Running these through the head is not praying. Non-contemplative meditation, expressed in the sentiment of what is often called, "the Lord's Prayer" is how to pray. It is the only prayer we have spoken by Jesus Christ.

[103] This is why I don't call this a self-help book. There really is no such thing as a self-help book. We either receive Supernatural help or else fall under the direction of the dark influence.

[104] If you have begun meditating as prescribed, then you will know exactly what I mean by Light.

[105] This is a decent characterization of the Non-Contemplative Meditation experience.

[106] You are being coerced into self-loathing, by an accusing entity within. This is the course taken by anyone who becomes depressed. The moment they get free from the Chattering Instigator they begin to heal. Recovery from depression is then rapid and thorough.

[107] The less negative energy it receives, the more selfless you become.

[108] We cannot save ourselves from resentment. It is a metaphysical phenomenon requiring a metaphysical rescue. No one can think or reason their way out of a supernatural force like anger. Neither do

knowledge or countermeasures stop us from hating. Prevention is beyond the ability of even the most prodigious genius. We do, however, become immune to the damages of negative emotional energy, like resentment, the instant we become conscious. In that moment, we are no longer subject to anger, fear, frustration, loneliness, or any form of resentful energy. They all just sheet off us like rain on a squeaky-clean car windshield. The answer to the resentment problem is to step back from thinking, Self's psychic umbilical cord to Its anger-food, and do nothing more than watch.

[109] Obviously, we need skilled doctors for repairs, to treat injuries and even sometimes to keep us going physically so we can avail ourselves to second chances.

[110] Some readers will experience instant relief from long years of suffering just this way.

[111] I mean seriously now. If I can figure this out, surely God already has. How could He ever hold this against you? See how easy it is for Him to forgive you. He knows it hasn't even been you who's hated and judged, but Something inside you. You already have His love.

[112] In rewriting this chapter, and coming upon this, I've since learned the tragic fate of the author of this work. He died young, in an airplane, from an emotionally induced heart condition. The night I was editing this page I brought it to my wife Nancy's attention and she cried. Not knowing this man or even being familiar with his work it was still clear that here was an individual who thought he had found the answer and a way to happiness. He hadn't. What he found was a way to suppress anger and to feel better without getting better. And it killed him, leaving a young wife and children. I've never heard of this man before now and I do not wish to disparage anyone's life's work, let alone that of another author, but please understand how serious this business of resentment is and how simple it is to resolve. You will see this same heartbreaking trend in all the POP-psychology presentations alleging to bring happiness. New Thought pseudo-

spirituality and POP-psychology fail in the long-term. Those who think they are being helped by it, aren't, and that will play out.

[113] Perhaps abuser is an ever more accurate word to use than user, but it would cause too many readers to stumble here and I do not want momentum to break with this idea.

[114] If you have begun meditating, then you've already experienced this quite strongly. It diminishes.

[115] It could be almost anything. Compulsive reading, entertainment, and sports obsessions are just some examples.

[116] Leaping out of airplanes, hopping into the boudoir with an illicit lover, even a weekend lost inside video games, anything pulling us out of consciousness is a distraction and takes us out of the present reality into some dark realm. No, it is not harmless. Perhaps it is unavoidable on this plane, but it is certainly not 100% risk-free.

[117] This led to all her children becoming obsessive drug addicts and alcoholics. I am the only one to survive.

[118] Later, I compensated for this weakness by becoming a cocky risk-taker, abrasive and too often overly demanding of my employees and business associates.

[119] In starting up the business I decided to knock on the doors of companies to try and sell my services. At 17, the prospect of meeting face to face with successful people I didn't know and asking them for their business and money scared the hell out of me. The day before my first professional level sales jaunt (Not counting wholesaling fancy fantail guppies to local pet shops when I was ten years old.) I told my future mother-in-law how scary it was. She suggested I might overcome the fear by imagining my prospects naked. Apparently, when approaching someone to whom she felt inferior, she'd simply imagine they were totally nude. I've since learned that this is an old standby gimmick. It's supposed to elevate one's low self-esteem by mentally demeaning others, thereby instilling confidence by comparison. I tried it once. The prospect's name was Arthur and he

owned a wholesale produce company in the South Bronx. He was
elderly, all of 5 feet tall, wore a dark, double-breasted suit and puffed
a huge Dominican cigar that stunk to high heaven. Arthur's
receptionist sent me into his office and I took a seat in front of his
desk. He was talking on the phone, ensconced in a high-back
executive chair that towered behind his head, puffing on his cigar and
barking to whoever was on the other side of the call. It was terrifying.
I immediately started picturing him without a stitch. Right then, there
was little old Arthur, suddenly naked, wrinkled and bizarrely running
his empire from a Naugahyde throne, his ding-dong dangling
between his legs, billowing huge blue clouds of smoke from behind
the giant mahogany power desk. This worked. He went from
intimidating to bizarre in a second. I got through my sales pitch
without a stumble. He signed up. I had finalized a deal. But I also felt
ashamed. I was not at all comfortable mentally belittling the poor
little guy in my mind. On the rest of my calls, I did well enough just
putting on a suit and sweating it out. I am so grateful to have this
example of courage in my own life. All I had to do was dress up, show
up, be honest, know what I was talking about cold, and work hard.
Plenty of good people said yes to my pitch. I learned the basics of
closing deals and established a fantastic business that taught me
immeasurably beneficial lessons I still use today.

120 And here is where your parents screwed up with you. You must
forgive them. Stick with me on this idea, please. Forgiveness is
coming.

121 We do not decide what is "right." We do not feel righteous. We just
naturally do God's will, which can never be wrong.

122 As you read this book you are going to discover an inner agitation
occurring at some passages. Some more than others. Hardly anyone
will be immune to this. When it happens, just watch the effect. It isn't
you. It's Something in you that senses the gig is up. Just observe the
temptation to become upset. Don't overreact. Just notice it squirm
and keep reading. You'll be perfectly fine.

123 To distinguish It's fear from our own emotionality, we will have to separate from It, to observe. Otherwise this insight is not possible.

124 The adage that, "The only difference between men and boys is the price of their toys," is a rather superficial and unfair indictment, wouldn't you say?

125 The healthy way to overcome hardships or to develop from the ground up isn't to compensate for deficiencies with emotional exhilaration. It is to find neutrality. Becoming objective first allows us to appreciate all we've been given, then allowing access to our own talents-gifts we'd otherwise never see through eyes blinded by egocentric desire.

126 Public speaking becomes more powerful when it's spontaneous and off-script. When I speak onstage to large or small audiences, I may use a talking point card to stay on track and within a time and subject arc, but there is no memorized portion. It's always organic. When done this way, I can speak effectively for an hour or up to twelve hours over a course of two or three days. Maybe more. (I've never had to go any longer than a three-day talk. Frankly, I hope I'm never asked to.)

127 You won't need to intellectually weigh pros and cons, trying to avoid making wrong decisions. You'll proceed forward, moment to moment, confidently making right life-choices, where even short-termed, wrong choices later turn out to be correct for the longer term. This is a boost to confidence so powerful, that until you've experienced and begun to live this way, it is difficult to imagine. Assuredness, shorn of an egoistic intellect is very powerful. This is how you get it.

128 The insight to see and not attempt to fix what's already been mended by time, God or others, comes with honest wisdom.

129 This is the reason why campaigns designed to eradicate drug addiction are never successful. Just Say No, the War On Drugs, Drug Czars, commissions or whatever new measures are soon to be

undertaken to battle opioid and other prescription drug abuse, will still coincide with widening addiction problems, not lessening. Government and privately funded crusades only address effects and never the cause. They'll try to develop means for preventing overdose deaths, an effect, but not anger, the cause. There will be public awareness, education, and outreach programs. We'll see anti-drug public relation campaigns and mass advertising. A new parade of conventional and unconventional devices, like legalizing, decriminalizing, classifying and reclassifying, will come and go. But the outcomes will always be increased drug use, not decreased, for the simple reason that the cause will remain unchecked. It may seem as though the epidemic is in drug use, but the true epidemic is not the drugs, but in the mass cultivation of the negative emotions, such as hate, residing inside every human being. If I had the ear of the authorities, I could show them how to cut the mass drug addiction in half overnight and nearly eradicate it within months. This is not hyperbole.

130 If you happen to be involved with a Twelve Step approach to recovery, then you'll appreciate that is the infallible Power behind that method and why it's so effective when done correctly.

131 Even if you weren't raised by a birth parent, if they died or abandoned you when you were young and you were raised by others, you still remained intuitively connected. Whether you realized it or not, the absence of either a mother or father, despite the practical presence of a substitute, is a metaphysically irritating thorn in the psyche of every child raised without a parent.Top of Form

132 Mindless being the opposite of mindful, filled with consciousness, grace and supernatural vision.

133 You'll find that this attitude often precedes depression. As it is applied to others there's a ricochet effect, turning judgment of others back onto the individual.

134 Be careful of reversing these roles. People who are too complimentary are to be observed with extreme caution too. So, don't seek out people who lavish praise upon you either.

135 The Ego entity residing in others is no dope. It knows when Its Adversary is present. An unconscious person will think it is they who are frightened or challenged by your presence. Just watch.

136 In case you haven't already guessed: Yes, vital elements of the Lord's Prayer are now becoming an aspect in your way of life.

137 Did anyone say, "Guardian Angel?" I just did.

138 A fascist regime can take totalitarian control at any time once people become so morally corrupt they project (elect) their own degenerate identities into public office.

139 This includes nicotine and caffeine along with the commonly prescribed pharmaceutical products.

140 The idea that saints are "perfect" is a widely held religious assertion.

141 He's had an "awakening," becoming conscious of his father's needs.

142 There's another angle to this narrative where the son's brothers become jealous of his reunion with the father. Despite all their good deeds, he seems to be better loved. I'm not one for pushing Scriptures on others but I highly suggest a read through once you begin meditating. You are likely to see things you've never seen before, in that story and many other biblical stories too.

143 Those who don't let go of the past, who're constantly reminiscing about the good old days and bygone eras or events are temporarily uplifted by the memories. Eventually, they become fearful of the future. During each second spent outside of the present moment, recollecting, they become agnostic, without God. In that state, minds and bodies deteriorate into a dark abyss of madness, dementia, and illness. Generally, we think of this kind of behavior as common when

a person gets old, but it can also become a trait in younger people. If you have a loved one, young or old, who's on such a path, please be sure to introduce them to the Non-Contemplative Meditation. Give them your copy of this book the moment you've finished reading it, or have one sent to them right away. Better yet, send them to my website where they can begin waking up immediately for no cost. Their lives will depend on this. They must come back to now. They will not make it unless they do. This is their only chance, believe me.

144 If you're in therapy or receiving guidance from anyone who's told you that it's okay to be angry, that its "naturally human" and right, then you need to discount advice from that person. They do not know what they are talking about and whatever their academic or clerical pedigree, that counsel will ultimately prove harmful. I realize how hard this can be for some to accept. If you've already bought into this popular idea in support of your own emotional states all I can say is, "Sorry," but also, "Let it go" it's a lie. Don't hate those who've been deceived. Just move on, free from judgment.

145 Therefore, we all must show our children how to meet meanness with grace, and why we must first have it in order to pass it on to them. The terrible circumstances that a victimized child suffers can always be traced back to irresponsible parenting. An over-emotionalized mother or father passes on their own inability to forgive. Unless one parent intercedes with love, showing a child how to properly meet stress, they enter the world ill-equipped for the inevitable cruelties they encounter.

146 You wouldn't have thought so. The very idea may even offend you. But it's true. This is what agnosticism really is.

147 This effect decreases as you become more aware through Non-Contemplative Meditation. If you've already been meditating properly for a while, then the voice in your head will not be as loud as it will be for individuals yet entwined with the thinking entity. The purpose here is only to show readers the mechanics of the mistaken identity and how it affects them currently. This is not a fail-safe test.

For some readers, thinking is so severely run amok and they so unified with the lower Self entity, that It will not allow them to perform DOSE. If that is the case, there is no need to panic. Meditating for a few days will rectify the situation. However, most people, typically tethered to intellect, will go through the task immediately.

[148] Never forget that judgment isn't limited to condemnation. It is also commendation. To condone or to revile are one in the same. Each is playing God. No human can survive either form of judgment.

[149] Studying the relationship between stress and the immune system presents challenges for the intellectual mind. It has not been a major area of research in the past. As of late, however, science has come to better appreciate the relationship between mind and body and the impact that stress has on the immune system. Still, the medical community tends to shy away from much meaningful discussion. That's because they have no understanding of the cause of stress. It is metaphysical, and therefore beyond their training and abilities.

[150] As you meet each intolerable situation and every flawed person with love and tolerance, you perfect your own imperfections. With each one met perfectly you are becoming perfected. Consciousness is perfection.

[151] Sure, we can all cite examples where cantankerous folk thrive on being loathed. They seem to get a thrill out of the irritation and annoyance they can usually raise in other people. But that's not them. It's something villainous within them with which they've identified and then project as their own personality. Such an individual is not acting himself. He's being used by a despicable spirit within to spread resentment, discord and ruin.

[152] Going along with the character defects in others, supporting their dishonest schemes or participating in their deceitful self-serving lifestyles for selfish purposes such as, "keeping the peace," is not what I am talking about here.

153 Can't say no to a bully employer? Lost your voice to a nagging spouse? To a spoiled child? To pushy, controlling people at work? Well, here's why.

154 Not that you won't know that you're being useful when you are. I am referring to deliberately performing for others to feel valuable, exploiting others need to generate a sense of self-worth-the epitome of self-centeredness.

155 This is the path nearly all entertainers travel. You can see why there is so much personal grief, tragedy and unsane lifestyle among those in the performing arts. It isn't the business that drives them. It's a profound inner need. There are a few who escape.

156 Respect and love exist safely only when you cease being the arbiter of worthiness.

157 As you recognize your own parents in this description, forgive them. If they are still alive give them this book, and then let it go.

158 Usually for impatience and bullying control over husband and family.

159 Give up anger for your mother and you will.

160 The corruption of every child begins early, at the hands of those who are supposed to love him but don't know how.

Emotional energy transfers from mother to child. This is how the seed of addiction is sown in all human beings. It happened to you. Both parents play a role. An impatient, angry mother projects her bitterness straight into her offspring. If severe enough, say, rage-fullness, then it may even penetrate the womb, reaching the unborn child. Now the baby is born already infected with a proclivity toward anger. Once born, mother's overall intolerance plus the failure of dad to preside with intervening love continues an affront against the child's innocence. For anyone beset by anger and fear—this is how it happened to you.

161 I am not a therapist, coach, counselor or a minister. I do not charge fees, there is no hourly rate, and I do not ask for donations. It's all free of charge.

162 It should come as a relief to realize that there is no such thing as good karma or bad karma and that fantasies like Law of Attraction are simply extravagant ruses invented by some clever people to dangle rewards for honoring godlessness. The universe is God's physical creation, just as are we all, deliberately placed into and apart from the endless void. All that exists is the creative substance of a single Creator. His handiwork does not get even if it feels violated. Nor does it experience pleasure when we honor it. The universe doesn't feel anything. While some may find theories like these captivating, they're still imagined notions manufactured in the minds of men for the purposes of instilling awe and fear in others. They are fantasies designed to control the gullible and to recruit guilt-ridden individuals into the folds of religious movements and cults.

163 And of course, that's nearly everyone. There are some people who are unbroken and have subsequently remained conscious for much of their lives. They are few. Once you awaken, they will become easy for you to recognize. Some of their names may surprise you.

164 If you close your eyes right now and look straight ahead, as if looking at the inside of your eyelids, you will notice tiny speckles of internal light. These are within you always. They're all around us, even right now.

165 In contrast, when you are not present, awake and aware, nothing is as it should be, no matter how desirable or pleasant.

166 Yes, angels and demons exist. No, your dead relatives cannot communicate or intervene with events. They're all dead, for now. Psychic mediums are not communicating with dead human beings. They are pawns for lying demonic entities.

167 Even I am confronted with the temptation to engage with the thoughts in my head. The remedy is to simply watch and observe

without getting caught in them—a theme repeated all throughout this book. This is so important.

168 This is when I immediately brought her back. I simply placed my hand on her forehead and reminded her how to return to reality. Do you realize how many people we all encounter each day who exist in a dream world like Nancy was in then? Well, you are one of them. Don't be insulted. Begin using the Non-Contemplative exercise right away. Put this book down for a while and go do it. Practice and begin reading again in a few days. I am not kidding. Better you should become conscious and well than finish this book.

169 Can you see now how life coaches, counselors, self-help gurus, even motivational speakers so easily gain the upper hand over people? How about self-serving politicians, entertainers, phony ministers, and preachers? These are ascended, approval junkies who've cultivated followings of feeder-devotees to serve a highly developed, Dark Self residing within them. In this way, they become masters at mesmerizing others, supplying Ego enriching illusions in the form of approval, just as they have already been mesmerized and inflated to believe they've been approved—by others, even by God. If you ask them it can be earnestly denied. This isn't an intellectual defense. It is a metaphysical, God-playing phenomenon they are not even aware is happening to them.

170 If you are "in recovery" from substance abuse, obviously this refers to a relapse episode.

171 It's an intentional redirect away from seeing the truth about the negative emotions leading to our obsessive behavior. Something needs us to remain ignorant on the subject, or else It starves.

172 The daily exploits of the real urban police on patrol regularly place them in harm's way. Every day cops meet with situations challenging the human ability to cope. All professional first responders, military and paramilitary, must be spiritually equipped to handle the injustices of a relentlessly cruel society. The exposure to them is frequent and endures for their entire careers. PTSD can be avoided

and reversed by learning to remain conscious and aware. You cannot be conscious and suffer from PTSD simultaneously. It is impossible.

173 It starts to kick in quickly.

174 Self is an opportunist. It pounces and gorges Itself on negative emotionality whenever It can. When you are inattentive, it sees the chance and makes It's move.

175 This is the point where bad habits and vices form. Smoking, drinking, compulsive sexuality, drugs, and overeating to name a few of the classics.

176 Doctors do not know what causes the deterioration of brain cells often associated with what they call Alzheimer's disease. I just gave you the chief one.

177 The muttering voice you hear inside your head is not God. It isn't Jesus. It isn't the dead. It is a coalescence of thinking language as a dark intelligence manipulates your thinking process to connive and influence you. Beware.

178 Ambitious book mongers, self-styled historians and students of spirituality take note.

179 Emotional need and physical dependency are not the same. One can be free from the emotional need for the psychoactive effects of a drug like nicotine, yet remain physically addicted. In effect, it's like being a non-smoker who still smokes, but doesn't realize he doesn't need the drug anymore to feel whole, yet remains physically a habitual smoker. Bill Wilson, spiritually awakened co-founder of "Alcoholics Anonymous," famously kept a smoking habit, despite having advanced spiritually over several decades. Wilson could have easily quit at any time. He just didn't know it. Many of the people I have helped quit smoking have found themselves in this same boat. However, once meditating, (properly) awakening and living consciously for a while, they've been able to easily get over their fear of the unpleasant effects of chemical withdrawal and simply detox off nicotine in a matter of a few days. Having recovered spiritually, there

is no more obsession for the drug to send them into a relapse. Contrary to what you may think or have been told, smoking is one of the easiest and simplest vices to break. It only seems difficult to anyone who's still living mindlessly, yet stuck in their heads and ruled by emotions. Get free of emotional bondage and then quitting is easy-peasy.

180 They might even take up a little of each, but in measured amounts to keep a low profile, within the limits of social acceptability. Sort of a vice cocktail, you might say.

181 Let's include multi-level marketing "businesses" and other Ponzi type schemes, whether financial, spiritual or religious.

182 Like God, angels do not communicate through voice either. Their guidance comes wordlessly too.

183 Dementia is symptomatic of an angry individual, usually suppressed, who's finally taken the deep plunge into the depths of the thinking mind. The great escape is hastened by pharmaceutical anti-anxiety medications and pampering. Many senior citizens prematurely placed into old age facilities can be saved from a tragic ending simply by waking up to reality, becoming themselves once again. If you have a loved one in this condition, please direct them to my Non-Contemplative Meditation so they can get free. It will save you and them a lot of unhappiness adding years of cognition and ongoing purpose.

184 It is also likely that he loses most or all his money to his financial gods.

185 If you think getting freed from anger and fear, losing bad habits or obsessions and never sinning means that one has reached perfection, then oh boy, are you in for a surprise. There are levels of human defectiveness to master, that exist on this side of sainthood, you haven't yet imagined.

186 I am loath to use the word instruction. I do not want to become your teacher or mentor. You should not use me as a spiritual guide.

However, I've been practicing exercising conscious awareness this way for nearly 40 years. I've done it wrong and I've done it right. I have worked with very many people who've done it wrong and right. I understand the consequences and I understand what works, not only through practical experience, but through inner understanding that only comes from conscious awareness. So please, just follow my lead here and do exactly as I say regarding the practice of this technique. Beyond that, I do not want to tell you how to live. I have a rather strong personality and presence. Attachment of the educational variety can happen without you realizing it. But if you find yourself "following" me too much, the conscious state of awareness that results from Non-Contemplative Meditation will allow you to spontaneously release from any hold my personality may invite.

[187] This is not a matter of a little is good, more is better and a lot is best. It's all or nothing. The "prescription" is right. It is in the exact dosage that will work for every human being who sincerely engages it. If you take less than prescribed, you can harm yourself as surely as if you take too much. Too little results in an extremely unpleasant state of twilight awareness and too much will put the overdosed into a dream that may never be escaped. As I have repeatedly brought up in this book, and much to the chagrin of my editors as well as my sensibilities as a writer, this is not a toy.

[188] I'm not a professional hypnotist and I am totally against commercial hypnotism as a solution to problems. I do however have a unique and deep understanding of how hypnotism works and I implore you to stay the hell away from it at all costs. I am the anti-hypnotist, not a hypnotist. If you are ever tempted to seek hypnotism to solve your problems you should first know that it does work, but only at great expense to your spiritual wellness, then in time, your physical life. If immediate gratification, like losing weight, smoking cessation, gaining confidence, getting rich, the classic egoist wishes, at the expense of permanent solutions, while losing your identity to the spirit of a hypnotist is okay with you, then go ahead and get

hypnotized. Nice knowing you. The nature of God-consciousness is anti-hypnotism. It solves your problems in an opposite fashion. This is metaphysical phenomena, the enormous dangers of which would require another book to fully explain. Perhaps one day I'll write it. Meanwhile, please heed this advice.

189 If you're meditating for a few weeks or months and began to experience an itch to cease using the recording, then you are not ready to. Stay with it. You'll know when it is safe to go commando, and it won't be for a while.

190 Another common pitfall along the same line is to learn and absorb what I write in my books and what I say in talks, thinking how wonderful the information is, agreeing with all of it, but without living consciously. When truth is in thought-form rather than revealed by awareness, it ironically becomes a distraction from truth itself. This is the danger of knowledge and study, even when it is of profound subjects—and what happens when you falter in the consistent practice of conscious contact through non-contemplative meditation. Again, there is that seductive inner voice that coos, "I've got it now." It isn't you saying that. It's not an original idea or observation. It's Something lying to you, that would rather have intellect rule your thought and behaviors, allowing the spirit to revert to back to its deteriorating state. This is the plight of religious types too.

191 Be wary of the voice that suggests, "You're there." You aren't.

192 Some people think that becoming self-aware somehow includes falling in love with your Self, providing your Self with approval, no matter what. That's ridiculous. Your Self is a liar. It is not realistic. It hates reality. Recognize It for what It is, and step back from accepting It's lies. Do not condone the bullshale It wants you to accept. It will mislead about your capabilities, your behavior and the world. It'll speak inside your head, telling you that you can do things you cannot do, and that you can't do things you absolutely can do—warping your view of success and failure. It is a cunning, deceitful dog and will

betray, preventing you from experiencing real progress in life-emotionally, relationally and even financially. You aren't who you think you are because you're thinking has come under the influence of a lying louse you think of as your Self. Thus, you're in a fallen state of unconsciousness and will not uphold the personal objectivity needed to discern true from false, right from wrong, or even friend from foe.

[193] There's a temporary, psychosomatic effect that even doctors and other scientists do not understand.

[194] It is never a good idea to become engrossed in trying to save people from their troubles. You can direct them to the Non-Contemplative Meditation and that is about it. If your own house is in order, they may take your recommendation. That alone will have the necessary effect on them. I regularly meet and speak with people all over the world who have problems with obsessions, substance and behavioral addictions, bad relationships with people and food, and who suffer poor health. As needy as they are, I do not become emotionally involved in their lives or tell them how to live and what to do. I hear their symptoms and based on those, counsel strictly within the metaphysical realm of spiritual well-being, reinforcing with them the God-consciousness solution. I do not prescribe therapies to them or diagnose illnesses. Non-Contemplative Meditation and God-consciousness is not therapy. It is the single supernatural solution to all problems. An individual either accepts the spiritual answer to all his spiritual problems or doesn't. The way to pass on the lifesaving message is through living example, not by preaching.

[195] As the populations of civilized countries continue to descend into the depths of their own stifled, internal anger, these methods will continue to grow in acceptance too. As fast as it seems to expand, the movement toward dharmic religions in the US and the UK has been slowed through the increased use of anti-depressant medications. As the truth of the harmful effect these drugs have is revealed,

contemplative meditation will increase in use. Yoga, contemplation, non-duality and pantheistic religions that deny God to promote Self are slowly replacing Judeo-Christianity in the west. This will mark the end of western civilization.

[196] These are the spiritual guides and gurus who nurture followings, large and small, and who are placed upon pedestals by parasitic sycophants. It can be a life coach with a small client base, a parish priest, a Twelve Stop sponsor. Perhaps a charismatic mega-church preacher, or a high-profile mystic cult leader. Think "Hay House," or the guest roster for the Oprah Winfrey show.

[197] These will be deep and personal revelations that are not discoverable through therapy, counseling or simple reflection and inventorying the events of one's past.

[198] I am not saying that I am perfect. I am saying I've learned how to meet the defectiveness of the world perfectly. Each time that I do, I move closer toward becoming entirely perfect. It's one perfect moment at a time. It takes a lifetime.

[199] This is explained in more detail throughout my writings, and on my website, as well as in my first book, *Real Meditation for Real Alcoholics: and those who love them.*

[200] If you have already read the Introduction to this book, then you've already learned more about this in that chapter. The upshot is that although I've experienced a share of suffering, personal loss and tragedy, I was spared much of the dissipation and degradation of spirit that many of my peers have experienced. I can see today how this has been a lifelong blessing. I do not feel special because of this. Just blessed in this regard. I have met others since who've been similarly blessed, and have a keen sense that there are more. Perhaps this book will reach some of those.

[201] I've since learned that it had been profoundly effective well before I was six years old.

²⁰² She had Hollywood star good looks and a personality to match. I guess that's where I get mine from. (sic)

²⁰³ If you're wondering if I also forgave my mother at this time for her role, no I didn't. Eventually, yes, but not yet. That would come years later, well into my adulthood.

²⁰⁴ That story is also in my first book.

²⁰⁵ During the early 2000s, I had been identifying as a member of Alcoholics Anonymous and attending their meetings to find alcoholics to work with. I am myself a recovered alcoholic and can rightly assert membership anytime I wished. That being the case, the opposite is also true. I've been able to rescind membership at any time. I am not a member of that beautiful fellowship, nor have I been one for a very long time. I do not go to meetings or attend *closed*, or *members only* AA functions. However, I like what they do and I continue to work with many AA members who wish to find and keep the God-Consciousness proposed by the co-founders of their fellowship and program. As an ex-problem drinker and former abuser of drugs, I find that many alcoholics and drug addicts are especially responsive to what I offer.

²⁰⁶ Alcoholics are only unique by merit of their symptoms. The root cause of their problems is the same as anyone else's.

²⁰⁷ When viewed at its original Hebrew root, the etymological perspective of the expression, "Being still," suggests we abandon our attachment to the activities in the mind. The Hebrew verb for this kind of stillness is 'rapah' (רפה). It is used all throughout the Scriptures. In the instances when I use "Being still," I'm referring specifically to stillness as 'rapah' appearing in Psalm 46. Here is the proposal to cease struggling against the whirlpool of thoughts that swirl like a tempest inside our skulls. Stillness is not quiet. Stillness is apart from the noise, to observe the noise in safety. We should never try to silence the noise. That's willful and would soon become a hypnotic obsession. But we can safely cease fighting to save ourselves

and still discover God's protection within through wakeful God-consciousness.

208 I suppose the number is in the many thousands by now. Hundreds directly via phone, email, cyber meetings, and social media. Then, thousands when considering the worldwide reach of my audience. *I don't mean to come across as braggadocious. I know how off-putting that can be. Hence this comment is placed way back here at the end of my book in this final endnote.*

***

A Very Special Acknowledgment

I'd like to personally acknowledge the support of Donna Marquise, Liz Holt Audette, Johan Aurvind, and Scott Robinson. These four individuals offered their backing through the initial crowdfunding campaign for *Go In*, floating the first edit of the original manuscript. I'm appreciative of their patience, waiting over three years for this book to finally be released and shall always be grateful for their early support of my life's work and unwavering belief in *consciousness* as a way of life. — Dan

Made in the USA
Middletown, DE
11 November 2023

42440155R00205